# Praise for *The Constant Choice*

"It is with incredible honesty that Peter Georgescu shares his personal journey of spiritual questioning to understand good and evil. *The Constant Choice* has not only enriched me, but also deepened my relationships. It has prompted in-depth discussions about good and evil, faith and belief, and the purpose of our lives on earth." —Linda Tullis

"I have always had problems taking the historic God on faith and subscribing to church dogma. Organized religion was spectator sport. When would I ever participate? When I read Peter Georgescu's incredible history and his journey to find his God, I finally got it after all these years. God is inside each of us, helping us do good, helping us conduct constant self-examinations of our actions, and helping us shape a life of compassion. Finally I'm a player." —Polly McTaggart

"Peter Georgescu's story is outstanding proof that goodness triumphs over evil. Those who survive desperate and evil situations are those who are kind . . . and possibly have a few guardian angels watching over them. These 'angels' reaffirm that there is tremendous goodness in the human heart and spirit. I found this treasure of a book both compelling and touching." —Margaret Sinclair

# THE

# CONSTANT

# CHOICE

An Everyday Journey From Evil Toward Good

PETER GEORGESCU

WITH DAVID DORSEY

GREENLEAF
BOOK GROUP PRESS

Published by Greenleaf Book Group Press
Austin, Texas
www.gbgpress.com

Distributed by Greenleaf Book Group LLC

For ordering information or special discounts for bulk purchases, please contact Greenleaf Book Group LLC at PO Box 91869, Austin, TX 78709, 512.891.6100.

Design, composition, and cover design by Greenleaf Book Group LLC

Publisher's Cataloging-In-Publication Data
(Prepared by The Donohue Group, Inc.)
Georgescu, Peter.
  The constant choice : an everyday journey from evil toward good / Peter Georgescu ; with David Dorsey. —1st ed.
    p. ; cm.
  Issued also as an ebook.
  Includes bibliographical references.
  ISBN: 978-1-60832-407-1

  1. Choice (Psychology) 2. Good and evil. 3. Self-preservation. 4. Conduct of life. 5. Georgescu, Peter. I. Dorsey, David, 1952- II. Title.

BF611 .G46 2013
153.83                                      2012944022

Part of the Tree Neutral® program, which offsets the number of trees consumed in the production and printing of this book by taking proactive steps, such as planting trees in direct proportion to the number of trees used: www.treeneutral.com

Printed in the United States of America on acid-free paper

12  13  14  15  16    10 9 8 7 6 5 4 3 2 1

First Edition

*To Barbara and Andrew, Sedona, Ali, and Mackenzie*

*To every thing there is a season, and a time to every purpose under heaven . . . A time to rend, a time to sew, a time to keep silence, and a time to speak.*

*—Ecclesiastes 3:1*

# CONTENTS

# WHY I WROTE THIS BOOK

MINE HAS BEEN AN UNLIKELY LIFE. AS A FIFTEEN-YEAR-OLD, off-the-boat immigrant with no understanding of the English language, no formal education, and fresh memories of the atrocities of a Soviet-style labor camp, becoming the very embodiment of the American dream was not the most probable outcome. In fact, as my life progressed, there were critical points at which my personal narrative could have unfolded in vastly different ways, including an early end. Throughout it all, my journey was influenced by the compassion of countless people, directed by the lessons of a hard childhood, and guided by a strong sense that there was a positive force propelling me forward. The knowledge of good and evil were my constant companions. The knowledge that evil existed in the world was incontrovertible and deeply personal. Yet also born of my experience there existed a growing faith in the promise of better, more enlightened choices that could shine light into dark corners and illuminate a better path.

I was drawn into events as a child that, for most people, are simply chapters in a book on European history. Being born in Romania, on the eve of the Second World War, was risky enough. Yet only a few years later I found myself, as a small boy, forced to work in a Communist labor camp, as a generation of former leaders, intellectuals, and anyone else who might pose a threat to the new regime was exterminated. My grandfather was one of these people, a national leader in Romanian politics and, as a result, a member of this doomed generation. He was put in solitary confinement where, one day, a guard kicked him in the mouth until he died.

My chances of making it through that same gauntlet alive were slim. But, after years of childhood captivity and abuse, that's exactly what happened. I landed in America at the age of fifteen, knowing hardly a word of English and having no education beyond the first grade. Yet I was a quick study, gifted with an admission to Phillips Exeter Academy, and I graduated with honors from Princeton and then Stanford Business School. Hired directly out of school by Young & Rubicam (Y&R), I began a career in marketing and communications as a trainee. Thirty-seven years later, still at Y&R, one of the leading advertising and communication agencies on Madison Avenue, I was running the entire company, as chairman and CEO.

Despite a life that may seem charmed to some, at least since 1954, I have struggled throughout the years to understand why evil pervades so much of human behavior. Let me state up front what I consider evil. I choose to paint this behavior with a broad brush. Acts of evil are deeds that when inflicted on others, with or without intent, cause suffering. Importantly, evil happens when harm unto others is committed without fair and morally acceptable justification. Some popular research data recently emerged claiming that human beings are moving on a kinder, gentler trajectory. The evidence is fewer wars with thousands slaughtered and fewer murders in towns and cities. Therefore, they say, evil is losing out and good is thriving. Yet all the evidence I have seen defies that analysis. Evil has simply mutated and changed garb. Evil is alive in business, in politics, in governments, and in nations. Sometimes it's overt as in Darfur, Sudan, Syria, or Al-Qaeda. Evil is still around us in the brazen thieves (the Madoffs), the bullies, the harassers. One in 4 women in the most advanced democracy in the world, the United States, suffers physical abuse from husbands or boyfriends. One in 6 young girls and 1 in 20 boys suffer some form of sexual abuse, too often from members of their own families.

I was born wired to keep asking questions and pushing hard until I was satisfied with a personal resolution to each quest. With some questions, well, let's just say I've been pushing for a long, long time.

It doesn't have to be this way. Evil is woven into our past, as a species, but it doesn't need to be a part of our future. History has blessed us with extraordinary messengers to show us the way to a better future. Their names are familiar, yet their messages are too often ignored. You'll likely recognize most of these names: Buddha, Confucius, Moses, Christ, Muhammad, Gandhi, Martin Luther King Jr., Mandela, and more. They all appeared in history to illuminate our way toward good.

But a culture of complacency and even cynicism simply shuts the door on historical leaders, and we move on with less insight, less knowledge, and fewer values, with a compass that points whichever way we want at any given moment. In fact, most of us, and particularly younger generations, have an indifference to history. As I looked at our collective future, at the world my granddaughters would inherit, this tendency filled me with genuine fear. This younger cohort feels history is boring, or worse, irrelevant. There is no wisdom to be extracted, nor insights to provide constructive context for the future. Life becomes one-dimensional: a continuous present tense, with no glancing forward or back. Let the future generations fend for themselves! How sad.

Winston Churchill's commentary on history is very revealing: "The longer you can look back, the further you can look forward." And the Pulitzer Prize–winning historian Arthur Schlesinger Jr. stated, "History is the best antidote to delusions of omnipotence and omniscience. Self-knowledge is the indisputable prelude to self-control for the nation as well as for the individual . . . It should strengthen us to resist the pressure to convert momentary impulses into moral absolutes."

Yet indifference to history is not the only hurdle we face. Perhaps my greatest concern about our future as a human condition is about what happens inside ourselves—how we think, how we reach out to the world around us, the instincts we choose to serve, and ultimately, our resultant behavior. On the one hand, we are witnessing an epic struggle with our capacity to imagine new environments, new institutions, new concepts, new technologies, new communities, and even new nations. On the other hand, our ability to adapt to these new ideas is glacial. Behaviorally we abhor change; we take comfort in the status quo. And the changes that have been adopted gradually over time have not necessarily been for the better. A good example of this is our democratic process. The Founding Fathers envisioned a beautiful ideal. It was a fair state of governance, with thoughtful checks and balances. Yet we seem to have retrogressed. The system's architecture appears as relevant and inspired as it was on that June morning of 1788. In practice today, we are faced with a dysfunctional, corrupt, contentious, and simply ineffective form of governance guided by self-interest. What happened?

Where are these "me first" impulses coming from? If these tendencies have always been with us but submerged in our subconscious or deliberately rejected for more altruistic behaviors, what has changed so drastically in our society today? Where is the institutional support for mature choice, for learning compassion, for developing a sense of commitment to the common good over selfish concerns as the ultimate goal in life? Unfortunately, in many ways, that support—in the form of family, community, church, and leadership—is lacking or has disappeared entirely.

Let's start with the traditional family unit. More and more families are single-parent households. More and more families have both parents or partners working. There seems to be less time to spend as a family and less inclination to talk about ethical and moral issues. Meals in the home are almost never sit-down events where discussion about happenings of the day takes place, where opportunities to guide behavior can be used as teaching moments. The extended family is no longer in the same home or even in the same neighborhood.

The community where neighbors were part of the larger family, looking out for each other's kids, is equally out of date. Church and Sunday school are no longer routines most of us respect. Sadly, institutional religions, with too few exceptions, have let their yearning flocks down. Most schools are afraid or reluctant to make up the gap in teaching morality or values. Even corporations are becoming much less caring or paternalistic. We're too often alone, without a working compass to choose a more balanced approach to life, where the common good and compassion have a chance against our more base instincts for satisfying our selfish, self-centered genes.

At almost every turn in my life, I learned that people look to leaders and observe what they do. Saying the right things is nice, but walking the walk is what really matters. So in today's world, where are the inspiring leaders? They aren't necessarily in organized religion. So many church leaders managed to turn their heads when the vilest crimes were committed against the vulnerable young. They aren't necessarily in business. In the first decade of the twenty-first century we experienced a global recession unlike any other since the Great Depression of the 1930s. It was a self-inflicted economic downturn created by selfish greed among the financial business elites. Inspiring leaders aren't necessarily in politics. During the attempts to recover from the recession, tribal warfare among political leaders continued to depress our economic and spiritual healing.

Add to these failings the pervasive effects of technology. Yes, technology can be good. Through it we can learn more, and we can share ideas and feelings with more and more people. Business and service activities can become much more productive and efficient. But there are also huge unintended consequences. If time with computers is growing, does it teach our children how to get along with each other or how to resolve conflicts with dignity and respect? Does technology inspire corporations to do better by their workers, or to demand higher and higher productivity while threatening to export jobs to lower-wage communities globally?

It is relatively easy then to conclude that our collective behavior reflects a loss of moral compass, a serious consequential diminution of our guiding values as decent, compassionate, caring humans. The most fundamental question of all is seldom asked: Why are we really here on this earth? What are we supposed to do? Are we making progress as humans?

Early on, I bought into the American dream of strong values

and wide-open opportunity. This characterization of the American scene is far from perfect, but in comparison to what I'd seen in Romania, it was entirely accurate. Living here felt like paradise on earth, and it still does. Yet the twenty-first century has been a bit of a brick wall. It has quickly become clear how our country and world have become mired in problems without easy solutions. We continue to face the threat of nuclear attack, and vast hunger punishes hundreds of millions of people around the world, while continuing violence and terror wrack places like Syria, Rwanda, and Darfur, as well as Sudan, Iraq, Iran, Afghanistan, Pakistan, and so many others. Tom Friedman, *The New York Times* columnist, says his generation had only one non-linear crisis to face, nuclear war. Now there are at least four: nukes; the deteriorating environment; our fragile, teetering global economy; and a growing culture of selfishness, greed, narcissism, and entitlement. At home I see deepening dysfunction in the body politic. The real constituencies for elected governments, whether local, state, or national, are less and less about the average voter and more about the tribes of lobbies and the money. It's no longer about the common good. It's about Red versus Blue. It's about a smallish group of "haves" who want to protect their economic gains at all costs. It's about an intolerant us, intolerance among religions and even within religions.

The real issue is we, the people. On the op-ed page of the *New York Times*, Tom Friedman said the solution to global problems isn't better leadership. "The real answer is that we need better citizens who will convey to their leaders that they are ready to sacrifice, even pay, yes, higher taxes, and will not punish politicians who ask them to do the hard things."

Exactly. And a great power that can't generate this kind of willingness to sacrifice and work together from its citizenry will not be a great power for long. The system isn't the problem. *We* are the problem. As Walt Kelly's comic-strip character Pogo put it, "We have seen the enemy, and he is us."

It has been said that from those to whom much has been given, much is expected. Likewise, the enlightened Benedictine Sister, Joan Chittister, in Erie, Pennsylvania, has asked us to "focus on our responsibility to give something back." So here I am, graced to still be around, this ordinary human having been blessed with the capacity, and even an obligation, to do more.

This book tells of events in my life that forced me to ask fundamental questions—sometimes asking them for decades— about who we are, what makes us human, and how we can possibly make the right choices. Why is the world filled with so much immorality? If we were created with a purpose, what is it? If God is in fact all-powerful, why did we suffer through Nazi Germany and the Khmer Rouge? Indeed, if we are the problem, as quite clearly we are, how can we also provide the solution?

If these questions sound familiar to you, read on. I'm not saying I have answers to sell. It's each individual's mission to find his or her answers. I can only share my own struggle, one man's quest to come to grips with existential doubts. But watch out. If you do find some workable answers for yourself, you may just have incurred a huge responsibility. You may find that you cannot remain a mere spectator, if you ever were, at the game of life. You, too, are likely to feel the call to become an activist, of some kind, helping to make the world a better place.

# INTRODUCTION

IT ISN'T EASY TO SEE WHERE I'M GOING. THROUGH THE WIND-shield of my Lincoln Town Car, the western New York State sunset, flickering through the poplars and pines along the road, is both blinding and illuminating. With all that light and shadow flashing past, it's hard to make out the next turn. It's all coming back to me, though. I've been this way before, many times. On this particular trip I am distracted, thinking about a moment in a hotel room four months before.

When the phone rang, I didn't want to pick it up. I was in San Francisco for a board meeting at Levi Strauss and Co., but my mind was on that impending call. Before it rang a third time, I grabbed it, just wanting to be done with it and hear the verdict. It was my friend Jim McCarron, who also happened to be my urologist. Before I'd left town, he'd done yet another dozen biopsies.

"Well," he said, "eleven out of the twelve biopsies were normal."

I braced myself for that twelfth one.

"The other one contained a Gleason Six Cancer."

"What's the next step?" I asked. "Surgery?"

"Let's get together and discuss the options when you get home."

Keeping a lid on my questions, I hung up. I was angry. Not at Jim, who's wonderful, but at the randomness of cancer. I'd known this was probably coming at some point, after a certain age, but somehow I hadn't prepared myself for the specificity of those words: Gleason Six. It sounded so impersonal, implacable. Why?

I felt I had so much left to do in my life, much of it of greater value than most of what I'd done until now. I wanted so much to give back to the people around me. I'd worked like a yeoman for decades, mostly making choices for good, giving up my weekends, often enough, doing what I thought was right, and putting myself into a position in retirement to actually make a contribution. And now this.

It isn't to say I was unprepared for the news. I'm a planner. You don't run a large company for years without thinking months and years ahead. Being ready to manage a cancerous prostate has been one of the many tasks on my preparedness checklist over time. In a way, I'd been training for this event as most men are likely to contract prostate cancer over time. Since before my retirement, I've been building a list of brilliant prostate surgeons. Whenever I heard about one of them, onto the list his name would go. The last and most recent name was Da Vinci. He's not a surgeon, though. He's a machine.

Early in this decade, this robotic device, designed for heart operations, was adapted for prostate surgery. With its extraordinary clarity of twelve-times magnification, the surgeon can see the actual prostate, its tissue and vital nerves. Yet, as with so many things on this little blue planet, there are caveats. Without a competent, experienced surgeon at the controls, Da Vinci is just a classy but empty name. I wanted a surgeon with some mileage.

Sitting in Jim McCarron's urology office in New York, we discussed several options. A "Gleason Six" is a cancer ranked six on a scale of one to ten, with ten being the most dangerous. Six is a moderate cancer but sneaky enough to break loose and wander around the body until it finds a new place to settle and raise its extended family of malignant cells. Having been on the Board of New York Presbyterian Hospital, I was well versed in all of this. By the end of his monologue, Jim said, "In your case, with an enlarged prostate, I recommend surgery. And at your hospital, you've got arguably the finest robotic surgeon in the world, Ashutosh (Ash) Tewari."

I'd known about Tewari for years, yet I needed to feel I was in good hands. So, when my wife Barbara and I met him, I locked my gaze on Dr. Tewari's face.

Instantly, my anxiety dissolved. The calm and inner peace radiating from this man belonged to a gifted physician. It suggested a man of God, a Buddhist monk. His voice was smooth and soft, a notch above a whisper, and it conveyed trust and confidence.

We chatted for no more than half an hour, and all the while, I was thinking, immediately, this is the guy. We're done here. I'll trust my life to him. Outside, after our talk, Barbara nodded. Yes, he's the one.

"Let's get this cancer and move on," she said.

---

What's interesting to me now, looking back at this crisis, is how the weeks *before* the surgery proved to be as significant for me as the procedure itself. I'd been diagnosed with a particularly dangerous disease and then told to sit around and wait for nearly two months to get rid of it. Let me point out that this period of waiting does not exactly induce a relaxed, welcome state of leisure. I understood the delay. The prostate had to heal from the biopsy and therefore seal itself, bottling up its cancer cells. That was necessary so that none of the bad cells would easily come loose and float into the bloodstream, only to lodge in my lungs, my brain, or my liver, after the prostate was removed.

But this delay meant I had all the time in the world for thinking. Just hearing the word *cancer*, you can feel your blood pressure rise, and the dread prompts you to cast a slightly dubious eye on everything you are doing, as well as on everything you've done. At crucial moments in my life, like this one, I've found myself standing back and wondering about my deepest beliefs about how each individual is influenced for good or evil and, accordingly, how each individual then influences humanity. The drive to write this book began to take shape during these two months of suspense.

Despite the dread, decades of visualizing best possible outcomes in childhood, in school, and in business had served me well, so I tried to shrug off the fears. Maybe the statistics were wrong. Besides, Dr. Tewari had a remarkable reputation, a brilliant team, and a fabulous hospital. Risks were minimal. Still, I couldn't shake the questioning.

As a child growing up in Romania, I'd been a traditional believer and an altar boy. But as I grew older, I wanted an intellectual model, a way of thinking about God that didn't conflict with science. I wanted an understanding of life that would give my own personal struggles a sense of meaning. My early model was simple and perhaps naïve. Our planet was populated by two kinds of people, the good and the bad, in endless struggle. But in the end, I believed, the good people would win. They would win because God was on the side of good, so good would always triumph over evil. Remarkably enough, this childlike model worked for me amazingly well throughout my youth and into early adulthood. Understand, I don't mean to dismiss it with that adjective "childlike." It was a powerful, benevolent—and, I think, partly accurate—vision of the world. Good does have an edge over evil. And we should all be trying out for that team.

This early, simplistic model of the world likely saved my life. It gave me the strength and endurance to survive the horrors of Communist Romania when I was separated from my parents for eight years and forced into physical labor in what were, at one point, life-threatening conditions of near starvation. Yet, later in life, after I came to America and was rising in the world of business, this model seemed less and less accurate. I saw good people tormented or ruined by others whose motives were clearly so self-centered, they inflicted serious harm. I saw how success can be achieved, and how goodness often becomes just as much a handicap as a source of strength. I found myself in a spiritual crisis far more perilous than the physical extremes of my imprisoned life as a child. I felt my belief in a personal, interventionist deity begin to disintegrate. And with it, the entire structure of my worldview, a picture of the world that gave me a reason to get up every day, work hard, devote myself to my family, and harbor hopes for a better future. My faith began to disintegrate because its foundations had eroded. My emotional life began to come apart, and my body began to break down.

All these struggles from the past came back to me as I waited for my surgery. I'd come through them and emerged with a new worldview, a new kind of faith in the potential of humanity, and an evolved belief in God. Yet now I found, once again, at the prospect of not surviving my surgery, my questioning had returned. Death had put his head through the doorway, looked me in the eye, and said, "Come see me later." So, like the good diligent worker I've always been, I began to scramble, retracing my spiritual steps in my mind—testing my beliefs and plumbing the nature of my faith to see if it still held up.

---

As a former CEO, I've had little time in my career for leisurely tours of the countryside, so I couldn't be happier than I am right now, rediscovering my way back to Chautauqua. Beside me, Barbara is relaxing comfortably. My wife has taken full advantage of her reclining seat, and it's such a smooth ride, she's probably half asleep.

This is our ninth end-of-June drive to Chautauqua, for the opening of the Institution's season, where we will stay for the full two months of lectures, concerts, movies, plays, conversations, and quiet dinners with guests. Our silver whale is loaded with the summer's provisions.

Part of the joy of coming to Chautauqua to live for two months in our little cottage, packed into rows of other modest homes, is never missing the material possessions that seem to crowd our lives. We keep coming back to Chautauqua, still hungry for something money can't provide.

Today our drive from Manhattan has taken longer than usual. The doctor told me I had to get out of the car every two hours, stretch, and then walk for at least a quarter mile. Still, I could use a rest stop, a *real* rest. It's the first time in more than six weeks that I've been allowed to drive. I love driving. Right now, it feels like a rare indulgence. But then, the closer we get to our destination at the western tip of New York State, the more everything feels that way. It's all a privilege, a gift. My recent brush with the possibility of death, and the surgery that followed, have given me a completely new perspective on what others might consider the tedious demands of travel and daily life. It's all a bit more interesting than before.

We're just crossing the high bridge over Lake Chautauqua, an hour's drive from Buffalo. Knowing we're only ten minutes from the grounds of the Chautauqua Institution, believe it or not, I get butterflies! After nearly a decade of these vacations, I still get that feeling in the pit of my stomach, a sense of warmth and delight, a sensation that means we're almost home.

You may wonder at this point why I love this place so much. It's a place where I've learned patterns of thinking essential to what I'm going to say in this book. It is exactly the place to go when a brush with death makes you think hard about what matters most in life. It's a place where people think about issues in ways that aren't always condoned in the media or even in universities. Granted, it can seem like a backward culture to many newcomers, a slice of the past trapped in amber. It's intentionally a bit cut off from our electronic, media-saturated lives. You come here to break old patterns of thinking and living, to find new and fundamentally open-minded ways of seeing the world. Chautauqua has come to strike me almost as an embodiment of my own lifelong spiritual quest—the state of questioning that represents the backbone of how I relate to the world. It's a place where smart and socially engaged people, with every manner of creed and philosophy and culture, gather to have good-natured, tolerant debates about issues that seem to have no easy answers. That's my element, and it's the fundamental chemical element, as it were, out of which this book was built.

As she has done at so many other crucial junctures of my life, Barbara led the way here, discovering Chautauqua nearly a quarter century ago. Her good friend Alice Neild used to invite her every year for a weeklong visit. Back in 1901, Alice's grandmother made her first journey to Chautauqua all the way from Dallas, and her family has returned every year thereafter. I was free to join Barbara and Alice on the weekend, but it was during the week, when I was always swamped with work at Young & Rubicam, when this place really came alive. The lecture series, Monday through Friday, from 10:45 till noon, for nine weeks every summer, is unique. Inspired by their weeklong themes, Barbara would phone to tempt me away from the office with raves about the lectures she heard on social justice, the growing importance of water in the world, the political crisis du jour from Russia to the Middle East, or even a parade of America's poet laureates reading from their work. You can't imagine how much I envied her at those moments. It was just the sort of experience I craved. Yet every year I would put her off with what had become my mantra: "It will be great to do, but in our next chapter, when I retire."

Well, my new chapter is upon me, and here I am pulling into the Chautauqua Institution gate at 7:00 p.m., nearly nine hours since we left New York City. My summer parking permit shows through the windshield, so the booth attendant can spot it without standing up from his chair. With a warm welcome and a smile, he lifts the barrier, and we glide slowly to our street. The speed limit is 12 mph here, in deference to the bicycles, pedestrians, and clusters of kids at all hours. Automobiles are a rarity on these narrow lanes. We're almost home now—our other home, our spiritual home—and yet something gnaws at me this summer. A feeling that began haunting me in my twenties, a questioner who whispers inside me, quietly calling out: Why? Why have I been so fortunate, and why can all that good fortune be so quickly and irrevocably taken away? What does it all mean?

My world, needless to say, didn't come to an end. Dr. Tewari did his magic, with the help of his assistant, Da Vinci, along with a team of nurses and other doctors, agents of mercy during my stay at New York Presbyterian Hospital. I recovered, on plan, as expected. My prospects are excellent. All the early indications showed that we caught the cancer, contained it, and got it out. And I had none of the dreaded side effects. Many more months of recovery lay ahead, but after only a few days in Chautauqua in that June of 2008, my sense of well-being rebounded, stronger for my having gone through the trials of cancer.

I felt energized and reborn. My sense of inner peace had returned. Yet my questioning had become a call to action: I intended to put my summer in Chautauqua to use. If ever there was a place and time to deepen one's understanding of God, to do an engineer's close inspection of the structure of my beliefs, this was it.

Everything begins on Sunday mornings here, so it's fitting that this is when I began pondering my own past, and all the ways I've tried to come to terms with it. Thousands gather at an amphitheater for the Sunday church service regardless of the weather. The whole tone of a week in Chautauqua is established by whoever is standing at the head of this ever-changing congregation. That tone is then often picked up every weekday, by whoever delivers the daily lecture from that same lectern, at the same time of day.

Chautauqua draws its audience largely from the Midwest— the often-derided Middle America, folks with a capacity and will to make a difference in their communities, their regions, and their nation. Teachers and ministers mingle with CEOs, people from the arts, and the small business owners who really make our economies work. It's a mosaic mostly of those unheralded American people who actually make things happen without needing recognition for it. These are informed people on whom nothing much is lost.

As Chautauqua Institution's brilliant president, Tom Becker, once told me, "I can't ever remember a speaker, after taking questions for half an hour, who hasn't said, 'Who are these people? I've never been asked such astute and challenging questions.'" Having spoken there myself, I have a rule of thumb: Never come unprepared to give a talk in this place. In a recent lecture here at Chautauqua, Justice Anthony Kennedy said that America's democracy and our freedom are completely dependent on a virtuous, enlightened, and committed citizenry. This is exactly what Chautauqua is all about.

The 10:45 a.m. lectures (and resultant discussions) during the weekdays are about seminal, contemporary issues that center on possible solutions to major social problems, in our nation and around the globe. This kind of questioning engagement, which resembles my academic training at Exeter, in college, and in graduate school, has always been a part of my professional life. It followed me into my career in business, where my work centered on creative teams of intelligent people inventing new ways to help companies succeed in their markets. So it has become second nature for me to examine intractable problems with new eyes, from new angles. I'm ready to dive in and imagine new possibilities, often because I look for any chance to seek novel connections between diverse fields most people would think are mutually exclusive.

Chautauqua itself looks like a little village someone has transported into today's upstate New York from maybe a century or half a century ago: small frame homes, packed tightly along quaint streets. Some of the major structures—the 1893 amphitheater and the huge Second Empire hotel—date back nearly to the origins of the place. Chautauqua has a long tradition of formal education and is imbued with a deep respect for spirituality and all the major faiths, with roots extending far back into American history. Early in 1874, a businessman from Akron and a Methodist minister from New York thought teachers and ministers of their day, as dedicated as they were to their vital missions, were simply not knowledgeable enough about the ways and happenings of the world. Reverend J. H. Vincent and his business pal Lewis Miller thought children needed a better, more enriching early education. So they created a summer school where teachers and ministers could learn.

Vincent and Miller wanted a location that would isolate their summer school from the distractions of home life. So they settled on a bucolic strip of lakefront, with gently rolling hills and magnificent trees, on the 17-mile shoreline of Lake Chautauqua, in the westernmost region of New York State. From Cleveland, it was a couple days away by carriage, a trip long enough to settle and focus a traveler's mind. A rudimentary camp owned by the Methodist church already exsisted, with roads cleared and rough basic cottages built in 1871. They eventually gave way to the slightly Disneyesque Victorian village, still standing today in the heart of the community. By the turn of the twentieth century, a 3,800-seat amphitheater had been built.

If you visited our house, near the corner of Ramble Avenue and Palestine Street, you might laugh at our ubiquitous red-white-and-blue theme. Inside and out, the house is a shrine to the stars and stripes. This seems corny, at first, or it may strike you as a little tongue-in-cheek. Yet it isn't a joke. We want you to know this is a thoroughly *American* household, and by that I mean it's a place that considers individual freedom of choice the most fundamental principle of all.

Here against this backdrop I've crystallized a lifelong attempt to see how my love of science—with its rational and fiercely empirical path to knowledge—could be reconciled with my reliance on something larger and more powerful than myself, through faith. I saw a way for me and my view of the world to marry science and faith, partly as a result of recent insights into one particular biological field of study and also because of the mental patterns of questioning and debate this place has fostered in me. My time at Chautauqua has helped me discover what is, for me, a surprising but deeply satisfying connection between the field of genetics and the admonitions of all the major religions. That connection is at the heart of what I hope to convey in this book and is based on a field of study that has, only in the recent past, begun to get public attention: epigenetics. My first encounter with this field came during a conversation I had with the brilliant New York Presbyterian heart surgeon and health advocate, Dr. Mehmet Oz.

We've known for some time that human life begins as a single cell equipped with all the genetic information an organism needs to survive and grow into an adult, encoded into what's known as the genome. In every cell of a human being's body resides this same identical genome. Yet despite the fact that all these cells have the same string of code, these trillions of cells somehow develop into a couple of hundred different cell types—building heart, kidneys, brain, and all the rest. What has only recently been discovered is that a cluster of molecules at the top of the genome, the epigenome (Latin *epi* means "on top of"), issues instructions to the entire string of code—thus determining what kind of cell will grow from the master code. Essentially, the chemistry of the epigenome tells the rest of the genome whether or not to develop a certain way and how much to amplify or dampen the volume on the instructions for its own growth and behavior.

Darwin's theory of evolution correctly contends that it takes many generations for a genome to evolve. Nothing in these new discoveries contradicts this principle, because the epigenome doesn't alter the structure of the genome itself. It simply turns parts of it "on" or "off." Imagine a player piano with a fixed number of keys, each with its own note. The sheet of "music" that runs through the mechanism causes only certain keys to strike at certain times, but the piano can produce a potentially infinite number of songs from the same finite set of keys.

Here's what's revolutionary about all of this. Research, mostly done in the past decade, indicates that individual human behavior can alter the way that the epigenomic "brain" controls the behavior of cells—and thus the body, including the brain. Repetitive behavior can alter the way an individual's genetic code operates. This is something that resembles evolutionary change within the span of a single individual life, and it's a genetically encoded change that can be influenced by individual choice. The data that supports this is persuasive and conclusive. Daily, habitual behavior can alter the way an individual's body ages, his or her state of well-being, and even the nature of that person's ethical choices. We're all familiar with how good habits can extend and enhance our qualify of life, but epigenetics demonstrates that these effects can be inherited by the next generation. The new behavior is stored and passed along as part of the way the epigenetic cluster of the genome instructs future cells in their growth and behavior.

An article in *Time* magazine by John Cloud ("Your DNA Isn't Your Destiny") sheds some light on what this does and doesn't mean: "It's important to remember that epigenetics isn't evolution. It doesn't change the DNA. Epigenetics changes represent a biological response to environmental stress. If you remove the environmental pressure, the epigenetic marks will eventually fade and the DNA code will, over time, begin to revert to its original programming." So far it has been shown that epigenetic changes can be passed along to several generations. As my wife Barbara often says, "The fruit doesn't fall far from the tree."

While we don't fully understand all the details of epigenetics and how and when it has an impact on an organism's life, the positive potential implications are spectacular. Cancerous cells may be influenced to stop dividing; obesity-driving cells could be dialed down. Specific drugs could be created to influence how these miraculously powerful molecules dictate their will on our afflicted bodies. This is all fact, now, not science fiction. In a small, phase-2 study of 45 patients facing almost certain death from an aggresive form of lung cancer, researchers at Johns Hopkins University have already shown that survival rates can be improved quite dramatically with the use of a drug designed to affect epigenetic changes instead of traditional chemotherapy.

Scientists have concluded that epigenetic changes start in the uterus with the fetus registering, in its cells, the behavior of the mother—what she eats, what she drinks, whether she smokes, the drugs she uses, how she exercises. In the twenty-first century, when changes in our world arrive at ever-faster rates, those tiny molecules might help us better adapt to this challenging environment. What epigenetics suggests is that the very structure of our bodies can be an ally—*a register of good behavior*—in our effort to better control our lives and our world.

Once I learned about epigenetics, many strands of my own thinking began to merge, which offered me a way to see the meaning in my own life experience and my quest for a way to understand it. For centuries, science and religion have seemed to be at odds. Stephen Jay Gould tried to keep them segregated in a way that wouldn't invalidate one or the other approach to understanding the nature of human life. He called them separate and distinct "non-overlapping magisteria." Each had its own authority and purpose, yet never would the twain meet. I disagree with this approach. Faith in God, and all the behavior that follows from it, has little to do with the propositional truths of science. Yet I think it's entirely possible that science, at some point in the future, might offer evidence that a faith in God actually reflects a profoundly proper way of relating to the nature of human life and the world. This is different from saying with certainty that "God exists." It's a way of saying that it makes perfect sense to have faith in what you cannot clearly imagine if that faith alters your life and the lives of other people for the better.

In some ways, contemporary science has begun to seem like a branch of faith itself, suggesting that scientists should be more than tolerant of those who believe in things yet unseen and unknowable. Science routinely now talks about dark matter as the most plentiful constituent of the universe, and it is, by definition, yet unseen and knowable. Quantum physics has postulated a number of paradoxes that don't jibe with common sense or human imagination, for example, that a particle can also be a wavelength. String theory talks about the possibility of anywhere from nine to twelve dimensions in the universe, but our minds can only visualize length, height, and depth. In other words, science now speculates about realities that are unimaginable, given the limitations of how our brains process experience. It would seem premature to rule out that science might end up confirming the paradoxes of religious mystics or the notion that the world that greets our five senses might not be all there is. Science is built on the assumption now that the world is far more than what we can see, hear, and touch. To say that faith, and even religion, is fundamentally opposed to science suggests that you have an unexamined and irrational grudge against one or the other.

As Karen Armstrong has pointed out in *The Case for God*, the whole battle between those who want to prove or disprove the existence of God misses the point. It's less about proof than practice. As the life of Jesus illustrates, the idea is to do good, not to wait for intellectual certainty. Good begets good.

Science can be an encouragement to those on this path, for studies have shown that those who consistently choose good can *evolve* to become different, better people. Does this mean as a species we could ultimately become more like the spiritual figures—Jesus, Buddha, Muhammad, Socrates, and all the others—who have taught various paths toward a higher understanding? I don't see why not.

Epigenetics, for me, represents a fact-based, scientific *analogy* for the sort of religious creeds that have connected everyday choices to grave and lasting spiritual consequences: the doctrine of karma for the Buddhists, or the Christian notion that the smallest choices in life have eternal implications. Science now says that the most seemingly insignificant habits—the accumulation of an individual's free choices, day after day—will register in the behavior of that individual's epigenome, which can eventually encode good habits into the behavior of future generations. What you choose to do, from day to day, actually does matter, and is, in a sense, permanently recorded in your own genetic structure. Choices that might seem inconsequential can have larger consequences than might be apparent in the life of the person making those choices.

Humanity's freedom to choose good represents, for me, *the* fundamental truth of life, partly because my own good fortune has depended so heavily on the choices other good people have made on my behalf. Many kind people have lifted my burdens onto their shoulders, helped heal my wounds, and taken me by the hand to safer shores. That force of good in all of us cannot be ignored any more than we can deny our own evil inclinations.

Are we able to choose to do more good than evil? I believe that if this is possible, it can change the fate of humankind.

This book is a result of my exploration of how individuals can align themselves with good through daily choice. My thesis is inordinately simple. If we better understand who we are as human beings, we should be able to make better choices in our lives.

So, with all of this in mind, I've felt compelled to explore and understand who I am, where I stand, how I've gotten here, and what's required of *me*, after having been given so much. The message of this book is to challenge others to seek answers to the sort of questions I've been asking myself since I first encountered evil as a child. Why are we here; what are we to do with this time we've been given on the planet? Why are we drawn into evil when so much of our nature seeks goodness? Why is evil still so dominant in the way the world works, when it seems so obvious that being good brings much richer rewards?

There's an old Cherokee legend that encapsulates much of the wisdom we need in our time. The story has it that an old Indian is telling his grandson about the battle that goes on inside people. "The battle is between two wolves inside us. One is Evil. It is anger, envy, jealousy, sorrow, regret, greed, arrogance, self-pity, guilt, resentment, inferiority, lies, false pride, superiority, and ego. The other is Good. It is joy, peace, love, hope, serenity, humility, kindness, benevolence, empathy, generosity, truth, faith, and compassion." The grandson asks, "Which wolf wins?" The old Indian replies, "The one you feed."

Over the next portion of this book I'm going to dwell for quite a while on how prevalent and common evil was in my experience of childhood, and I'm going to descend into the story of the increasingly horrific experiences I had. After having said how important free choice is, how crucially we need to keep choosing the good, I offer my childhood as a lesson in how nearly impossible it is to escape evil. Nothing in my experience or thinking for many years, even as an adult, has enabled me to understand why evil should be so pervasive; that thought sent me down a path to understand how this could be.

I have suggested already how science confirms the wisdom embedded in traditional religious injunctions to be good. Yet for many years, especially when I was suffering under the evil of Romania's ruling elite, I had no way of comprehending why ordinary people so quickly descend into viciousness. Questions about the nature of evil and good have taken me a lifetime to answer. Flashbacks flood into my mind as I sit in the Chautauqua amphitheater listening to Jared Jacobson's organ, the largest outdoor instrument of its kind in the world, booming out an opening hymn for Sunday morning's assembly. Often Barbara and I try to find seats just outside the protection of the amphitheater's roof, in a sitting area nestled under the shade of a tall oak tree in the open air. When the organ gives way to a choir of 150 singers, I gaze up at patches of blue sky and white clouds and give my attention to the nondenominational service. With my thoughts on my first encounters with evil as a child in Romania, it seems appropriate that Dr. Joan Brown Campbell, our resident minister and the head of the religion department at Chautauqua, quotes from Psalm 56: "Be merciful unto me, O God: for man would swallow me. Mine enemies would daily swallow me up: For they be many that fight against me." And then: "Blessed is the man that walkest not in the counsel of the ungodly nor standeth in the way of the sinners, nor sitteth in the seat of the scornful." Blessed indeed, because the scornful do seem to keep multiplying.

Her words from the Psalm pierce me with painful memories, because I became obsessed with evil at a young age and therefore have struggled to understand the nature of it all my life. Listening and gazing up at the sky, my mind tumbles back to Europe and the horrors that took me by surprise as a child in Romania.

# CHAPTER 1

# SEEING EVIL FOR WHAT IT IS

THE DAY THEY TOOK MY FATHER AWAY IN 1941 MUST HAVE felt like any other day. I was a little two-year-old, full of fun, living with my brother, Costa, and my grandparents in the Romanian village of Lipova in Transylvania, where Romania shares its border with Hungary. My parents, still in Bucharest, the capital of Romania, had sent us there for our safety. So when the police arrested Rica Georgescu at his home, I was far away, probably playing with toy soldiers in my grandfather's enormous library or helping my brother water the rose garden. On that particular day, I likely felt safe, happy to be living in that little village. By sending us to Lipova when World War II began, my parents had hoped to shield us from Hitler and the Romanian fascists. As it turned out, they kept us from seeing our father being led away to prison.

So, in a strange way, the day of my father's arrest may have been quite happy and pleasant for me. Soon enough, I was told about it, and the long puzzlement of my life began. But my first thought, when our mother described how he'd been taken to prison, may have been that I couldn't immediately see any difference in my world. My father had been gone from my life already. All of this took place in 1941, when the war was just getting started, and Costa and I had been living without him for weeks, maybe months.

According to my mother's recollection, she arrived from Bucharest and sat us in the kitchen to say our father had been arrested. Even at that age, I must have felt my mother's warmth and charm. When I was older, I recognized how extraordinary she was with her intelligent eyes, a penetrating gaze, and a talent for immediately seeing into another person's character. She also had a gift for conversation, and she used it to help my father many times while he was in prison. Obviously, at that age, I was blind to her heroism. I can recall my mother now from my encounters with her as a teen and an adult. Looking back, I know my impression of her, then, was of the woman she became as she rose to the challenge we all faced.

"Did he do something bad?" Costa asked.

"No. He's a very good man."

"But if he's been good, how could they take him away?"

I didn't know it at the time, but I would keep asking that question for the rest of my life.

"Because *they* are bad people," she said. "Don't worry. He'll be fine. He'll be free someday."

Even though I was too young to understand my father's arrest, I believed her. And she was right, although at that age, my hopes had a shaky foothold. As I got a little older, I had a simplistic, youthful assurance that good and evil were easily recognized and that eventually God would intervene, in this world, on behalf of the good. Therefore my father would be saved. My faith foretold a happy outcome for my family because we were good. I didn't see that my father was persecuted *because* he was good.

These earliest experiences of the darker side of human nature were showing me one of its most subtle and significant characteristics: evil is often hard to see, especially when your personal life doesn't appear to be immediately disrupted by it. Evil can be at its worst, and most dangerous, when you don't even know it's changing you and your life. In a sense, my first encounters with evil were in situations where it was reorganizing my world and I wasn't even aware of it—a situation I was to face again and again both in Europe and America. It's a fundamental challenge of human life: to choose against evil, you first have to recognize it.

Living apart from one's parents was not an unusual arrangement in our family. It was becoming something of a tradition for us. We Georgescu men came of age through exile and separation from our families, against a backdrop of war and political turmoil. Much earlier, with social upheaval on the horizon in Romania, my father's own parents knew how vulnerable the Balkan states would be in the event of war, so they'd sent my father to a boarding school, Warwick Academy, outside London. His full name was Valeriu, but it had morphed into a more intimate Valerica, shortened eventually to the nickname Rica. He grew up in England, developed a British accent, and came to identify completely with the values of personal liberty and individual rights. He was raised to believe in freedom, alongside children of the British upper class. Although he spent most of his youth in Great Britain, far from his parents, he intended to return to Romania after the turmoil of the First World War subsided.

With some of the richest oil reserves in Europe, Romania then had a lot in common with Saudi Arabia today. As a student, my father knew he could use that oil as his ticket home, so he studied petroleum engineering at the University of Birmingham. When he graduated, he fulfilled his dream by taking a job with Standard Oil in Romania, assigned to manage oil fields in Ploesti. He commuted to his work from nearby Bucharest, a sophisticated metropolis known as the Paris of Eastern Europe. He hadn't been there for long before he met a young woman named Lygia Bocu, just back from the Sorbonne in Paris. At the time she was being courted by Prince Nicolae, the younger brother of King Carol II, who ruled the nation more or less as a figurehead, in the manner of British royalty. Even though, if she'd surrendered to this romance, she could have become something like the Romanian equivalent of Princess Di. She chose a life with my father, a mere oil executive.

A cynic might say she was a clever lady; she chose the *real* power. Others who knew her better would have recognized it as true love. My brother, Costa, was born in 1934. As a young man he would turn out to be serious, brilliant, bookish, and pious to the point of wanting to be a priest at an early age. I was something else entirely. Born in 1939, a skinny imp full of antics, a little clown, I was the one with the unruly imagination, the playful one my mother showered with love. When war began, my father's Romanian job with Standard Oil of New Jersey (later Esso and Exxon) kept him in Bucharest. My parents sent Costa and me to live with my maternal grandparents in Lipova.

My family, on my mother's side, was intimately connected to what was going on at the highest levels of government. We were virtually a part of the royal retinue, even though our mother's lineage traced back to peasant stock, not the aristocracy. We had deep ties with the Peasant Party, whose leader, Iuliu Maniu, had headed the Romanian government until King Carol II set up a dictatorship in 1937. As the second world war started, Ion Antonescu took over, supported by the Iron Guard, a fascist movement that assassinated its opponents and seized power just in time to align Romania with the Germans. Maniu went into hiding and established connections between members of the Peasant Party and the Allied forces, especially England and America.

Willingly drawn into the resistance, my father, with Maniu, helped set up a radio transmitter that became a key link between the British in Turkey and Romanian nationalists aligned with the Allies. That radio was crucial to an effort to organize an uprising. The transmitter looked like a pile of spare parts, but when certain wires were connected, it worked perfectly. But a Romanian girl who learned about the radio by sleeping with a British agent in Istanbul, had been sleeping, as well, with a member of the Gestapo. She tipped off the Germans about the transmitter.

My father was arrested and charged with treason, and he spent the rest of the war imprisoned at Malmaison—the Bad House— still working clandestinely with the OSS to defeat the fascists. He was, in fact, a resistance leader from his cell during those years. All of this may sound thrilling, but I remember only the great void of his absence—the withdrawal of someone who could have carried me on his shoulders, taught me to fish, play soccer, and then, later, to fly a plane and drive a car. He could do all of that and more, but we had so little time together when I was growing up that he had few chances to tutor me about anything. During the war years, I got to know him mostly from his photographs.

My mother, as well, became a distant figure, spending so much time in Bucharest, working secretly with my father to help free her people. It was the beginning of a pattern that never went away: The grand opera of my parents' life always seemed to take place somewhere far from mine.

As someone working for an American company, my father would have been killed if Antonescu, the Romanian fascist dictator, hadn't been so circumspect about all possible outcomes to the conflict. He represented himself as loyal to the Germans, but he hedged his bets by keeping my father alive. It was a shrewd way of showing the Americans how much he had sympathized with the Allies, all along, in the event of a German defeat. Meanwhile, my father continued helping the resistance with Frank Wisner Sr., an American OSS operative who would emerge later to become one of the four founders of the Central Intelligence Agency. My mother smuggled messages into my father's cell, on slips of paper hidden in cigarette packs and matchbooks, and then she memorized whatever he told her for delivery to Wisner and the Romanian nationalists plotting a coup against the German forces. It was an effort aided by the Allied intelligence network based in Turkey, led by Wisner.

Antonescu's shrewd intellectual duplicity reflected Romania's uncertain identity and position in the world. On a vacation in Syria a number of years ago, I finally achieved a clear, simple vision of Romania's predicament. Our guide was telling us about the fate of his country, how for thousands of years the Persians, Romans, Turks, Greeks, Crusaders, and the usual assortment of barbarians had all trudged through Syria on the way to somewhere else. As a convenient stop along the Silk Route to the Mediterranean, it became a kind of way station between East and West. Our guide summed it up: "Everyone goes through Syria to get to the sea." With few exceptions, the Syrians simply adapt to whomever has the most influence over them at any given time, because they are tiny and ill equipped to defend their borders from greater powers. Foreigners were welcome to fight other foreigners on Syrian soil. Who were the Syrians to say no?

It's the curse of the country at the crossroads, and I realized this was precisely Romania's curse. It was one of many countries in the world serving mostly as a route, a corridor, between empires. Antonescu, like others before him, was being realistic about his nation's situation. In his view, Romania didn't have the power to say no to Hitler or Stalin or—deeper into the past—the Austro-Hungarians and Turks. Romania was a pawn on a chessboard with powerful rulers installed on squares far from Bucharest, beyond its borders. Yet Romania was even more than a passage. It had something Hitler wanted to fuel his war machine: huge oil reserves.

So, without making excuses for the man, it is understandable that Antonescu may have had a reason to behave the way he did. At one point, he reprieved my father literally from a firing squad and, at another time, refused to surrender him, against Hitler's orders to deport him to Berlin for interrogation. Antonescu protested that my father was a Romanian citizen and Germany had no right to arrest him. That was Antonescu's privilege. He won that argument, and my father survived, yet again. All this time, with Antonescu's full cooperation, Germans streamed across Romania, pausing briefly, at their discretion, on their way into Russia. Antonescu was a master of *realpolitik*, and although he was loathed by many of the people, he may have simply been doing what he thought was in Romania's best interests.

When I was older and still a child in Romania, it seemed so easy to single out the bad ones: those people who mouthed destructive political agitprop, children who informed on their parents, and the militia who arrived in the night. Yet now, so many decades later, I look back and realize Antonescu himself represents the *real* conundrum of a human being's darker impulses: a man of so many mixed motives, good and bad, that he was easy to both defend and despise. In his brief rule over the country, he demonstrated how difficult and intractable evil can become, and how hard to escape, because it's so often woven into the behavior of someone doing things absolutely essential for survival. On one hand, in his mind, much of the evil he did may have been inescapable because it actually allowed Romania to survive as a sovereign nation. On the other hand, most of what he permitted was clearly evil. There were more than 300,000 Jews and Gypsies, who'd been destined for the extermination camps, to testify against him.

At the time, in that chronic state of political crisis, these horrific events came to seem like ugly necessities to many Romanian people, as they had for the Germans who fell under Hitler's sway. The pressures of the day blinded people to the fact that the ends cannot justify the means, that establishing and maintaining political and economic order couldn't justify the evil of what Antonescu was doing. Another leader might have been able to see the prospect of ethnic cleansing as an atrocity and face squarely the challenge of maintaining some kind of political integrity at great expense, but Antonescu was focused primarily on his own power. And all those who went along with him were undoubtedly clinging to the benefits of milking the system he created. To do that, they had to blind themselves to the evil they were doing, to see it as simply an ugly necessity. The ugly necessity is never simply a necessity. It's a choice.

Antonescu may have sought protection from the Allies with his Machiavellian maneuvers, yet he proved his loyalty to the Germans with assassinations, persecutions, and cleansings. In one instance, he let the Iron Guard break into a prison where they seized and shot dozens of people suspected of plotting against them. Another time, they raided a Jewish ghetto in Bucharest and killed hundreds of men, women, and children, hanging their bodies on hooks in a slaughterhouse.

Meanwhile, my father was held under low security, thanks to his skillful manipulation of his captors. He arranged for the chief jailer's two girlfriends to obtain jobs in the oil industry, which gave him the freedom to operate while in prison. As the unofficial dean of the place, my father was able to keep books and papers, had a sitting room in addition to his cell, and had the ability to communicate with other prisoners—partisans, British Army officers, a whole crew of people sympathetic to the resistance. At one point, he had the company of sixty Americans who had been shot down over the oil fields. Almost all Allied prisoners of war were held at Malmaison prison.

My mother, working just as hard as an agent for the resistance, would visit him in prison as his courier. Early on, when she arrived, she had to endure intense interrogations. But as time went on, she brought fresh clothing and supplies to everyone, as well as pots of food and boxes of apple pie for the Americans. She was such a frequent guest that they would let her in and forget about her. She was able to smuggle news and plans and ideas back and forth between the prison and resistance headquarters in Istanbul.

In 1943, midway through my father's imprisonment, our grandmother called us into the rose garden and said she'd just gotten wonderful news from Bucharest. That incident is still one of my most vivid memories from early childhood. Our mother had contacted a Gypsy fortune-teller in the mountains to ask about our father's fate. The fortune-teller had requested something owned by my father, and she'd dispatched a driver to deliver one of his handkerchiefs to the Gypsy. With it in hand, the fortune-teller phoned our mother and said our father would be freed on August 23, 1944. He would be alive and well, and we would be reunited.

None of us had any way of knowing the Gypsy would be right. Yet, as soon as I heard this news, I was overjoyed. Without hesitation, I believed it would come true. I suppose partly because my mother and grandmother and brother believed it, but also because it felt true. Absolutely convinced that our father would survive the war and be released, on a Sunday morning, we celebrated his freedom while he was still being held, sharing hot milk and special cakes our grandmother had baked. As it turned out, we were right to celebrate. A year later, on that exact date, our father was released.

Skeptics would dismiss our confident hope as a minor case of magical thinking. Yet our unquestioning faith in the good news even now strikes me as something more than that. It was a willingness to trust in something we couldn't explain or understand. We felt its veracity—something real had been communicated to us, and we accepted it as a gift. Even now, I don't think I was wrong to feel the joy I felt and still feel now, after all these years. I tell you about this particular event, not simply because the predictions just happened to come to pass, but because I still feel something more was at work.

After a year of planning, organizing partisans inside and outside Malmaison, the plot to overthrow Antonescu culminated in a successful coup. In June 1944, when the Allies secured Normandy, it was time to act. They mobilized sympathizers inside the government, army, and in key industries. King Michael, Carol's son and successor, spearheaded the uprising.

On August 23, 1944, all the key people in the government and army, who had been plotting secretly with the resistance, emerged and arrested Antonescu. The coup succeeded in Bucharesti without bloodshed. (After the war, though, Antonescu was convicted of collaboration with the Nazis and executed.) At this point, the resistance took over the palace, with troops dispatched to Ploesti—my father's oil fields—where they began to drive German allies out of the country. Lines of communication were cut, bridges were closed, railroad stations seized, and the oil fields were reclaimed—all within a matter of hours. The prisoners at Malmaison were set free. It was Bastille Day in Romania.

Risking his life, King Michael addressed the nation over the airwaves, saying that he was establishing a democracy. Romanians rose up and liberated their country, fighting bravely, losing 150,000 soldiers in eight months. But, as it turned out, all those deaths were for nothing. Only a few years later, the Soviets moved in and Romania sank into subservience and fear once again, this time for forty-five years.

As Barabara and I walk back to our house after the morning church service, I reflect on how far apart the world of occupied Romania was from the American principles and culture that have made Chautauqua possible. With its tradition of education, imbued with a deep respect for religion and spirituality, Chautauqua has roots extending far back into its history, roots which grew out of the idea of making a fresh start. In Europe the past is everywhere, in the architecture, the memories, the religion, the politics. The past is inescapable. But America and Chautauqua both share in this spirit of starting over with a clean slate.

The pattern of America's emergence was recapitulated in my own life. The corruption of European politics was left behind for the fresh and seemingly innocent opportunities of American soil. Of course, innocence is the first thing to be lost in the evolution of political freedom. Pick any presidential race over the past half century and you'll see how the freedom to vote gets warped by special interests and the same kind of self-deception that laid the groundwork for so much suffering in Romania. Yet Chautauqua is actually a good argument for American exceptionalism. Our political system makes a place such as this possible, and it's a crucible for new thinking, new hopes, new dreams—new possibilities that are fundamentally good and essentially American. As corrupt as our political system has become, on so many levels, it is still an expression of the highest and most honorable values. There's goodness built into our system in a way that largely wasn't the case in human history until America emerged. Even though Chautauqua may seem like simply a thinking person's theme park, an alternative vacation for those who still like to read and think, it's actually a place where people struggle quietly to understand and act on the most urgent issues of the day. It's a laboratory where liberty and hope keep themselves alive and untainted, where they refuse to lose their innocence, and where no one ever suggests that the ends will justify the means.

Like everything else in America, Chautauqua had humble beginnings. Yet its first assembly was a huge success, with 20,000 people in attendance. After the first summer of 1874 and the following year, Rev. Vincent invited a friend, who happened to be president of the United States at the time, to visit the camp. President Ulysses S. Grant must have taken a long time to reply. Vincent's partner, Miller, who also knew President Grant, scrambled to order a prefabricated house for him, which was built in Ohio and then delivered in pieces, by rail and steamboat, for reassembly on a tent platform. It was a clever ploy on Miller's part; he took up residence in the house after Grant left. In the following years, as reports of the president's attendance spread, more and more people thronged to the lake, and Chautauqua's houses and buildings went up rapidly, built on the old tent platforms.

Thomas Edison, one of the inventors of the lightbulb, came to the Athenaeum Hotel to see one of the first public structures in America to utilize the new, mysterious phenomenon of electricity. His pals Henry Ford and Harvey Firestone would spend days with Edison discussing and debating issues of their time. Edison loved Chautauqua and became a familiar resident, having married Miller's daughter, Mina.

The lecture series became famous soon after the amphitheater was built. Susan B. Anthony, a leading suffragist, argued women's right to vote from this very platform. By 1900, Chautauqua had founded the largest book correspondence school in the world. They counted more than 800,000 members. Slowly, arts moved in as well. The New York Symphony Orchestra, which later merged with the New York Philharmonic, played there in the summers of the 1920s. It was where FDR made Chautauqua famous with his "I Hate War" speech and George Gershwin composed some of his best music while sequestered in one of the claustrophobic wooden practice shacks. Then came the Opera House, generously endowed by the Norton family of Chicago, as well as the repertory theater and Jean-Pierre Bonnefoux's dance company.

A first-time visitor here may be taken aback. We're a bit frayed at the edges. There's always some paint in need of scraping, and our village has a slightly frozen-in-time quality that can seem a bit unreal to the newbie. On the surface, many spots in our little questing community seem as if they haven't been touched up much in the past hundred years or so. Those staying at the Athenaeum, our grand old hotel on the lake, will discover rooms only now almost completely modernized and remodeled.

Walk down any street and you'll see one porch after another, with wicker furniture, rockers, and vases full of gladiolus and, here's the key, people sitting together, eating, drinking, talking, listening, and thinking. It's a form of community diametrically opposite to the one I suffered through as a child, a world where ideology led to divisions, strife, war, and death. As a child, I watched Romania endure a death struggle precisely because it lacked those qualities so ubiquitous here at Chautauqua. Our community's unique, eccentric charm takes you quietly by surprise, offering one small epiphany after another. This place really is proof that the evils of the past can be left behind for the sake of a new beginning—a life dedicated to good.

---

I had an inkling of this truth in my own childhood, during a brief idyllic and joyous time after my father's release from prison. My brother and I returned to Bucharest, and I finally got to know my parents. I experienced two years as the son of a celebrated couple, heroes of the war. I'm convinced that a confidence in good, a faith in its presence at the heart of our best motives and behavior, depends for most people on being able to witness it in the character of one's parents. Shielded and nourished by good parents, you instinctively feel the good in others and the world around you. If your parents are good, it will be hard to shake a sense that goodness is the heart of life, even when you don't see nearly as much of it as you'd like in the behavior and events around you. Just being a good person is the greatest gift a human being can give to his or her child, because children learn to depend on that goodness. They absorb it over the years and, at some point, begin to rely on it in themselves. Having been blessed with good people for parents and extraordinary grandparents and brother, for much of my life I've never doubted the central role of goodness in the human character.

Almost immediately after being released, our father borrowed a small airplane from King Michael and flew himself to Lipova. He landed it in a field, where a friend picked him up and drove him to our grandfather's house in the center of the village. He wanted to share with us the exhilaration of freedom he'd just experienced, so, that same day, he bundled us up and drove us to the field and told us to climb into the plane. On a hot August day, with the fragrance of a summer field around us, he started the propeller and took off, giving us a view of our newly liberated country, from thousands of feet in the air—showing us little toy houses on hills, a carpet of trees, the landscape like a rumpled bed. He took us beyond the clutch of gravity. For years, my parents told the story of what happened after we came back down: I climbed out of the plane and tugged at my father's trousers and told him I wanted to fly planes when I grew up. On the way back, he let me sit on his lap in the car, pretending to steer, and back at my grandfather's house I said I'd changed my mind. I wanted to be a chauffeur. The world was suddenly full of endless possibilities, thanks to my father.

After saying a long goodbye to our grandparents, he flew us home to Bucharest. We lived there for two years with our parents. In the first winter together, one of the longest blizzards Bucharest had ever witnessed, the snow piled nearly as high as the sill of my second-story bedroom window. So I dragged a toboggan up the stairs and opened the window for a long slide down the drift. It was magical, something from a storybook, riding that powder to a cushioned landing in our yard. The whole two years felt that way, as if I had been singled out to be included in a world of privilege I'd never known before. My father continued to let me "drive" whenever he could. Sitting on his lap and steering, I acquired enough premature confidence in my own maturity that once, when I was six, I remember stealing a cigar from my father's humidor and lighting it upstairs in a closet. I managed not to burn down the house, yet I was sick the rest of the day. That caper was indicative of how bold we felt, as the children of these two particular people, at this point in history, in this secure place. We knew they were heroes, special, and this gave us both courage and a certain illusory sense of privilege. My father's history had shown me how he was able to do nearly anything he set *his* mind to, and my pride in my parents was a powerful resource, a reservoir of confidence. Now, finally, their freedom and power involved me. It gave me a self-assurance that was tempered by my knowledge that everything could be lost, in a moment, at any time. Someone could simply knock on the door, and our whole world would disappear. Sure enough, evil was soon to take control of our lives again.

———

For most of those two happy years in Bucharest, my parents hoped Romania would remain free. Along with the rest of the underground, they had wanted Britain or America to send military forces into Romania, to prevent the Russians from moving in as the German forces collapsed. But it didn't happen. We were told later that if only a couple hundred British paratroopers had dropped into Romania in 1944, it would have made Russia cautious enough to stay away and thus would have transformed the fate of our country over the next four decades. Yet, despite pleas from my father and others in the new government, the British and Americans kept their distance, and the Russians were able to move into the country unopposed, quietly infiltrating Romanian society.

My father knew the momentum of events was not on our side when he went to Moscow in September 1944 to help craft an armistice, which would allow Romania to pull out of the war. Afterward, he was deeply disappointed with the terms. He saw how the Soviets viewed Romania as a conquered enemy, an ally of Hitler, similar to Mussolini's Italy. This didn't bode well. All of this was a direct consequence of Antonescu's tactical duplicity. He'd done a good job of convincing everyone he was freely joining forces with the Nazis. Yet, this ignored everything my father and others had done at the risk of their lives on Antonescu's watch. The Allies could have stepped forward and pointed this out to the Russians. But they didn't. My father, and others, felt betrayed that the West didn't speak up about how much Romania had done on behalf of the Allied cause, helping to undermine the fascists.

Over the next two years, power continued to shift throughout Central Europe. Romanian advocates of democracy, like my parents, were still hoping the West would influence Russia to keep its hands off Romania. Everyone in Romania was watching and listening, as the war in Europe neared its conclusion. The Big Three Allied leaders—Churchill, Roosevelt, and Stalin—met at Yalta. Their negotiations were kept secret and the full impact of their agreement was not made public.

Still in the dark but suspecting the worst, a year later in 1946 my father attended a crucial meeting in Bucharest. All the country's leaders were there: Maniu, then serving for a second time as prime minister; King Michael; and my father, because of his strong ties to America in his role with Standard Oil, his service in the resistance, and his perfect English. They had been granted an audience with W. Averell Harriman, the American diplomat, who was a central player in determining the shape of postwar Europe.

During his visit to Romania, Harriman stayed at my parents' house and was treated as a friend and ally, although my parents were careful not to ask him the sort of questions that would be raised at the meetings.

Maniu was concerned about Russia's influence over our country. Having proven their heroism in the final stages of liberation, the Romanian military would be willing to fight Russia, to preserve Romania's freedom. But Maniu and the others needed to know where America stood. He informed Harriman that certain details had been leaked from the conference at Yalta, and Romania believed Harriman had helped Roosevelt design a secret agreement to divide Eastern Europe with the Iron Curtain, setting up free nations to the west and Soviet satellites to the east. Where would Romania be, once this land had been divvied up?

"We are ready to fight," Maniu said. "The Romanian army is mobilized and armed. If what we've heard is true, say so. We'll stay on alert and defend ourselves. If you are willing to guarantee our safety, then we'll disarm. We'll focus on rebuilding our country, but we need to know it's safe to do that."

He got no response from Harriman. So he said, "If it's impossible to respond without violating whatever agreements you have, then say nothing. We'll do what we must. But if you can tell us what happened, please do it."

Harriman took a moment and then said, "It's understandable that there should be rumors about what was said at Yalta. But these notions floating around about 'spheres of influence' in Europe are absolutely false. I spoke to President Roosevelt myself immediately after Yalta, and he told me all that was decided. America and Britain will stand behind Romania, and we'll guarantee your right to free elections."

Maniu wanted an even more unequivocal response: "You're saying we can disarm without fear of the Russians?"

"Absolutely," Harriman said. "You have my word."

Romania disarmed.

Within two years, the Russians had taken control of a defenseless country, and neither the United States nor any other Western nation offered any resistance. It's almost impossible to imagine that Harriman was unaware of his own duplicity. After all, he was a top aide to Roosevelt and present at the Yalta conference.

In later years, my father often tried to contact Harriman in New York to ask him directly what had happened at the talks, but Harriman never agreed to a meeting.

Maybe he truly couldn't imagine what horror he was about to endorse with his false assertion. I believe he had some motivation, grounded in postwar statecraft between the United States and the Soviet Union, and like Antonescu, he simply did what needed to be done and looked the other way. But the possibility that he actually didn't know the implications of his actions, in some ways, is even more troubling. Making a moral choice requires you to see the true nature of your behavior, and human beings are highly skilled at ignoring the reality and consequences of their own actions. At times, maybe it is impossible for an individual to fully realize he's doing evil.

Most likely Harriman made what could only have been a conscious choice to deceive the Romanian leadership, with disastrous results. He lied. The moral ambiguity of Harriman's actions reminds me of how my grandparents insisted we stay in Romania, despite the political darkness surrounding them. Both situations led to dire outcomes, and yet the choices couldn't have been further apart, in moral terms.

In the 1950s, my mother wrote a first-person article about our family, telling the story of what happened to my brother and me as children in Romania. I don't know if she ever published it, although at one point I'm sure many magazines might have bid on the story. Our family had become the cynosure for news organizations around the world by this time. For some reason, she may have thought better of the effort and put her thin sheaf of memories away. She'd typed it on onionskin, the sort of paper writers would use in the day of typewriters to make it easier to erase and correct mistakes, although she didn't seem to have erased much. These thirty sheets of paper have a fragile, transparent quality now, and you can almost feel the tremor of her anguished hope in your fingertips as you hold the pages. She wrote the story before she had any idea what would happen, ultimately, to her children in Romania. She wrote it as a plea for the world to stand as a witness to what was being done to Romania. The words have faded a bit since she typed it, but her emotions haven't been diluted.

Barbara has stored this manuscript for many years, along with other artifacts of my personal history, in a zippered garment case under our bed. She pulled it out not long ago and showed me the piece. Glancing through my mother's story, I noticed one small aside: during that brief, happy two-year hiatus in our lives, the eye of the storm, as it were, in Bucharest, my father had suggested sending the children away to America for schooling.

Given what was going to happen to us in Romania, it actually might have been the best possible choice, almost prescient on his part. It would have set up a wonderful coincidence of good fortune for all of us, if my mother and brother and I had gone to live in America, because shortly afterward, my father would be summoned to New York City by his employer, and we would have been reunited at exactly the right historical moment. Our move to America would have achieved what my parents wanted, immediately: putting us far, far away from the political turmoil they suspected was looming, sheltering little Peter and Costa from the storm of Russian hegemony in Eastern Europe. It also would have carried on the family tradition. Rica's parents had sent him to England for schooling, safely distant from the instability of the European scene before World War One. He had grown up there, without much contact with his parents. Sending us to America would have replicated this tradition, if my father had stayed in Romania to run the oil fields.

Presumably, in this scenario, the three of us would have been reunited with my father quite often, during his extended business trips to New York as an executive for Standard Oil. All in all, it offered a reasonable way to lower the risks for at least those of us who emigrated. Yet, in her typescript, my mother goes on to describe how her parents reacted to this proposal: "Their grandparents wouldn't have it; they had grown so attached to the boys."

Clearly, my grandparents loved us too much to let us go to America, and they may have simply wanted to protect us from the unknown. They knew their homeland; they didn't know America. And yet, by drawing us into their custody, they helped set in motion everything that was to follow. I am completely certain that my grandfather had no idea that by keeping us in Lipova they were putting us at risk—even though he had to have known what was happening to Romanian society, how the Russians were moving in everywhere. In Lipova, under the Nazi occupation, our grandparents had never been at risk, so he had little reason to think this new political infiltration would put us in danger. By holding on to us and showing us all their love in the time we spent with them, they had an indelible impact on our character, setting an example and helping to shape the adults we eventually became. Yet that same love for us, ultimately, put our lives at risk.

How does this wash, in moral terms? Intentions don't count, because people must be held accountable for what they do, not what they intend. Aside from the question of how you judge it from the outside, imagine how difficult it was for my grandparents to know, for sure, the consequences of clinging to us. And that's the deepest problem: how to know your own motives, and even worse, how to know whether your intentions and actions will actually lead to good results. Could they stand back far enough to know their own motivations and understand the level of peril we faced at that moment in history? They were good people, acting out of love, and yet, as I will describe, I nearly died, as a result of this love.

It seems to me there's something cautionary in all this for anyone who employs words like *good* and *evil*. To call my grandparents evil would be absurd. And it feels just as absurd to characterize their desire to keep us in Romania as evil. To question whether their attachment to Costa and me was good or bad seems impossibly complicated and nuanced: it was good, seen from one angle, and terribly mistaken, maybe selfish, seen from another angle. It was hardly evil, and yet it led to a terrible ordeal.

What's most daunting about all of this, though, is how, when you contemplate that moment, you begin to see the difficulty of knowing, at the time we make any choice, whether that choice is good or bad in a moral sense. It may be made out of an almost desperate affection and care; but what feels absolutely right and rooted in love can turn out to be destructive and perilous.

Over the years, the more I recall Harriman's behavior, and Antonescu's, the more it has come to demonstrate how evil so often infiltrates the lives of people who believe they are trying to do good. Under the pressure of social and political forces, as well as plain old generic self-interest, when something big is about to be won or lost, evil works its way into choices through self-deception, rationalization, and denial. Instinctive behavior takes over at the expense of clarity and self-knowledge. At the root of it all was simply dishonesty. Antonescu and Harriman may have thought that a greater good was served by a lesser evil—that those who suffered in Romania mattered less than the interests they were protecting. But that doesn't excuse what they did. If they'd been honest, Romanian history, and my own life, would have been altered in incalculable ways.

At any given fork in the road, the challenge is to select the good path, and avoid the evil one. But how do you do that without knowing clearly where either path ultimately leads? Given this ambiguity, what happens, as a whole, to moral judgments of human behavior? Striving to make moral choices is hard enough as it is. Passing judgment in hindsight or from afar on the choices others make is far more difficult, if not impossible, to do with confidence. When evil actually reaches into your home and begins moving members of your family like chess pieces—when you're actually touched by it—there's no doubt about what it is.

# CHAPTER 2

# OUR UNCERTAIN MORAL NATURE

IN 1947, MY PARENTS LEFT ON WHAT SEEMED A ROUTINE business trip to New York City. They packed enough to stick around as long as Standard Oil needed my father, a couple of weeks at most, with surplus space for the presents they would buy us. Costa asked for a pullover sweater. I was even more specific. "Mommy, I want one of those baseball caps with the colored buttons on top. And lots of ice cream," I said, according to my mother's story.

Although the ice cream would have been a bit difficult to deliver, logistically, it wasn't complicated for them to be away and return for a happy reunion. Travel was simply a requirement of my father's career. So my grandparents arrived by train to act as surrogate parents for the duration of the trip. As it turned out, my parents left just before the Soviets staged a bloodless coup and assumed control of Romania. Communists had moved into various levels of business, the government, and the military. As a result, while my parents were in New York, they were declared enemies of the state and stripped of their Romanian citizenship. If they'd returned to be with us, they would have been arrested immediately.

Once again, on the surface, nothing changed, except that the weeks without my mother and father stretched into months—and then years. The family tradition of separation between parents and children was renewed, once again, in a way we'd never anticipated. The old heartache of being apart from them returned, only this time more painful because I could compare it with the happiness of our two previous years in Bucharest, when I'd sat on my father's lap, steering the car, and I'd dreamed of flying a plane. I'd seen a whole world of tantalizing possibilities open up simply because I was under the wing of these two wonderful people, these parents I was only getting to know, and now they were gone.

My grandparents assured us that somehow it would work out, but whenever I looked at Costa's face, I suspected otherwise. Soon enough, our grandparents quietly decided we should retreat to their home in Lipova and continue our schooling there. It was the same village we'd been visiting as long as we could remember, but in subtle ways it was entirely different. What we were taught in school and the way people talked became odd and unfamiliar, everything tainted by distrust and paranoia. We hesitated to say certain things and had a sense of being watched and judged, although the feeling was merely subliminal and instinctive at first. By keeping to our personal habits, our faith, and family rituals, we kept our hope and sense of identity alive.

My grandfather stood in for my father, and I sought the comfort of his strength. Staying close to him immersed me in Lipova's

Eastern Orthodox Church, a church he'd helped to restore. As a famous political figure and a respected journalist who owned his own printing press, Sever Bocu seemed almost a different breed of man. He was taciturn, dignified, and at six and a half feet, much taller than the average Romanian. (My son, Andrew, is just as tall—the gene skipped a couple of generations.) When people passed this distinguished, gray-haired gentleman in the street, their hats would come off. It wasn't just a matter of touching the brim.

A spot in the front of our church was reserved especially for my grandfather, and I quickly became a part of the ceremony. Before long I was carrying candles in elaborate services full of mystery and beauty. I remember all of it vividly: the swinging censers hanging from thin chains giving off billowing, pungent incense, as well as the shining gold-leaf artwork of our icon-covered walls, and the soft brilliant robes. When the consecrated bread was offered to the faithful, the priest always held out the first piece to my grandfather, a gesture that symbolized how much the people of our town and our entire country felt they owed him.

This pride in my family's heritage was only strengthened when I learned about an ancestor who was a national hero on the order of William Wallace in Scotland, having led a peasant rebellion against the Turks many centuries earlier. Only eight years old, I was assigned a text on Romanian history. In the seventeenth century, the Ottoman empire became our new landlord, as it were, and they took control of almost every aspect of peasant life. Christian worship was forbidden. People were allowed to store only enough food to survive. All personal freedom was curtailed. It was a foreshadowing of a fate Romania was to suffer again in the twentieth century when history repeated itself.

In the Banat, the region later governed by my grandfather, an earlier peasant leader became famous for leading an uprising when Romania was still ruled by these Turkish forces. Because the rebels wielded only pitchforks, clubs, knives, and bows, they were quickly suppressed. The Turks imprisoned or killed many who were involved. Having captured this leader, they chose to make an example of him and, to get the most out of their effort, sent emissaries to surrounding villages and towns and brought back thousands to witness the execution in the village square.

Bringing their prisoner out, they strapped him to a platform before a huge circular wheel—ten feet wide, weighing tons—made of oak planks secured with iron bands. Slowly, using horses, they dragged the wheel over his body, crushing him from his feet to his head, making sure he was alive to feel the pain as long as possible. In my history book, at the end of the story were the words, "The hero's name was Pavel Bocu." When I went home that day, I asked my grandparents and they said, yes, our family had descended from that peasant leader. The story strengthened my pride in the courage of my ancestors, although it also might have demonstrated, which was lost on me at the time, that goodness can cost a man his life.

This knowledge only solidified my innocent vision of good and evil as distinct entities: the white hats and the black hats. I was unaware of how evil works its way into view from the inside out, as it were. Unseen, it takes root in our daily lives and then slowly twists its way into the minds and hearts of those who accommodate it. At first, nothing seems to change, so subtle are the ways it can warp what people think and feel and do. I couldn't see what was right in front of me because I believed that evil was something "out there," something *other* people commit-ted, the ones who had consciously abandoned everything good. I didn't realize that evil is far more subtle and universal.

———

My grandfather drew my attention to Jesus, a far more consequential victim of a public execution, who became my hero during
those years. In hindsight, it's clear to me that a key strategy for my
emotional survival was to be completely blind to the significance
of his death. In my mind, Jesus became a kind of superman: an
invulnerable God who stood up to iniquity at all levels. The way
I envisioned him, if he'd been alive in Romania, he'd have defied
the Germans and then swept the Russians out of our land.

I realize now, of course, that this isn't the actual Jesus, or the
figure most Christians worship. It was my emotional response to
this Biblical messiah. That may have been the only way I could
face the darkness around me, by fantasizing my God into someone who would personally defend my family and me. He would
save us, not only spiritually, but also physically, in this world,
here and now. I created stories in which Jesus was the conquer-
ing hero and I was his knight with my wooden sword. All by
myself, I would enact little plays in the forest just outside our
village, at an age when most American boys would have been
playing cowboy or soldier. To me, Jesus stood for all the goodness in the world, and when he said he brought a sword, I took
him literally, imagining him the way Michelangelo did for the
*Last Judgment*, dividing the wheat from the chaff. But imagining
him right now, not in some vision of a mythic apocalypse. This
was a vision of Jesus, and of God, that sustained me for decades,
long after the ordeal of my childhood in Romania, and it was
only after repeated encounters with evil, of a far more subtle and
more seductive kind, that I found myself questioning the way I
envisioned God.

We missed our parents, but the separation of children from
parents was a patrician commonplace—a boarding school culture, in a way—and we knew this. Our father seemed to have
turned out well, growing up in England, away from his parents.

Still, this was different. Our grandparents worried about our separation from my mother and father, as the months began to add up, but they didn't burden us with their fears. They sheltered our happiness the best they could, but bit by bit this protective shell began to crack.

It started with little things. Tipping a book off a shelf in class, I would open it and find tiny slips of paper had been pasted over every mention of King Carol or King Michael. Weeks later, it escalated. Students were told to inform on people they knew who said anything against the Communist Party, including their parents, brothers, or sisters. One day my grandfather came into the kitchen and said people had confiscated his printing press.

Unfamiliar teachers replaced the ones we knew and trusted. Over dinner, my brother talked about how these teachers were working with students to spy on people in town, keeping the militia informed about any suspect behavior. Some students were forced to participate in "voluntary" work programs, and everyone was warned against engaging in "superstitious" behavior such as prayer and worship. Suddenly, people we knew, other students and adults, would turn away from us in a hallway or on a street. People walked past my grandfather now without making eye contact, let alone tipping their hats. Some of these early indications that a culture of fear had descended are now the most chilling to contemplate. Up was down, and white was black. The long heritage of heroism and leadership in our family was now, apparently, a stigma, a cause for shame.

———

It wasn't until I faced what probably seems like a minor injustice at school that the transformation around me felt like an attack.

It may seem amusingly ordinary to anyone else, looking back on it, half a century later. Yet it devastated me because it threatened more than my own personal survival. It began the long, slow fracture of my entire worldview, where good was ultimately rewarded and evil punished, and Jesus was my superhero. In a way it was deeply threatening because it showed that my belief in being rewarded for hard work and merit was fatuous. Therefore, in a sense, any effort to achieve something in life and to be good, for that matter, might amount to nothing. Evil had infiltrated even my classroom and I could now *feel* it.

The time for the annual academic competition arrived. Classes in our school vied for distinctions. I'd always been near the top of my class in academic performance, and in the early rounds, I earned the right to represent my entire class in the next stage of competition against three or four other sections of the school. We competed on a full range of subjects: history, science, arithmetic, and literature. At this stage, before the next round of competition, as an award for our achievements so far, I was to accept a prize for my entire class. The morning of the presentation, one of our principals took me aside and told me that I couldn't receive the honor I'd indisputably earned. I was from "unsound social origins," so someone else would have to take my place. It was my job to pick someone else to receive the award or it would be given to another section.

I knew immediately that none of this had anything to do with my worthiness, that it was unjust and politically motivated, part of the entire fabric of lies, denial, and manipulation that was infecting our entire society, all in the service of the ruling power. At the time, it seemed there was no way to oppose the power of these lies or the way the Communists warped the facts to strengthen their hold on us. There was no appeal. I was helpless, and my actions meant nothing.

The alarm goes off at 7:30 a.m. It doesn't ring. It chirps in an electronic way that makes me want to silence it as quickly as possible. Which, of course, is the point. Barbara looks over and says, "Time to get the girls off." I've been awake for a while already, reliving all these events from my childhood, retracing the long, gradual spiritual path of my life. But with a look around our bedroom, which is not large, but has a vaulted ceiling that always gives me a hint at the freedom of movement I feel everywhere in this village, I realize how blessed I've been since I came to America.

It's a typical morning for us in Chautauqua. Downstairs, in a pair of warm-ups and a T-shirt, I put out boxes of cereal. Our three granddaughters will be out of bed and on their way down shortly. It's just another morning, but I can't wait to see their eager, happy faces. Mackenzie is 6. Ali is 10. And Sedona is 12, going on 20. Their parents entrust them to us for a week or two every summer, a chance for us to show them our undivided devotion.

I can hear them moving, two floors up, as I open a box of Honey Nut Cheerios. Beneath the shimmering surface of this happy morning in Chautauqua, my memories swim—and I feel a deep gratitude for my life now, against the backdrop of my childhood in Romania. That past is often present in many things I do even when I'm not conscious of it. No one here is smuggling treasonous notes into a Nazi prison. No one is praying for just one more small loaf of bread to get through another day. This has to be one of the safest places on this planet, and one most dedicated to peace, cooperation, and morality.

Here in America our grandchildren live in a just world, full of the sort of order I didn't enjoy. How many of us in America are even conscious of the values built into the freedom they enjoy, the goodness inherent in the system itself? Our little decorative scheme, the red, white, and blue all over our Chautauqua home, constantly serves as a subliminal reminder of the blessings we and our family enjoy here.

The girls wander into the kitchen quietly, showered, dressed, and ready for a morning at the day camp. Unlike her younger sisters, Sedona doesn't hop out of bed on time. She loves to sleep late but gets up with the other two, because she loves camp. After breakfast, they head down to the garage for their bikes, and we help them with their helmets.

"Do I have to?" Sedona asks.

"It's the rule, honey," Barbara says. "We don't want you to get hurt."

"But my hair."

"You'll look fine."

When she turns 13 in a few months, she won't have to wear it. She's counting the days, marking them off the calendar. What a luxury to be able to focus on these civilized, privileged choices: whether or not to wear a bike helmet and when to get up in time for day camp. I rest my hand on Mackenzie's shoulder as she wobbles out of our tiny driveway on her bike and into the street. I climb onto my own bicycle and pedal behind her, not close enough to make her self-conscious, but I never let her out of my sight. Being the smallest sister, she can easily fall behind, and so many other kids are on their bikes heading the same way now. I want her to know I'm there, if she needs me, only seconds away—as a grandfather should be.

My memories of Romania aren't all bleak. One of my happiest moments returns to me as I pedal back to our house, alone. My father woke me up and led me out of our mansion on a secluded street with the name Gregoria Mora, in Bucharest.

Waiting for me on the walk was my first bicycle. Small enough for me to pedal, it didn't have training wheels. This was typical of my father, the infinite quality of his expectations. He trotted behind me down the lane, past the hedgerows, a hand on my shoulder, always there to keep me from falling. He held me up, showing me how much he cared, until I didn't need it.

---

As unapproachable as he might have seemed to someone who didn't know him, our grandfather wouldn't hesitate to cater to a little boy's emotional needs. He may have had a legendary career, yet he was as tenderhearted as anyone. As a slight, small boy of five or six, I was afraid to have my hair cut because the barber had once nicked the back of my neck with his scissors.

I remember how my grandfather walked hand in hand with me, sat beside me at the barber's, resting his hand on my arm as I winced, listening to the scissors whispering around my ears. He may have been pious and dignified, a legendary freedom fighter risking his life for the sake of his country, but he was a deeply compassionate man who, if anything, felt the suffering of others more intensely than most of us. Accordingly, I loved him with a deep respect, admiration, even awe—all at arm's length. There was an Old World formality and distance in our relationship unlike the casual warmth and friendship I share with my granddaughters.

Years later, when I was an adult, I visited my parents where they were living in Geneva, Switzerland, and my father pointed out to me, a few miles away from their apartment, the building where my grandfather negotiated with the Allies on a peace treaty at the end of World War I. That's all he told me. Here's how Vasile Bogdan, a Romanian historian, fills in a few of the genuinely heroic details:

At the beginning of 1918 Sever Bocu and other important personalities from Transylvania established, in Iasi, the new "Committee of the Romanian from Austria-Hungary" with the aim of going to Paris to sustain politically the union of the Romanian provinces. The journey to Paris was a long nightmare, as he had to travel with a false passport across half a continent devastated by war. When he gets first to Odessa and then to Kiev, the cities were under German occupation, and he was running the risk of being arrested and deferred to the Austro-Hungarian authorities and executed. From Kiev he goes to Moscow and St. Petersburg, which were experiencing the Bolshevik Revolution. Through incredible hardship he manages to reach Finland and then Sweden where, embarking on a British ship he leaves for Britain. After another ten days in London, he arrives in Paris, as he noted in his Memoirs: . . . "I had done this journey in the Apocalypse, from Iasi to Paris in 87 days."

My reaction was that it might have been easier, although a bit less dramatic, to get from Romania to Paris by simply drawing a straight line on the map from the Banat to the City of Lights, but that route must have been impassable, politically. This account makes clear how my grandfather's life had already become a legend to the people of Romania, and he seemed to live constantly within the confines of his public persona, even in his bearing with us. In my earliest days, I'd always sensed that my grandfather was an important person. My grandparents were not only the wealthiest people in Lipova; they were the most prominent and, until the coming of the Communists, the most widely respected. As a leader of the Peasant Party, and for a time governor of our region, my grandfather was a national political figure. Thanks in part to his work in Paris when the old Austro-Hungarian Empire was dissolved, Transylvania and our home district of the Banat became part of the new Romania. Grandfather was repeatedly elected to parliament, was appointed to several Romanian cabinets, and later served as a representative of Romania in Paris and Geneva.

Between the wars, Romania enjoyed a brief era of prosperity and democracy. Under a constitutional monarchy, during the 1920s, Romania made progress toward land reform, the expansion of civil liberties, and the modernization of the economy. Sever Bocu was associated with all these advances. And when, in the 1930s, Romania took several long steps backward, thanks both to the specter of her powerful fascist neighbors and King Carol's inability to resist the lure of dictatorship, Sever Bocu resisted all these trends in his writing and his statesmanship.

---

On a chilly May night in Lipova, in the house where I had been living, still awaiting my parents' return from America, I awoke as someone grabbed my shoulders and yanked the sheets from my bed. The glaring light from a lantern stung my eyes as he snapped, "Get up and get dressed."

I could make out three officers in jackboots. The fear I saw in Costa's face unnerved me. Only eight years old, I admired my brother. Throughout our ordeal so far, he'd lived up to his usual posture of stubborn hope and defiance. Now he looked helpless and stricken. Even Costa couldn't protect me. Still, we had our grandfather to defend us. He would stop this.

"When you're done, come to your grandparents' bedroom," the officer said, in a commanding but matter-of-fact tone, as if he'd been living with us for months. We dressed, the socks shaking in our hands as we aimed our toes into them.

When they led us down the hall and through the doorway into the master bedroom, I saw eight uniformed people standing in that room, all of them in those jackboots. They had thrown their guns on the bed. We'd seen them in the past, in the streets of Lipova, where they used to acknowledge us with a nod. After all, everyone in that town knew who we were.

Until now, we'd considered these intruders decent, ordinary people who simply wanted to get along with whomever happened to be in power. They had families. They wanted to survive. It was smarter for them to keep their heads down and submit to the new bosses than to risk everything by speaking out. We, too, had learned to be very cautious about what we said and how we answered questions in school. Yet now none of them would look at us directly.

Much of this I remember vaguely, as I was too young to register the larger political meaning of what was happening or to even recognize, physically, what was taking place. My brother, Costa, some eight years after these events, in his early twenties, wrote down a detailed account of our lives in Romania. His manuscript, like my mother's, rested under the bed in our Manhattan apartment where Barbara has stored everything about my childhood. In presenting this scene, and in several other places throughout this book, I've consulted his story, rich with specifics, thanks to his prodigious memory.

"Why are you so impatient? I would have opened the door," my grandmother scolded the officers. Thinking back on that criticism now, it's almost funny, as if she were talking to one of us. Oddly enough, they put up with it. Even in this horrible situation, it was impossible not to respect and fear her. Even these uniformed men found themselves honoring this stoic old woman's reputation.

There was a story everyone knew about our grandmother.

Near the end of World War II, in 1944, when the Nazi domination of Romania collapsed and our father was freed from detention, Romanian troops were marching back through the province to reclaim all of it from Hitler. The Nazis had held a town across the Mures River from Lipova, and they'd driven the Romanian infantry back to our side of the water. Our men were ready to retreat and surrender Lipova without a fight. All alone, our grandmother rushed down to the river and exhorted them to hold the line and save our village. On her own, this elderly woman gave them the courage and determination they needed, and they defended the river until reinforcements arrived. For this and other feats, our grandmother had become a local legend, a folk hero. I have no doubt it was true. It would have been just like her to do that. The point is, everyone in town knew that story, including all the men who had invaded my grandfather's bedroom, so when my grandmother asked them for papers, they simply looked at the ground. They didn't talk back. A man named Adalbert Toth, a Hungarian, was in charge. He said, "Be quiet. We have orders to search your house."

"Do you have it in writing?" my grandmother asked, fixing him with her gaze, without missing a beat. Without answering, Toth smiled, as if to say, "Nice touch, Mrs. Bocu. But don't be silly."

All the while, fully aware of what was actually happening, our grandfather, Sever Bocu, stood his ground with quiet dignity, displaying his respectful and kind demeanor. He was part of the intelligentsia, a reactionary, a believer, an enemy, a man who could command the loyalty of peasants everywhere. In other words, they saw him as a powerful subversive, near the top of their blacklist, even though he was nearly eighty years old.

My grandfather would have recognized the Pyrrhic quality in what my grandmother was doing: shaming them, reminding them that in countries governed by the rule of law, they would need a court order, and due process, to search a home. And in her understated indignation, she was also showing them that moral laws were being violated here much deeper than any statute. They were betraying everything Romanians had fought and died for, as a people, over the previous decades—national unity, rights for peasants, freedom, and self-rule. Our grandfather had been a key figure in the establishment of all those things. He watched our grandmother with love in his eyes. Her bearing, her simple questions, and her goodness itself brought the evil of what they were doing into painful relief.

Although he was a national hero to the farmers and the working class and anyone else who cherished democracy, our grandfather was powerless now. Even so, he seemed too noble to be touched by this intrusion. I think of Jesus in the garden of Gethsemane when the soldiers came for him. I imagined he had the same look in his eyes: *Nothing you can do to me matters. You won't find what you're looking for here. My treasure is elsewhere.* Good would win; evil would lose.

Our grandmother was a little more sophisticated in her assurance that these men wouldn't harm her. They weren't depraved, just cowardly and selfishly obedient to the new social order. Plus, they were smart enough not to harm the wife of a legendary Romanian patriot and man of letters, someone who was respected and loved by all the people of the village and the province. Why else would they sneak through our garden, having climbed a ten-foot wall in the middle of the night, rather than simply come through the front door in full view of everyone on the main street? They knew what they were doing was wrong. So she was going to stare into their eyes and make them face the truth of what they were doing, even if that awareness wouldn't stop them.

"We haven't got any papers, and we do not need any," Toth said. "Mr. Bocu, get dressed. You're going with us."

"Show me your papers," my grandmother insisted, but they weren't listening.

"How do you put up with this, Bocu? You'll be your own man soon," Toth said. "Where is your telephone? We know you have one."

In our grandfather's study, Toth found it behind a stack of books, and he cut all the wires. When he returned, he took my grandmother aside, as the others were busy watching over my grandfather. He pulled out a sheet of paper and said quietly, "Here is your written order. You understand? I'm sorry. I am. But it has to be done. We're only making sure your husband can't cause trouble. You see? They're afraid of him, his influence." Toth showed decency and a semblance of compassion, but still he served a much larger evil, seemingly contradictory behavior all in one man.

I knew nothing of this moral complexity at the time. Our grandmother told us later there was a long list, names of those to be arrested as enemies of the people. One was a former prime minister, ninety-six years old, who had to be removed from his home on a stretcher. Toth gave her a look as if to say, *What can I do? This must be done. Someone else will do it if I don't. His name is on the list.*

The others spat on the floor and muttered insults about America and Americans—it was something they all did, day after day, in our village, this clucking about America. It was all an act, a way of showing their loyalty to a larger contest already under way between the Soviet Union and the free world. They knew our father was in America, working for Standard Oil, and so he was, like my grandfather, a threat to the new regime.

They began to dismantle our house, overturning anything

they could move, one room after another. As a Romanian book about my grandfather puts it, quoting from a written account by my grandmother, "bayonets cutting through flower pots, digging the soil, emptying marmalade cans in storerooms . . ." The local police in this group kept quiet, probably ashamed. Yet once in a while one of them would shout some insult about America, like a dog barking at the night.

They found a box containing our grandfather's military medals.

"These trinkets will go to Resitza," one of them said, referring to a Romanian munitions plant. "They'll be melted down and molded into bullets to kill imperialists."

Yet another stock phrase they'd learned from the Party.

Almost all these men looked ill at ease with their duty, announcing these things to each other almost as a routine part of their role playing. Human nature hadn't changed; only the uniforms were new. My brother, Costa, saw one of them steal a box of sleeping pills from my grandmother's nightstand and slip it into his pocket. They rifled through all our cupboards, drawers, and closets, and looked under cushions and carpets. They found nothing: no jewels, no weapons, no American dollar bills, no subversive communications. Finally, they found my grandfather's old battered safe and gathered around, gloating as they unlocked it, yet they discovered only a bundle of our grandparents' love letters, tied with a ribbon.

They asked her about her jewels. She ignored them. They kept haranguing her about jewelry, valuables. Was there another safe in the house? Finally, she said, "Follow me."

She led them down to a front room, which my grandparents had turned into a museum, an exhibit of her vast collection of peasant costumes and embroideries, a visual history of the people my grandfather had championed all his life. This room celebrated and helped preserve the heart and soul of Romania, the spirit of an entire people. It was a testament to everything that had given meaning to my grandparents' lives. Turning on the light, she said, "Come in. Take a look at my jewels."

A few of them were visibly astonished at the beauty of what they saw. It obviously had taken a lifetime to collect these artifacts, and it was clearly not about hoarding anything of economic value. It was an act of love for an entire culture's tradition, a way of keeping alive the heart of the Romanian spirit, era after era, as one greater power after another left boot prints on its hills and valleys. Yet, under one foreign ruler after another, the peasants had secretly preserved the spirit of their culture and had remained true to themselves as a people. The officers who saw my grandmother's collection of intricate embroidery had to have recognized all of this. They came from peasant stock themselves, and putting on those jackboots was a betrayal of everything their families had stood for and struggled to preserve—all of which they could see on full display in this museum. When Hungary had ruled over the Romanian provinces, my grandfather himself had been expelled from school because he had refused to wear Hungarian colors.

Two of them suddenly became sick and rushed outside. They were human beings, after all. The rest kept silent, out of respect. The membrane between good and evil, benevolence and cruelty, was, and still is, so thin and permeable.

Captain Toth came in and broke the spell. He was dark, slender, with a thick mustache, in his early thirties, and if I'd been older I would have recognized him as an opportunist, a careerist, someone who knew how to make the best of political upheaval, no matter who was in charge. He ordered my grandmother to help her husband pack. He gave her a deadline, of course. Nothing ever happened under the Communists without a harsh, if not impossible, deadline. My grandfather had fifteen minutes to say goodbye to almost eight decades of a life, fifteen more minutes of life as a citizen.

To fill his small satchel, she had to search hard for clothing, because shirts and underwear and pants had been tossed everywhere on the floor and furniture. Then she rushed to the pantry and brought a chunk of ham, a pound of sugar, a loaf of bread, and managed to slip into one of his shoes most of the cash they'd hidden in the house: no more than the equivalent of $30.

Meanwhile another lieutenant took a group of his men into my grandfather's enormous library. It was nearly a public institution, housed in one wing of the house. All he could say was, "What is the use for all these books?" With nowhere else to search, they went outside and pointed to a birdhouse my grandfather had built: a 30-foot pillar with a cone-shaped roof, and a long lightning rod mounted at the peak.

"See!" one of them said, "this is where they have their transmitter."

"Oh yes," said my grandmother, sardonically. We'd followed the group outside. "You're right. That's how we communicate with American imperialists."

One of the officers climbed an unstable ladder he'd leaned against the pillar and, once he reached the top, called down, "Just feathers."

We all went back inside and found my grandfather packed and ready.

Toth said, "Say goodbye to your wife and grandchildren."

My grandmother took a crucifix down from the wall and held it out to my grandfather: "Sever, this cross will save you." His eyes filled with tears, something I'd rarely seen, and he brought the crucifix up to his lips.

"Bless you, dear."

"Silly people," Toth said. "That cross will do nothing."

Coming over to hug Costa and me, my grandfather said, "Take care of yourselves and your grandmother. God will watch over you."

We had no idea how much these words would fuel our behavior and thoughts and hopes over the next seven years. He had addressed us both as men. It was two o'clock in the morning as they led our grandfather out of the house. Later, we learned he was taken first 20 miles away, to a prison beyond the Mures River, the river my grandmother had helped our soldiers hold against the Nazis. He would never be released and would die in a prison in Sighet, a town in the northern part of Romania. In his book on my grandfather, *Sever Bocu*, Bogdan sorrowfully puts it:

> Sever Bocu dies in the prison of Sighet in 1951. A secret prison, a tomb. They didn't know where they were, they seldom saw the daylight. One day they made him wash the floor of his cell and the guard kicked him wildly in the mouth with his boot until he'd cracked his skull. That was the cause of his death.

A premonition in Sever Bocu's words highlighted his life's credo: "If I were to die by the hand of a scoundrel, I shall die, but the idea whose torch I carried a lifetime will never die."

––––––

Our family had become a target. The precise catalyst for this assault has never been clear to any of us. I've always assumed they recognized my grandfather as a threat, simply through his reputation and character and beliefs. Later, I learned of another force that may have been at work. The Kremlin wanted to drive all American and other Western business operations out of Romania, so, given this purge, my parents could never have returned. They would have been seized immediately. Yet Romania itself badly needed an American loan to buy grain and relieve a food shortage after two years of drought. A Romanian Communist official asked the U.S. minister in Bucharest for a loan to help relieve the shortages. He got nowhere. There could be no help while the government blocked legitimate American business, specifically Standard Oil.

Ironically, this official then contacted my father, in America, asking if he could help expedite an American loan for his homeland. Apparently, this request came immediately after my parents arrived in the United States, before their Romanian citizenship had been revoked. Playing along, my father inquired about the terms. It became clear that the intermediary, the man approaching him for the money, would skim a large percentage off the top of the loan before it ever got to the hungry people who needed it. Therefore, my father refused to participate in the graft because it was a cheat, and he suspected most of the money would be diverted. It was how the Communists worked. It isn't clear to me how deeply my father considered whether or not his perfectly ethical decision would affect us, who were now at the mercy of the Communists. I suspect he knew his decision might be used against us, but in the end, he was true to his values and did the honorable and right thing. Learning of all these actions later, it was another lesson that principles matter and that often the right and honorable choices come with a price.

———

It should be clear now why "the problem of evil"—the bland phrase applied to it by the philosophers—became one of the central obsessions of my spiritual and intellectual life for nearly fifty years. I kept asking how my faith in God could be squared with the reality of evil and human suffering, and also how manifestly good people not only suffer evil but often either commit it or set it in motion, unwittingly. It's easy to forget that the man who kicked my grandfather to death may have been a loving father of half a dozen children.

The problem may partly be the word "evil." It's been invested with so much significance that merely uttering the word is often a complex kind of behavior in itself. It's a way of branding an enemy. When evil is out there, in opposition to you, it can be quite vital and energizing. There's nothing like an honest fight against the bad guys to make you feel good and alive. We'll probably never quit telling murder mysteries and detective stories and tales of dragon slayers, James Bond villains, and G.I. Joe because all these myths reconfirm a comforting vision of the world: Evil is out there, and it can be defeated. It was my vision of the world, as a child with Jesus Christ as my G.I. Joe. But there's another reason those stories keep coming back: When we tell them, we're saying evil is most definitely *not inside us.*

This was my worldview in Romania. In some ways, with my suffering and deprivation during those years, I was surrounded by more evil intent than at any other time of my life. Yet I retained my most unsullied experience of good. I believed in it, I prayed to it, and it saved me. I was surrounded by evil, but it was all outside me, in other people. The good guys won, and I was one of them. As a result of that victory, both geopolitical and personal, I arrived in America just in time to make a generous living from the greatest period of industrial growth in history. But I hadn't left evil behind, in Europe. It was waiting patiently for me in America, having assumed a more insidious, problematic form.

The ones I had to watch out for here didn't thump into the

conference room in jackboots. They wore double-breasted suits and quiet leather brogues. They worked hard. Half the time they were doing something I admired, setting the right tone for a client call, getting us to work all night on a pitch, or helping me earn a nice year-end bonus. But eventually the moment arrived, under pressure, when nothing much in the way these people looked or sounded had changed, and yet everything was different.

Unlike the perennial myths that urge us to believe in the good and stand up to evil, my encounters with the dark side of American life were often hardly distinguishable from the productive routines that enabled me to buy a home and fly to the Caribbean for a vacation. To just *see* evil as it happens and know it for what it was: I began to realize this was the greatest challenge. Especially when it was in my own heart.

It was more than just seeing through the camouflage of social conventions. The whole notion of evil became hard for me to pin down and understand. At all stages of my life there were destructive psychological forces all around me, but calling them evil didn't seem to illuminate them or make them any easier to resist. We think the word *evil* describes something we instinctively understand—bad, destructive behavior—in an objective, impartial way. It's just a noun, clear and familiar as daylight, the use of which seems essential to our survival as a civilization. And, up to a point, you can't argue with that. Evil signifies what we oppose, all the behavior we consider wrong and antisocial and disruptive and unjust. It describes behavior we prohibit, as a society, to ensure order and happiness.

That's certainly part of it, but in the West, it comes with centuries of religious connotations that make the word more of a weapon than a noun. You aim it at people to shame them and control them. In our Western culture, we use it to stigmatize practices, not just prohibit them with rules and statutes. The word itself carries the weight of divine judgment. With the word *evil*, we say, "You are wrong, and I am right." For many people, the banishment of Adam and Eve resonates in that word. And so we see a story about a serial killer or a pedophile on television, and we brand them as evil to reenact, emotionally, that moment in Genesis, when an angry God disowns and exiles his two sinners. For those who use the word this way, evil can become a malignant spirit or force personified by the devil or some other dark spiritual entity. Fundamentalists aren't the only people who accept this view. C. S. Lewis believed it. Even someone who for most of his life behaved as if he were pals with some kind of mischievous devil—Norman Mailer—seemed to endorse this view, in old age. Evil, or the devil, is simply a way of personifying or objectifying a fundamental force in human action.

There's little room in this for an understanding of "evil" behavior as simply unproductive, self-defeating, and in some ways, built into our nature as human beings. Socrates believed that evil was the by-product of ignorance. Those who understood good would simply shed their wrongful behavior. St. Augustine believed evil was the ontological absence of good, a kind of void within the world and the human heart. Yet in the Hebrew Bible, the word for sin actually means to make a mistake—to miss the mark. You've taken aim at happiness and goodness, and your arrow has slightly or completely missed its target. There's an assumption of forgiveness and hope, and practice, no less, built into that understanding of the word. It's almost a practical term.

As a child, my perils were only about to begin. I had begun as a witness to evil, a little boy who could only stand aside and watch as other members of my family suffered. Now I was about to be drafted as a player into this contest and struggle and become an active opponent, in my own childishly Christian way, of the people who were destroying my family.

# CHAPTER 3

# WHAT REALLY MATTERS IS PERSONAL, NOT POLITICAL

WE KEPT HOPING OUR PARENTS WOULD RETURN, BUT MONTHS of patient waiting became years. Unknown to us, living and working in America, they were spending large sums of money, trying to arrange for our rescue. One day, a professional smuggler arrived at our doorstep, with a three-day stubble and an odd odor, claiming my parents had paid him to usher us out of the country, but our grandmother didn't believe a word of it. She wouldn't let us go. My parents had in fact paid him, and he wasn't the first in a sequence of consultants, operatives, and agents who promised to save us for a fee. My brother, just a teenager, was inclined to take a chance and go with this stranger, so he was visibly depressed by our grandmother's refusal to let us go. But he didn't speak up. As time went on, I could tell his hopes were beginning to wane, but mine never did.

Life seemed to return to "normal" for a while after my grandfather was taken, or at least it fell back into the predictably surreal regimen of our lives at school. At the start of the year in 1948, we realized that out of thirty teachers, only three trustworthy ones remained. All the rest were replaced by members of the Party or those completely cooperative with the new regime. Our new principal, George Gorun, made the teaching of Russian mandatory. Students were subjected to frequent interrogations: "Who are your parents? What is their income? How much income tax do they pay? To which political party or other organization did your parents and your grandparents belong? How long have they been associated with such groups? Do your parents or guardians sympathize with democracy? Are they ever critical of the regime?"

It was as if we'd passed through the looking glass. We hid our true thoughts and feelings. Were our parents and grandparents supportive of the new regime? We said we had no reason to believe otherwise. Our teachers asked us to address them as "comrade teacher" rather than "sir" or "ma'am." Once, a teacher tried to reprimand a student in my class and he snapped back, "Do you want me to report you to the Party?" Incredibly, our teacher backed off and never disciplined that child again.

My brother knew another politically shrewd boy who essentially took control of his own parents. He was twelve, from a well-known family in Lipova, and one day he came to school and reported on an uncle who had been listening to Voice of America on the family's radio. When his parents heard of what he'd done, they disowned him and threatened to send him away from home if he didn't straighten up.

"Don't even try it," he said. "You want me to tell the Party that you're teaching me to be disloyal to Communism?" They backed off, and he essentially lived like an adult, doing whatever he wanted.

Our grandmother, Maryellena, nicknamed Michie, had to watch every penny for us to survive. Our parents sent us a monthly check to help with expenses, and although it seems hard to believe, considering the social oppression surrounding us, for a while the Communist authorities delivered these checks to us faithfully. Unbelievably, certain principles of fairness and justice seemed to prevail, although, as my experience of Communism deepened, it seemed harder and harder to discern any justice in the system whatsoever. Corruption spread throughout every organization.

As former members of the bourgeoisie, with "unsound social origins" through our links to American business, we weren't entitled to ration cards. Friends would give us supplies and food, and we tried to produce everything else we needed in our garden, but everything else had to be purchased on the "free market." Prices, therefore, were three to five times higher than those charged for anyone with a ration card. The only consolation was that the quality of everything in the free market was far superior. Everything was taxed at a punitive rate. Discriminatory real estate taxes ate up much of the money our parents sent us.

In class, there wasn't a single subject that wasn't politicized. Science textbooks were filled with contempt about the "decadence of western science," while at the same time portraying superior efforts in Soviet science to advance the conditions of workers. Ironically, during that period, Stalin's pseudoscience was destroying agriculture and causing widespread famine throughout Russia. In one way or another, all of our required reading portrayed life in the free world as one of ruthless exploitation, racial discrimination, and widespread poverty. Our textbooks described history as nothing more than a long struggle between the masses and the ruling class, thousands of years that culminated in Russia's October Revolution. French was taught, but no one read Corneille, Racine, Voltaire, Balzac, Flaubert, Victor Hugo, or Baudelaire. An example of "French" poetry was represented by the Communist "Internationale," the international Communist labor anthem, but in French rather than Russian or Romanian. We were warned against "religious superstition." Going to church was discouraged, and we were ordered to avoid worship and prayer.

In this kind of circumstance, your entire life becomes a pose, a provisional role you play. You were always hiding your thoughts and feelings, even with trusted friends, because there was no way to know who would overhear the conversation. The way people spoke or acted became unreal. You simply assumed it was all a calculated front, in response to the pressures applied on everyone to behave a certain way.

In retrospect, this subtle, gradual change in people now strikes me as closer to the real nature of evil than any of the more dramatic episodes in our youth: our father's arrest, my grandfather's abduction, the abusive interrogations still to come, and most of what awaited us, as workers for the Communists. People around us became susceptible to what can only be called organizational evil. They simply went along with the system that had sprung up around them, doing whatever it required and instructed them to do. They did it to such an extent that they didn't even recognize the sickness inherent in what they were doing.

People who found a way to fit into the Communist system didn't question the completely hypocritical way in which the ideology created almost a parody of capitalist inequities. The privileged few got all the food and supplies and luxuries, being high up in the Party, while the masses were near to starving. Simply change the terms—substitute the term "Party bosses" for "greedy capitalists"—and you have a clear picture of the injustices Communism supposedly had swept away. The new regime created a surplus of administrative, bureaucratic jobs, doing little to promote industry and siphoning most of the profit from commerce. What the Communists produced, ultimately, in Romania wasn't the promised utopia, where everyone was supplied according to need and no one was allowed to keep more than his or her fair share. What we witnessed under Communism was not just the worst aspects of capitalism, by another name; it became an ongoing system of evil justified by an idealized philosophy.

What I didn't see at the time but now realize in retrospect was that all the atrocities that became politically commonplace in Romania as I was growing up stemmed from the simple tendency to do evil in the service of honorable or at least practical ideals. Communism at its theoretical core actually represents an effort to institutionalize Christian principles: to put the welfare of all people before the interests of the privileged few, to share the wealth. As Jesus put it: "Give what you own to the poor and follow me." Yet this honorable ideal, as a political system, falls apart rapidly because it requires human beings to carry it out. Human nature undermines good intentions every day.

Even with capitalism and free enterprise—the expression of some of the highest ideals, founded on individual human liberty—human nature can intervene and you can end up with a social and economic structure that pools most of the wealth into the hands of the privileged few. In essence, you can end up with a democratic parody of the British aristocratic order that the American Revolution attempted to overthrow.

For me, the problem is essentially the evil side of human nature, which can be addressed personally, but not through organizational means. It can't simply be addressed politically, or economically, or socially. It is very personal and unique to every one of us.

Several months after my grandfather's arrest, a uniformed officer rang our doorbell.

"Who are you?" he asked my brother, who happened to answer the door.

"We live here, comrade," Costa said, doing his usual impersonation of a happy citizen under Soviet control.

"My name is Major Ciurea. I have an offer that may interest you."

Costa invited him to come in, and we sat in the parlor. Our grandmother had joined us by now, hearing voices.

"Do you want to join your parents?" he asked.

He was a younger man, and he looked newly recruited into the Party ranks, with pale skin and dark hair he'd combed carefully back from his forehead.

"Of course," we said, in unison.

"I'll give you two hours to pack," he said. Again, we were given an unreasonable deadline, to keep us off balance, obedient. "You are to leave with your grandmother," Ciurea said.

"I don't understand," our grandmother said. "You're saying they can go to America? How is this supposed to happen?"

"You are to go with the children to Urziceni by train. From there you will all go by bus to Galatzi," he said, referring to a port on the Danube River. "You will be able to visit your husband, Mrs. Bocu, and the children will be able to say goodbye to him before they depart, by sea, three days later."

In a hurry, we packed six suitcases with clothing, but our grandmother insisted on packing as much food as possible. With the help of Maria, our family's loyal and trusted helper, she wrung the necks of four chickens, plucked them, and had time enough to broil them. She deposited them, still warm, along with bread, cheese, sugar, and tea, in one suitcase that served more or less as a pantry for us. Knowing to be prepared for anything from these people, she was also careful to pack three woolen blankets.

When we were climbing up into the train, our guard asked, "Did the children bring their schoolbooks?"

"What?" she asked, startled.

Costa gave me a crestfallen look. He knew exactly what this meant.

"Why would they need their schoolbooks in America?" she asked.

Instead of an answer, the officer closed his eyes with frustration at his own stupidity, knowing he'd given away the ruse. He then quickly changed the subject.

"They aren't letting us go," Costa whispered to me.

"Come on. Get on board," the officer said.

We got to Bucharest before noon the next day, and we had to wait another six hours for the train to Urziceni. In keeping with the topsy-turvy, unpredictable character of our country now, we were escorted to a kind of club, exclusively for the use of the militia, near the train station. Some were playing cards, others were drinking, while we were shown into a small office and the door was shut behind us.

Through the wall, we could hear our handler joking with the others. When he came back in, he said, "At Urziceni, you will have two heated rooms for the night. The next morning you will take a bus for Galatzi, so that the children can see their grandfather before sailing. Should you get to Urziceni before nine tonight, you'll leave this evening and spend the night with your husband at Galatzi."

All these elaborate lies about our ostensible journey did what they were meant to do. We forgot his slip about the schoolbooks and began to think maybe we were being released. It was all so involved. Why would he put this much effort into a lie? He had complete power over us; he didn't need to explain anything, just tell us where to go next. It seemed no one would be so cruel as to call up these visions of freedom for an old, good-hearted woman and her two innocent grandchildren, unless he was telling the truth. So, as he left us to our little room, our hopes were revived by our own innocence. We couldn't have imagined doing something this devious and vicious. How could another human being do this? He had to be telling the truth. With no other furniture, we napped by stretching out on a pair of wooden tables.

An hour later, we went to the train station, boarded again, and arrived at Urziceni that same evening. We were beginning to doubt everything again when a horse cart arrived for our luggage and us, and it took us to the local station for the militia. They told us their orders had arrived too late for action that evening, so we were to stay the night there. Again, we went into a little office, with broken windows and doors loosely attached to their frames, and a little stove for warmth. That night, I hardly slept. I remember one particular older militiaman who kept coming into our room quietly, to keep stoking the flame in our stove, mindful of our comfort. He would tiptoe into the room and never leave without a caring, compassionate look around the room at the three of us.

Throughout our entire ordeal in Romania, there were always these nameless guardian angels watching over us, people motivated less by their own self-interest than a spirit of goodness, urging them to look out for us. Sometimes these people would show compassion to us at the risk of punishment or arrest, even though we were strangers. In the morning, our grandmother asked about our departure for the port, and a Lieutenant Dinu said, "Your departure is delayed. You may stay here as long as a week."

"A week? How can that be?" she asked.

"You didn't let me finish," he said, tilting his head back, looking down at her with a slight smirk. "Or it may be a month. Or even a year for that matter."

At that point, Costa resumed his flat, indifferent gaze: the usual, protective mask he wore. All the lies they'd told us—but why? Was it just to see the look on our faces when the truth finally emerged and feel the pleasure of their power over us? What could an aging woman and two boys have done, if they'd told us the truth?

He led us to a house only a couple blocks away, a little cottage on Strada Scantelia, named after the Communist daily newspaper that had begun publication in Bucharest. The place was a shambles. We had two cramped rooms, walk-in closets more or less, filthy and without any plumbing. Cracks ran in webs across the ceiling, and the walls appeared to have been made from troweled mud. The doors and windows didn't seal out the cold, with daylight visible around the frames. Nothing would open or shut properly. The room was infested with roaches and bedbugs. Our only furniture had been shoved into one corner of the first room, an old iron bed, with a mattress of grass, a kitchen table, and two chairs. Our only bathroom was a tiny wooden shed in the backyard, with a hole in the ground and a bench.

The commander who had brought us here announced, "This is to be your home. You are not allowed to write to anyone during your first week here; later you will be allowed to communicate with your family in Bucharest." At that point, he listed the prohibitions. We were not to leave the room, meet any local people, speak to anyone, take walks, or leave the house for anything but food and necessities.

"The boys cannot attend school," he said.

My brother wasn't able to hide his anguish at those words. It's interesting, looking back, that one of the greatest causes for Costa's anxiety was his desire to complete his secondary education. More than anything, he wanted to learn, in all subjects, and have a diploma to show for it. Despite the radical ways in which the world had changed around us, he craved excellence in academic disciplines that clearly had no relevance now. The less we understood, the better, in the eyes of this regime. Yet he never gave up this focus on his education, which was the only way, it seemed, he clung to hope. He was very sensitive to the power of the darkness that had descended on our society, so aware of how futile it would be to resist it directly. The whole ordeal seemed to alter him in some decisive way, forcing him to shrink into himself in a way that hobbled him, socially, as an adult. And yet, privately, personally, he clung to his education, never giving up on his search for genuine learning, real literature, and rational understanding.

In the end, Costa suffered emotional wounds from our captivity more lasting and crippling than mine. But he showed me how to fight back against our oppression in a nonviolent, personal way. He chose good, and I followed his example. With a couple of books he had brought along, he took to his studies, trying not to lose ground. He kept his mind alive and his heart free, despite the encompassing reality of an evil political system designed to enslave our thinking and control our feelings. His secret, personal regimen of learning represented Costa's initiation into all the skills that would enable him, in later life, to become a brilliant analyst for the Central Intelligence Agency. He learned how to survive by using his mind while he was a prisoner—researching, analyzing, hypothesizing, testing, consolidating diverse information, and finally understanding. And these habits of learning led him into a career where these skills were absolutely crucial and valuable to a political system based on freedom rather than solidarity. The goodness he clung to in his personal system of values made him a better person, and that, for me, was his greatest example.

At this point, we were penniless. We had no idea how long it would take for our family members in Bucharest to locate us and send us food and other necessities. Those four hastily broiled chickens our grandmother had packed into a suitcase lasted us a long, long time, as did all the other provisions she'd brought.

After three weeks of complete poverty, some money arrived from our relatives in Bucharest and then a few blankets. I'd never had a Christmas more thrilling than the moment of those deliveries. Now, on my grass mattress, I would have an extra blanket to pull over me.

An officer of the state kept all our paperwork and escorted us to the post office or the state bank, watching over every transaction, with all the diligence of an auditor. In his small book, he would record the amount of our tiny deposits, so the state knew exactly how much money we were saving. Apparently, they would share this information with our landlord, a man named Moscanu, and his wife, because as soon as we had some money and were able to buy food and other necessities beyond the barest need, the woman would tax us by coming into our little room to "borrow" some rice, sugar, oil, or tea, which she would never replenish.

As difficult as our plight seemed, we knew, in some ways, we were actually lucky at this point. Thousands of others that summer, along the Yugoslav border, were killed while trying to escape. In a nightmarish echo of what had happened during the Holocaust in Germany and Poland, these people were herded into cattle cars at the train station, shipped under guard to the steppes south of where we were now living, and left in empty fields to die without food, water, or shelter.

---

One day, we were surprised to be summoned to the local security station. This was unusual because until then we'd had contact with only the militia, the ordinary police. The station was a small, one-story private home, rebuilt to function as a compound for the secret police. The structure itself was designed to instill fear in anyone who walked past it. Brick walls eight feet high had been raised around this building so that no one could see what was going on inside. It was frightening to be led through a gate in that wall, waiting as the police officer rang the bell.

A heavy iron door with a tiny aperture, a little square porthole, slid open.

"What? Who are you?" someone asked.

The door opened and the first thing we saw was a police dog, a German shepherd, snarling and leaping in the air, struggling against the chain around its neck. The guard snapped at the dog, and it relaxed, settling into a corner. These trained Soviet dogs were everywhere in Romania now.

Passing through a hallway, we were told to sit in a bare interrogation room. It was a classic scene with a single pendant lamp casting a cone of incandescent light onto a table. A security agent came into the room brusquely and immediately began peppering us with questions: "Where are your parents? Why had they not returned to Romania? What communication did we have with them? What had they sent us? What had we sent them?" We answered in general terms and my brother pointed out that our parents had been denied citizenship. They wouldn't be allowed to return. Wasn't he aware of that? After writing down our answers, he went to a telephone on the wall and barked into it a report about us.

At this point, someone we would come to know came into the room: Lieutenant Vasilescu from the central headquarters of secret police in Bucharest. He wasted no time introducing himself or getting to know us. He already knew plenty.

"I have orders," he said. "I'm to move you to other quarters. Go home and start packing. In four hours, you'll be settled into your new home."

The invariably ridiculous deadline, and the constant compulsion to completely unsettle us, once we had managed to make a small, temporary nest out of the broken-down cottage we'd been given, was becoming a familiar pattern. Rushing home, we managed to get ourselves packed in time, and we were taken to new lodgings on Strada Stalin. We actually had a single electric light, and by now this seemed an incredible luxury, although power failures became so frequent that we more often used kerosene. For washing, we used an enameled iron bowl and had to carry water from a well in back.

One day, I was playing with some kind of improvised toy blocks in a corner of the room and noticed the glint of something metallic hidden in the molding. I reached down and plucked at it with a fingernail, prying it away from the wood, but when I tried to lift it up for a closer look, I realized it was attached to wires running inside the wall. I called my brother over.

He put a finger to his lips, and led me outside.

"They're listening," he said. "We need to watch what we say, even here."

———

Overall, our time in Urziceni was a bit of a reprieve. It was, in some ways, a time in my life that crystallized my faith in good, in the fundamental goodness within all human beings, which can become incredibly strong in those who choose to nurture it. The authorities allowed us to have contact with a small group of people, usually elderly couples and widows, evidently anyone they felt would have something in common with my grandmother. As a result, we found ourselves surrounded by dozens of guardian angels, acting as individuals, with no official role in the political system. They would often drop off gifts of staples: eggs, cheese, fruit and vegetables they produced on their own land. Apparently, they knew my grandmother was Sever Bocu's wife, because they acted as if it were a privilege to provide us these needed goods. We appreciated their kindness and affection especially because they themselves had little to spare. As time went on, and more of the townspeople heard about us, we began to receive gifts like these from unknown people.

At a time when the food supply was getting tighter and tighter, these people helped make it possible for us to survive. Yet they had nothing to gain by caring for us.

In that terrible winter, they saved us from freezing to death. Firewood, always plentiful in the past, used in the smaller Romanian towns as the only heating fuel, was now rationed like everything else and off-limits to people like us, who lacked ration cards. So in the coldest month of winter, during a heavy snowstorm, one of our peasant protectors brought us a wagonload of firewood. He took great risks bringing that wood to us. Violating the artificial strictures of the Communist economy might have landed him in a forced labor camp. Even so, he came to our rescue and looked deeply happy to be giving away that valuable lumber.

---

The two o'clock lecture program has become one of my favorite events in Chautauqua. My take on that hour is that it is a search for spiritual understanding. My sense of the program's mission under its director, Joan Brown Campbell, is to explore the sources of religious belief to help bring morality into the public square. This strikes me as a daunting task. There is little doubt in my mind that our values determine much of what we do in our lives, in every realm of our experience. Values are the underpinning of a successful business culture, a thriving family and marriage, and even an enduring sports team.

Yet values, when mandated and manipulated by organizations, can result in violence. Diverse religious beliefs can be twisted to serve the selfish aims of individuals or communities. Dictators, autocrats, and radical zealots will often cloak themselves in a warped version of religious faith, and so will those with an economic mission. And there are even more subtle ways in which religion and ideas of God can be manipulated to support self-centered agendas. Often it can be hard to discern quietly authentic spiritual leadership in the cacophony of voices that use religion to strengthen power and wealth. In his essay, "Reflections on Gandhi," George Orwell said, "Saints should always be judged guilty until proven innocent." Christopher Hitchens liked to fling broadsides at nearly anyone who professed to serve God by serving humanity, including Gandhi and Mother Teresa, and as heavy-handed as he may have been in selecting his targets, his skepticism wasn't entirely misguided. The most vocal proponents of a God-inspired mission can be people who deserve the greatest scrutiny. One of the reasons I love Chautauqua is that faith is professed here virtually without any partisan agenda.

The theological lectures at two o'clock in the afternoon, at the outdoor Hall of Philosophy (as well as my conversations with Joan, the charismatic and inspirational leader of the Institution's Religion Department) have had a profound impact on my quest for understanding the relationship between human beings and a spiritual reality that can give meaning to life. The tolerant Methodist leaders who started Chautauqua welcomed all religious groups on campus. Several small churches sprouted here. Over a dozen denominational houses were also founded.

Though its roots are still deep in the ecumenical Christian mission of its earliest tent meetings, the community has been drawing more and more Jewish and Muslim residents, representing their religions through organizations and programs. The Edith Everett Jewish Life Center has been completed, Sunday morning Christian services are nondenominational, and almost every gifted preacher in America other than the too-busy TV evangelists have preached here. We have begun to incorporate Buddhists and Hindus, and in due time I would expect all spiritual paths to find a home here.

So, at two o'clock, I'm lying on my back on the grass lawn just outside the Hall, a kind of miniature Parthenon, consisting of a roof supported by pillars rather than walls, with a small amphitheater of benches and a stage. It may be small, but it *does* seat hundreds of people under its roof, with space in the grassy surroundings for another throng. To get a coveted seat near the front row in front of the lectern, you need to arrive at least half an hour early. Those of us who want to remember what it was like on a spring day in college, stretched out on the lawn with a volume of Cicero or Emerson, can arrive almost whenever we like, and recline on the grass to gaze up through the leaves of silver maples as we listen to the speaker. Recently, the talks have been amplified through large speakers aimed toward the people to make it easier for the leisurely listeners to catch every word. From my comfortable, casual spot on the turf, this has become one of my favorite moments during a Chautauqua summer, watching the white clouds tack across patches of blue sky, as I listen. It's a clarifying, meditative ritual for me.

The Reverend Peter Storey, a Methodist minister from South Africa, has come to upstate New York to talk about the evils of apartheid and the virtues of compassion. A distinguished man who fought to abolish discrimination in his country, he had been a key member of South Africa's Truth and Reconciliation Commission, chartered by Nelson Mandela and Frederik Willem de Klerk, to bring justice and healing to their society. Personally, he had seen how compassion could defeat hatred, prejudice, and injustice. His words bring back recollections from both childhood and my later years in marketing. In his lecture, quoted by the *Chautauqua Daily,* he said:

> I come from a country that has become known throughout the world for its commitment to one of the most uncompassionate ways of life ever seen. I know there came a moment when the people of that nation reached out and touched one another in a new way. They touched the fringes of what it means to live compassionately. Because of that miracle in my own homeland I'm a profound optimist about what this message can do around our planet. I believe people can change because deep down they want to change. They need leadership to tell them to turn away from the ways of hate to the ways of compassion. Those of us committed to faith need to take care that we're on the right side of history. People time and again have used religion to advance political and ideological visions of death. I hope anyone who preaches any message about compassion will ask the question, "How many people have died because of the *way* I believe what I believe?"

Barbara and I have traveled to South Africa with some regularity since 1982. Young & Rubicam's global client, Colgate, had a huge business in the country and needed Y&R to open an office there to serve their needs in African markets. So we purchased an agency in Johannesburg and Cape Town and transformed it into an office for Y&R. Luckily for us, its anchor client was Pick n Pay, Africa's version of Walmart, which turned out to be a highly progressive organization. The Pick n Pay founder, Raymond Ackerman, and his wife, Wendy, were principled, value-driven individuals. Often in defiance of South African government regulations, they operated by the highest possible principles, hiring Africans and minorities in defiance of segregation, giving anyone qualified an opportunity for dignity and hope.

The Ackermans became a personal inspiration for me. When he and his company took a stand on human rights for black South Africans, the leadership of Pick n Pay was harassed and criticized by politicians sympathetic to apartheid. They were also vilified for their decision to violate the law by promoting hardworking black South Africans to positions they deserved in the Pick n Pay organization. Over the years of Raymond Ackerman's leadership, his company educated, and housed, tens of thousands of employees. In the past three years alone, still a vital figure for change in South Africa, Ackerman and his company increased the number of black franchise owners of Pick n Pay stores from 10 to over 120. The company has world-class human resource practices, with partially paid maternity leave for nine months. And its social investment spending, a practice Ackerman instituted long before it became a fashion, is one of the highest in South Africa.

When, in the late 1980s and early 1990s, a misguided movement in the United States demanded that American businesses pull out of South Africa, I refused to cooperate with the mandate because I believed Y&R could follow the lead of its main client in South Africa and work for change by staying in business there. To pull out, as a protest against apartheid, would have done more harm than good for the nearly four dozen Africans we employed at the Y&R office. These hardworking people, who had devoted years to their service with Y&R, would have simply lost their jobs. I knew there were better ways to protest racial segregation than to put people out of work. So I came to New York City to persuade management not to pull out. I walked through the pickets outside our headquarters on Madison Avenue. From the floor where we conducted a five-hour meeting to convince management we needed to stay in South Africa, I could look down at the protests still going on in the street.

Apartheid was simply one among many examples of tribalism, a way for the greedy and powerful—in this case a corrupt minority—to maintain its dominance and control over a larger and weaker group of people. The rich, white English and Afrikaners would not cede their power to a black majority and risk losing the power they had accrued through decades of rule. Bigotry, with all the attendant discrimination and cant about racial superiority, offered the powerful few a way to morally, and even spiritually, justify the oppression of those they were exploiting. What was most unsettling for me, at the time, was how many of these oppressors were deeply religious people, mostly Christians who believed they were following Jesus in their way of life, blind to their own hypocrisy.

Years later, all of this was put into perspective for me in a conversation I had with Margaret Thatcher. In the early 1990s, I attended a gathering that draws representatives from almost every advertising agency of any significance, the annual convention of the Four A's—the American Association of Advertising Agencies. We were going to have the privilege of hearing a keynote address from Mrs. Thatcher, the former prime minister of Great Britain. Our agency's chairman, Alex Kroll, who was also chairman of Four A's at the time, had invited her to speak about the new geopolitical world at a time when the global economy was emerging as a transformative force in American business. Alex had invited me to join him for breakfast with her.

Leaping in where your average fool would race to the nearest exit, I volunteered how, as a European-born individual, I felt confident that Europe would soon complete the vision of a successful European Union. I fully expected a nod of approval.

Instead, the Iron Lady put down her fork and gave me a reproachful look, as if she were dealing with a noisy child. "The Europeans may collaborate economically, but they will never, you hear me, NEVER, forge a united Europe politically. Never. What you don't understand, young man, is that Europe, like the rest of mankind, operates on the principle of tribalism. And those tribes in Europe will never, never agree to give up territories and put themselves under the power of a different tribe. That is just not part of the human condition."

I realize that I had learned these lessons as a child in Romania, without quite being aware of what I was seeing. The Communists, like religious zealots, espoused a perfectly coherent political philosophy of sharing and compassion for the common worker. In reality, in their behavior, Communist individuals simply used the new economic order to reinforce the inequities of the capitalist system they claimed to have overthrown. The Communists did not invent the lust for power or the need for creating a culture of absolute obedience to the tribe. You were in the group, willingly or not, or else you became dispensable. Those who were or could become threats to the tribe had to be exorcised. In their worldview, like others before them, the end did justify almost any means.

# CHAPTER 4

# BEWARE OF FORCE

POWER AND FORCE ARE NOT THE SAME THING. POWER CAN be good. Life requires it. Creativity grows out of it. Love is a tremendous power in the world. Force, on the other hand, warps that vital energy into something harmful. It enslaves.

Having lost sight of the dignity of the other, a ruling state or an organization of any kind uses force to sustain order. Force not only destroys the tribe's enemies, it will almost always destroy the tribe itself. In the meantime, those outside the clan will become its victims.

I learned much of this, without realizing it, during the next few years in Romania. At the time, I hid from the truth of all this, clinging to my simplistic view of good and evil, yet I was about to experience how deadly the use of force can become, especially when it is employed by an organization that seeks to control what its citizens can say, think, and do.

The darkest and most dangerous period of my captivity was set in motion by an innocuous letter in the mail. It was from the United States legation in Bucharest and apparently it had escaped the attention of the police, probably because it bore no return address. The letter, written in Romanian, invited Constantin to appear at the legation for a hearing about our visa application. Someone in the militia learned about the letter, possibly from someone at the legation, and so we were called in for questioning.

"When did you receive the letter from the American legation?"

"Exactly a week ago," Costa said.

"How did the legation know you were in Urziceni?"

The interrogations we faced during our captivity increased as time went on, and they always proceeded along a certain rhythm, with refrains and crescendos and moments of calm, almost like a concerto. It was an art to these people, breaking someone down, extracting a confession. Our interrogator would abuse us, curse us, yell and threaten, and then back off and sound reasonable and friendly. He would take every possible point of view on some event he wanted to know more about, explore every possible angle, and then move on, only to return to the same event and line of questioning, again and again and again. This time, the questioning went on for hours. Apparently, the prospect of our getting a visa was a terrible threat to our captors. An interest in our well-being was being shown at levels of the government they couldn't control, which suggested their hold on us represented a source of power for *someone*.

Having exhausted every possible angle, our interrogator gave up and said: "From now on, you are forbidden to write to the American legation, to your parents, or to any family members anywhere. None of this should bother you. Why would you want to be with your parents? They have abandoned you."

"No, they haven't!" Costa shouted. "They aren't allowed to come home."

Eight hours after we'd been taken in for questioning, we arrived back at our room and told our grandmother everything that had happened, and the look on her face suggested we would soon be facing worse. In the morning, the stress of what we were enduring must have helped to trigger an unstoppable nosebleed: her bed and the surrounding floor were soaked with blood. As we scrambled to find towels to help staunch the blood, someone knocked on the door. It was another security agent.

"You have four hours to pack up all your things," he said. "You're leaving with your grandmother."

He told us our ostensible destination, a mountain town, a resort 50 miles north of Bucharest. Shocked by this news, we agreed it wasn't an unpleasant prospect. One of our uncles resided there. As best we could, we packed yet again and arrived at the train station shortly after midnight. We helped our grandmother, sick and cold in the December night, onto one of the wooden benches in a third-class car. We soon realized we weren't going to a resort in the mountains. Our train was headed to a larger town to the north, near the border with the Soviet Union, in the Romanian region of Moldavia.

––––––––––

We arrived in Botoscani only a few days before Christmas. Botoscani had never been a dynamic place, but it had become an economically balanced community, an overgrown village. It had no large-scale industrial development. Instead it was a strong agricultural base supplying the mills with the grain needed to grind flour. Before the Communists took over, it had become one of the primary sources of the entire country's food supply. Botoscani flour was famous throughout Romania. It had also become a trading center for the region, where people from hundreds of surrounding villages assembled to buy and sell their goods. And it also had an array of smaller businesses: breweries, vegetable oil refineries, tanneries, and candle factories, as well as two textile mills. It had developed a small, healthy, self-sustaining economy.

Under the Communist economy, everything began to come apart. Trade with the surrounding villages collapsed. Much of what was produced in the region went directly to the Soviet Union. Only a small fraction of produce from the surrounding fields was sold in the state-owned stores, marked up by a factor of ten. Municipal offices and security forces grew exponentially. Meanwhile, bread lines stretched endlessly in the streets, where people would wait for hours to claim a small loaf, for as long as the bread supply lasted.

The privileged class would flaunt their privileges, so social unrest was universal and often not successfully contained. Spontaneous rebellions and even semi-riots broke out at times. The ordinary citizen could hardly afford a few vegetables, eggs, and a bit of cheese. Every week, the Communist elite, however, would carry away a whole turkey, a few chickens, dozens of eggs, quarts of cream, and ten-pound wheels of cheese. It would take a skilled worker an entire month to earn what one of the wives of Party favorites would spend in a single morning at the market. Even so, when peasants served them, they would use pressure and threats to force special discounts in fees for work being done to their property.

Our guards led us to a one-room wooden shack that must have served as a storehouse or workshop at one point. It had a mud façade, and its doorway gave directly onto the street. The windows and door were loose, most of the glass shattered or cracked, and every time we walked across the floor, our shoes raised small plumes of dust. At first we thought there was no floor, only dirt. Our interior walls were mottled with mold. Spider webs clotted the corners of the room and every nook in the window casements. It was furnished with a few pots and pans, a washing bowl, a chamber pot, a single chair, no table, and no beds, only a pile of hay in one corner, to serve as a mattress. The shack had no running water, no kitchen, no bathroom, only a public water tap a quarter mile away, down the street—and once again, an outhouse, in back, built around a hole in the ground.

In later years, my brother and I always referred to Botoscani, but particularly this house, as our "work camp." It was the home of a middle-aged couple, the Rappaports, who undoubtedly had no desire for tenants but had been ordered to house us. A door into the rest of the house was nailed shut. In all our time there we hardly exchanged a dozen words with our landlords.

Having by now managed to stop her nosebleed, our grandmother, weak and dehydrated, inspected our new home. It did have a small stove, but she saw that its flue was blocked with creosote, so it would be impossible to heat our room.

"I don't think this place has been used in ten years," she said. "We can't make a fire until the chimney is cleaned. We'll have to bundle up."

With the temperature outside well below freezing, the shack was as cold as a meat locker. So, needless to say, we were fully aware that this new home was punishment for having received a letter from the American legation. It was also a way of hiding us again. Since someone at the legation knew where we were being held in Urziceni, we'd been smuggled to a town many miles away. We couldn't understand why the government considered us such a valuable commodity and yet treated us like cattle.

We attempted to improve our living conditions. Using some makeshift pillowcases and some hay, we created a bed for our grandmother. We swept the place, filled the cracks in the ceiling with mud, and stuffed the holes in our windows with old newspaper. From our landlords, we borrowed a loaf of stale bread, and we tried to make it last as long as we could, supplemented with boiled potatoes and sugarless tea. Fortunately, our grandmother had brought along our oil burner and about a gallon of kerosene, which we could use once someone had swept the chimney. Costa and I huddled together, side by side on the floor, fully dressed, using our overcoats as our own comforters, wrapping jute bags around our heads to conserve our body heat.

Within days, the militia showed up at our door and told my brother and me to get dressed. They led us to a station where we were introduced as new workers. "Comrades, this is Constantin Georgescu and his brother, Peter. They come from Urziceni. Their parents abandoned them and went to America years ago and have never returned. Apparently, they like it there. They are enemies of the people and have never stopped working against the interests of their homeland. They sabotage the republic by any means. It has become their primary occupation. These two, their children, begin work with us today. They must learn what it's like being a workingman. Today will be their first lesson."

Someone in this little assembly said, "Make them sweat blood."

The head of this unit was a simpleminded sort, with a high-pitched voice. As an aside, he told us he'd once served in a mountain army regiment under one of our uncles. My first job was sweeping the streets. I remember people passing me on their way to work or play or school, some of them pausing to stare or point. I was convinced they all knew my whole story and were mocking me: "There's the boy whose parents betrayed

Romania! He'll never go to school or play with the other children again!" Choking back tears, I'd never felt such an intense sensation of humiliation, grief, and rage at the lies people were telling about my parents. It bothered me more than anything I had to endure myself.

For our next assignment, the head of our unit led us outside, handed us a handsaw and an axe, and pointed to a large pile of logs.

"Get to it, comrades," he said.

We hacked and sawed all day until we could hardly lift our arms.

In the evening, on the way home, Costa found enough energy to speak a few quiet words: "They're out to break us. They want to see us crying and crawling. They want us to beg for softer jobs so they can call us the pampered sons of a capitalist. Let's show them we can take it. God will help us."

I was determined to prove to our captors that I could do *more* than what they expected, not less. I was going to show what I was worth to them.

"Don't tell our grandmother about any of this. Don't make her worry."

---

Though he was just under six feet tall now, Constantin weighed around 130 pounds. I was even smaller, at five and a half feet; I couldn't have weighed more than 100 pounds. Our meager diet virtually prevented us from putting on much muscle, and our bodies had begun to burn the muscle we already had. In our first five days in Botoscani, we were unable to gather together a single full meal. We each ate three boiled potatoes per day, and an occasional bit of bread. For sleep, we had our eight hours on the dirt-coated floor, fully dressed. Days passed this way, one day the same as the next, the hunger never abating, the work never letting up.

Each day at work, we were assigned to a different foreman who loaded each of us with tools weighing nearly 50 pounds. I had to carry tools that weighed half as much as I did: a foreman's toolbox in one hand, and on the other shoulder a pickax a spade, and a large wrench for opening water mains. We were in charge of clearing the streets. Residents would simply empty their garbage and sewage into the ice-covered gutters, where the pile would freeze into jagged formations as solid as rock. We would chip away the mess with our pickaxes, only to be faced the next day with another new heap of frozen refuse. Whatever we were able to loosen from the gutters, we moved by hand to a corner curb, where we piled it until the sanitation crew picked it up, many days later.

Occasionally, we had to repair broken water mains. This was even tougher. First, we had to hack away a thick layer of snow and ice, and then attempt to break up the pavement and dig a ditch deep enough in the frozen ground to reach the pipe. At that point, we'd help the foreman repair the pipe, and then he would relax while ordering us to fill the hole with all the dirt we'd piled beside it.

In this town of approximately 30,000 people, only eighteen men were assigned the nearly impossible task of servicing the sewers and water mains, and a third of those were supervising the other dozen workers. All labor was done with hand tools, without trucks or carts or wheelbarrows. We repaired not only the public infrastructure but also the water pipes, faucets, and drainage systems in buildings and private homes. The wives of the elite government and Party officials, now living in the finest homes, were among our best customers. We learned how other workers did private work on the side, often at rates much higher than their wages. Although it was against the law, the management tolerated it, precisely because the people being served were the ones in power. They wanted special attention, and they were willing to pay for it, tipping generously. They knew that the quality of the work would suffer if they didn't have a reputation for paying well, and a few days later the job would have to be done again.

As if this labor out in the streets wasn't draining enough, our foreman, a fellow named Furnica, singled me out for bullying, constantly nagging me about extra chores, no matter how well I did my assigned work. In the early weeks, when I would set out for the day's labor, Furnica would escort me into the street and then make me guard all the tools as he went into the state liquor cooperative for an early morning drink. Once I'd developed my skills sufficiently, he set me off without supervision and took on an entirely managerial role, nagging or collecting fees and tips for what I'd done.

Costa and I had become accustomed to our work, but eight hours of digging and walking with a heavy burden was almost always followed by two or three hours at indoctrination or union meetings. We were burning more calories than we were able to eat. We would come home every evening utterly worn out and often without enough strength to eat supper, our one substantial meal of the day. We never got to read and seldom got to talk to Grandmother because we had to go to bed early to get up at four o'clock the next morning.

They wanted obedience. It was a motive in nearly everything they did to us. First of all, we weren't simply given work designed to break our spirits, we were also called from our home and interrogated as criminals on a regular schedule.

Although I call these sessions "interrogations," they weren't a serious attempt to extract information. It was impossible that we could know anything of value to them. Too young to be sub-versives in anything but our glum disbelief in the social disorder around us, we did our work with diligence and kept to ourselves. Summoning us into a small room to sit under the proverbial dan-gling lamp gave them a chance to play with our minds. Their likely objective was to break us down and, therefore, have lever-age against anything they feared our parents would do in oppo-sition to the new regime, from faraway America. Basically, they belittled us, criticized us, and lectured us.

They worked in pairs, sometimes wearing military garb, which frightened me. Those jackboots had become a subcon-scious trigger for internal anxiety and panic. With my head bowed, I'd endure an hour of their screaming, name-calling, and accusations. No one touched me. It was all mental, but by pounding on the table or kicking the walls, they created a sense that their emotions might ratchet things over the threshold into violence.

To hear these men spew this invective and yet season it with small, intimate details of what I'd done earlier in the day or the week before—they seemed to have seen or heard every moment of my life—weakened me with fear. They could quote my words back to me from three days earlier, getting off work, implying a subtle layer of meaning I hadn't intended. The comprehen-sive extent of their informant network showed how quickly ordinary people turned against their own values, families, and friendships, in order to earn a fragile sense of security in the new order. Yet, never—not once—did they ever quote anything we had said at home. They hadn't been able to rig a listening device in our little shack.

As painful as these sessions were, the bullying left me wounded in a particular way for the rest of my life. Any sort of bullying or even just heavy-handed authority would unnerve me with the first stirrings of panic. At the same time, this sensitivity made me fight harder and helped strengthen me. They were unable to break me because I had a faith in my view that good would triumph and confidence in my own skills as a worker, which I thought would earn their respect. Neither could have been further from the actual reality of what was happening to me, but they gave my struggle a sense of meaning and purpose that nourished and preserved me.

As a Communist worker, I was given the blue ration card because the work I did was exceptionally difficult. This little card, with its differentiating color, became my only solace, my source of self-esteem and identity. I invested all my pride and ego into that card. It marked me as someone special, not only a survivor but also someone who was tough enough to do a strong man's work at a boy's age.

The Communist ration card became an emblem of my worldview and my faith. Ration cards controlled access to food for the vast majority of Romanians. Every day, you went to the store with your card to get your allotment of food, which was meager: only so much milk, bread, rolled bacon, cheese, cornmeal, and perhaps some vegetables or fruit. Cornmeal was our main starch, mixed with water to create something like polenta, which we ate at almost every meal. The cards were color coded, yellow, green, and blue, and you reached a new level of achievement based on the degree of difficulty of your labor. Just as if you were a Boy Scout rising to a new rank as tenderfoot or star or eagle, you would have access to better rations. The fact that my card one day rose from yellow to blue, when they changed the nature of my work, gave me the illusory hope that even more "promotions" might follow. So even during these interrogations I willfully misinterpreted the experience as a test, an exam, a way of proving my mettle. I would show them I could withstand any assault and go back to work even harder as if nothing had happened. And that, surely, would stir their sympathy and respect, and earn me better work.

"Say what you will," I would reply calmly to them. "I'm a good worker, and I'm going to get better. I don't care what you say about me or my parents. Just watch."

"Your parents!" one of them would shout. "They've abandoned you. They don't care about you. Where are they now? Living the good life in America. How can you be loyal to them when they haven't done a thing to help you?"

As furious as this made me, I simply gazed at the table and refused to respond. They wanted to spar with me, and I refused to show them that anything they could say would weaken me. My naïveté and my age made all of this possible. If I'd been a little older, they might have been harder on me, and I might have been unable to keep up this façade. Yet they never showed sympathy for me, and if they felt it, they didn't give any indication.

In reality, I was terrified of them. My stomach ached, my pulse pounded, and this continuous, contained panic often caused me to hyperventilate. The interrogation sessions themselves left me feeling as drained and exhausted as a full day's work.

———

After months of this, Furnica told us we were now to work underground, in the sewer mains. With only a pair of rubber boots and a lamp, we followed our foreman down into a manhole, clinging to iron rungs as we lowered our bodies into the dark shaft. Someone else lowered our pickaxes, shovels, and pails to us, where we stood shin-deep in thick sewage blocking the drains.

"You go left," he said, pointing to my brother, then looking at me. "And you go right. When you get to a blockage, break it apart and carry it up in your buckets."

As if the stench and the cold weren't bad enough, we had to walk continually stooped over, bending at the waist, for hours and hours. Rats swarmed around our feet, and sewage seeped through the holes in our boots. Very early in this forced servitude, I applied my worldview to my own predicament. In the background, of course, was my personal God who would reward me for being good and defeat my enemies because they were evil. Now under the employment of my enemies, this meant in order to be saved I had to prove I was good, which meant, in this context, skilled at the manual disposal of human waste. I would prove myself to God. Built into all of this was my confidence in the classic Puritan work ethic as well: not only would God be pleased and reward me, but my employers would be persuaded as well and at least put me to better use. The universe, and more important, the social and political organization of Botoscani, would recognize that it *needed* me.

So Costa and I lugged our sewage back to the manhole shaft, 60 pounds of sewage, not so much carrying it as dragging it. One hour stretched into two, three, four, five, six. We'd hand our full bucket to another worker waiting, with a shaft of light falling on his shoulders, and he would hand us an empty bucket to carry hundreds of feet into the dark recesses of the sewer main, where we would hack another load loose from the sewer walls and fill our buckets. At the end of the day, at the municipal works garage, there was no way for us to clean up. Our feet and legs and shoes were caked and stinking. Hanging up our tools, we were handed a single glass of skimmed milk, the special reward for anyone required to work underground. In one small way the Communists confirmed my worldview, my belief that I would be rewarded for my work. The day we went underground was the day I received the elite, blue ration card. It provided me with more rations at a time when my work almost completely eliminated my appetite for food.

At the end of the day, we were too tired and disgusted to eat. Walking home, people who saw us coming would cross over to the other side of the street, covering their mouths with a scarf or handkerchief, keeping their nostrils as far from us as possible, without going entirely out of their way. When we walked back into our apartment, our grandmother gave no indication of how we smelled. She just behaved as if nothing had changed. We washed as best we could, with what little water we had at our disposal, and fell onto our piles of straw.

Day after day, we did the same thing, nauseated by the stench, sore from the weight we carried, and after work we dragged ourselves home through the dark. These were not what we think of as sewers today. They had no man-made water supply and would be flushed clean only in the spring, during the rainy season. In subzero weather, the sewers would become a huge, septic labyrinth, clogged with excrement. And always, because we were only boys, we had to clean the narrower sewers, only three to five feet wide, never the ones in which you could stand up straight while walking through them.

Again and again, we were sent down into the sewers as part of the make-them-sweat-blood campaign.

———

My memories of this labor remain dim and get more fragmented as time passes. Sometimes, I would bring home remarkable discoveries. The revolvers and swords and medals I'd found: treasures tossed into the storm drains as the Communists took over, evidence of old allegiances that might have led their owners to imprisonment.

By nature I was a happy kid, not just a believer in goodness even during the worst kinds of suffering, but a playful boy ready for adventure. My brother watched as my smiles disappeared and my manner turned into a kind of robotic obedience. We'd spent so long struggling to put together just one full meal a day for ourselves, and yet now, even when the food was available, our appetites had disappeared. I lost pound after pound, and after only a couple of weeks underground, I began to look the part of the forced-labor camp inmate. It was how things worked now: the Party didn't need to kill you outright; it simply worked you to death, forcing you to burn more calories than you could eat. What kept me going was my naïve vision of a world that rewarded goodness.

"Take it easier," Costa would say to me. "I can do more than you. Take more breaks. Let me pick up the slack. I've heard things. This isn't going to last. That letter from the legation? That was just the start. They'll release us. I know they will."

I knew he was just improvising, trying to keep my spirits up. The loss of my smile worried him as much as my loss of weight. Now, home was no escape from the rigors of our work. Because we couldn't wash up thoroughly after a day's work, our apartment smelled as repulsive as the sewers. The scent had settled permanently into the fabric of our overalls and the leather of our shoes. Hanging them on the stove to dry out when we got home, they fouled the air of our little room, and yet our poor grandmother never showed the slightest hint of how hard it had to be for her to breathe that air. Sewing up the holes in our overalls, she never made a face.

Eventually, I developed a high fever and collapsed when I got home from work. Putting me to bed, our grandmother tried to summon a doctor, but no one could make a house call, so she and my brother watched over me the whole night. In the morning, a doctor arrived after Costa had set off for the sewers.

When the physician told her I had pneumonia, she was almost relieved. Even though my work had weakened me, it was a more encouraging prognosis than she'd feared. Tuberculosis was the equivalent of cancer back then, so she believed this diagnosis was almost a blessing.

It took me some three weeks to fully recover, time enough to begin eating properly again and regain much of the weight I'd lost. But it was clear to all of us that the conditions under which we'd been forced to live had nearly killed me. By staying alert to the gossip around him, Costa learned that our grandmother wasn't alone in fearing for my life. The local government and security officials had panicked when they learned I was bedridden with high fever. Once again, it became obvious that they had paradoxical motivations. They wanted to make us "sweat blood" but also to keep us alive. Our mysterious value to the government of Romania once again emerged, which struck us all as supremely ironic, considering how they were treating us. Apparently, Costa discovered, it was against the law, even in Communist Romania, to force a child under the age of fifteen to work underground. As I recovered, they realized they had dodged a bullet and quickly reassigned me. This time I got to dig holes in the countryside for telephone and electric poles.

Then Costa, too, received something of a promotion, when they transferred him to work in the bus garage of the town's public transportation department. Though he disliked the job, it was work I dreamed of doing as soon as I visited him there. I wanted badly to work on the big REO bus. I would have been proud to develop skills as a mechanic or transportation engineer. The truth was, I simply wanted to know how a bus ran.

The 1953 winter in Botoscani was brutal. Snowfall was so heavy that most streets were impassable for months, because our public works didn't have enough equipment to keep more than the main thoroughfares cleared. "Equipment" signified primarily a shovel in the cold, chafed grip of a fourteen-year-old boy. Romanians had never heard of snowplows or salt trucks. So while it may have been an act of mercy to fish me back up to the surface of the planet for a day of labor, my muscles weren't thanking anyone for the favor. Wet snow weighed nearly as much as sewage. But I could stand up straight now. That was a relief. And while my world was wonderfully aroma-free as well, my body was just as sore and spent by the end of the day. I constantly had to check my toes for frostbite, and the pace was relentless. Our highway department consisted of half a dozen workmen, an equal number of supervisory staff, and a small boy charged with filling the bed of a truck with snow and ice in a matter of minutes before moving a little farther down the road to do it again, as the garbage collectors do it today.

As bad as clearing snow was, my next assignments were hostile. They seemed almost intentionally life threatening. First, I was assigned to work for the Electric Distribution Division as an apprentice lineman on high-tension wires and the array of transformers spread throughout the town. I learned how to sleep while walking through the streets carrying a huge ladder on one shoulder. I was bringing up the rear, with the ladder, while the worker ahead of me bore the weight of the front end. Worn out from the previous days of work and sleep deprived, I would close my eyes and actually fall asleep in a trance-like state, still walking and leaning on the ladder to stay upright, waking up when we'd arrived at our assignment—the way truck drivers sometimes discover they've driven miles in a state similar to sleepwalking.

In these ambulatory catnaps, I'd give my brain enough rest

to get through the day of work. Meanwhile, when I regained normal consciousness, I'd realize it was so cold that my breath had condensed on my upper lip as a ridge of ice. Usually I was the one helping to dig a hole for a new power pole because my partner wouldn't allow me to risk working on the wires themselves. Always the workers, peasants, and ordinary townspeople, regardless of their political allegiances, recognized our humanity and protected it. Those in power almost never did. The funny thing was, I resented this prohibition. After all I'd been through, I considered myself the equal of any adult.

The worst assignment of my entire captivity began soon after this apprenticeship with the linemen. I was ordered to get up at 4:00 a.m. every day and be responsible for turning off all the electrical transformers before dawn, and then, in the evening, turn them all on again. It was part of an attempt to save power and prevent daytime blackouts. These huge switches were housed in square metal cabinets, about four feet wide and deep. In the dark, these boxes seemed like something you might see now in a horror movie, impossibly dark inside, with the glow of capacitors or meters glimmering in a dark recess, not putting out enough light to show me what to touch. They hummed, too, a deep, repellent mechanical drone that seemed to fill my head and rumble in my chest, making it hard to concentrate. This was not a good state to be in while groping into a cavity full of exposed wires, any one of which could stop my heart at the wrong touch of a fingertip. Somehow, though, I managed to find the handle, pull it, and watch a dozen streetlights wink on, or off, depending on the time of day. Every morning I prayed the moon would shed enough light to help me see the lever inside those boxes. It seldom did.

Occasionally, my hand grazed the wrong projecting piece of metal, and a searing jolt of electricity rocketed through my body, knocking me onto my back. Eventually, I'd come to, finding myself stunned and sprawling on the icy pavement, with the growling black transformer still glowering above me, ready to swallow my arm again.

Moving through the town on a kind of nightmarish scavenger hunt, from one to another of fifteen transformers, took me on an early-morning six-mile hike. Then I put in a full day's work doing repairs for all the favored "customers." At the end of the day, I did my six-mile circuit of the transformers again. So, essentially, I walked half a marathon every day. After that, my team was on call for emergency service and repairs, and we received a constant stream of them, since the government had invested so little in the system.

A 24-hour stretch was equivalent to three working days of eight hours each. If the Communists had actually cared about labor and the workingman, we would have been given three days of rest. Instead, we were allowed a day off, and then we were back for another long shift. Each of us was putting in nearly ninety hours of work per week, without extra pay or overtime. During my first month, I was exempt from this forced march, but once I'd finished my apprenticeship, I was working 24-hour shifts and contending, again, with a state of continuous exhaustion.

———

Robert Wright, in his recent book *The Evolution of God*, has a wonderful section on how, in many cultures, village populations never grow beyond a few dozen people who seldom venture more than a few miles from their homes. What we call evil doesn't exist in these villages because it can't take root in such an open environment. No one has inordinate power over anyone else. Everyone knows everyone else so intimately that deception and self-deception become impossible; for practical reasons there's no privacy. Religious behavior has nothing to do with morality in these cultures, because these people don't need morality. There's nowhere and no way to hide what they do. If someone were to steal a valued possession, there's no way to use it. Everyone would see. Stealing makes no sense.

In more developed societies with populations easily given to conflict, such as nations or corporations, behavior we consider evil seems to arise with great fluency as an adaptive strategy, a way of achieving a purpose that seems to override one's sense of what's decent. It arises because it's possible in ways it isn't in smaller groups. In a world of strangers, no one knows who you are, and this anonymity breeds a new sense of license. Base instincts—aggressive behavior, greed, misuse of power against other people—can arise easily in this kind of environment.

Some years back, I came across a story about a famous experiment at Stanford University. Though the scientific rigor of its methods have since been questioned, this experiment, conducted decades ago, showed how quickly and easily people become blind to the moral ramifications of their own behavior. In this case, the behavior was torture. Philip Zimbardo, a psychologist, created a prison setting where he tested two dozen male college students—all of them volunteers—on their willingness to inflict pain. He gave these students one of two roles: guard or prisoner. He asked the guards to allow no one to escape and to commit violence. The prisoners he simply told to be prisoners.

Artificially, Zimbardo created a depersonalized, alienated world in a group about the size of one of Wright's villages. He had guards wear uniforms and sunglasses, while prisoners wore stocking caps and overalls and were given numbers, sewn into those overalls. They were also forced to wear a symbolic chain around their ankles to brand them as captives.

Guards were told at the start never to harm a prisoner. In a video recording of the proceedings, Zimbardo tells the guards, "You can create in the prisoners feelings of boredom, a sense of fear to some degree, you can create a notion of arbitrariness that their life is totally controlled by us, by the system, you, me, and they'll have no privacy. We're going to take away their individuality in various ways. In general what all this leads to is a sense of powerlessness. That is, in this situation we'll have all the power, and they'll have none."

From the earliest stages of the experiment, the participants were all psychologically manipulated to believe in their roles. Those chosen to be prisoners were "arrested" at their homes and "charged" with armed robbery. The local Palo Alto police department assisted Zimbardo by arresting his prisoners at home and transporting them to the police department for fingerprinting and mug shots. At this point, they were driven to the mock prison, strip-searched, and given new identities.

Almost immediately, behavior got out of control. The guards began to humiliate the prisoners to enforce obedience. Their role was simply to maintain order, and they did whatever it took to achieve it. Among the prisoners, rebellions broke out, leading to a riot the second day of the experiment. In response, the guards volunteered to coordinate their efforts and put in extra hours, attacking prisoners with fire extinguishers.

As a way of preventing future revolts, guards created meaningless tasks to occupy the prisoners, asking them to repeatedly sound off with their numbers, not their names. If anyone made an error, he was smacked or his mattress and clothing were confiscated, so that the prisoner had to participate naked. Sexual acts were simulated, as a way of humiliating some prisoners—reminiscent of the abuse at Abu Ghraib.

Zimbardo was criticized for not shutting down the experiment when the prisoners had begun to coordinate organized escape plans. In his role as prison superintendent, Zimbardo himself became so psychologically enmeshed in the experiment that he proposed moving the entire mock prison to the local police station to maintain order, at which point, the police decided to opt out. Apparently, they realized they never should have been involved to begin with. The guards ultimately identified so deeply with their artificial roles that they protested when the experiment was called off—and this happened only when Christina Maslach, a graduate student Zimbardo was dating, and whom he later married, objected to the conditions of the prison when she came in to conduct interviews. She was the only person who questioned the morality of the experiment itself. It ended after only six days, when it had been planned to last for two weeks.

Zimbardo published a book to explain his findings, called *The Lucifer Effect: Understanding How Good People Turn Evil*, in which he argues:

- Nearly everyone can be easily induced to harm another person for his or her own survival.

- If you strip away routine and familiar social pressures, a person's character counts for little when it comes to this willingness to do evil.

- People follow the herd. If others are committing evil around you, you are likely to join in.

Not long ago, a *USA Today* article, "An Expert Asks: Do We All Have an Evil, Dark Side?" by Marilyn Elias, pointed out that Zimbardo now sees key similarities between his experiment and behavior found in some military prisons in Iraq. When you relieve a guard of his or her ordinary identity, with all of its inherent accountability—as in giving a soldier a uniform and a mission—that person can easily inflict suffering on another person, almost without provocation. Something as simple as a mask or a set of sunglasses can provide a sense of anonymity strong enough to remove most moral inhibitions. Take away these conditions, put a person back into a familiar social environment where secrecy and depersonalization are eliminated, and inhibitions kick in. Then evil behavior becomes much more difficult to induce.

When I read of Zimbardo's experiment, it was hard for me not to remember my grandfather's torture, his being kicked to death in that lonely prison in Romania. Given the right circumstances, evil can emerge, unless we've trained ourselves to be acutely aware of our own actions and remain skeptical of them. Although the experiment has been faulted by some as unethical and even unscientific, a few participants later explained their behavior by saying they were role-playing to please Zimbardo. Yet it confirmed my own sense of how human beings behave. It didn't explain *why* this is the case, but it felt like the clearest crystallization of what I'd seen throughout my life in the behavior of people around me and in myself. It created, in my mind, an accurate picture of the human psyche and its fragile grasp on what we consider the most simple, fundamental mores.

---

Months passed in Botoscani, and my strength and spirits slowly began to fade, until one cold, damp morning. I have vivid memories as I write these words of our hovering around a radio in a work shed. Listening to the radio was beyond a rare treat. We never had one in Botoscani. Curious about why everyone was so transfixed by the broadcast, I moved closer and elbowed into the group. It was March 9, 1953, which happened to be my fourteenth birthday. There it was, a birthday present to cheer me up and buoy my spirits. Iosev Vissarionovich Dzhugashvili, better known as Joseph Stalin, had died. The radio extolled the virtues of this "great man," as the announcer, in a low voice full of gravitas and sorrow, proclaimed the terrible tragedy Stalin's death represented for the liberated millions of proletariat in the Communist world and for oppressed workers the world over.

My own delighted response to the man's death didn't exactly jibe with the announcer's eulogy. Although I didn't have a clue about the breadth of the atrocities this madman had committed, I despised him for what he'd set in motion in the land around me. I held him personally responsible for my family's current plight: our grandfather's arrest, my parents' exile, and our own forced labor. For years, we'd heard nothing from Grandfather Sever. He'd died in solitary confinement in 1951, though none of us knew it, at that point. Nor did we hear from my parents. The money they kept sending had ceased to arrive, intercepted or stolen by some Communist official. Our famous great-uncle in Bucharest, Ionel Manolescu, the celebrated actor and my grandmother's brother, could not get his messages through. We simply existed in an isolated cocoon, just putting one foot in front of the other, day in and day out.

Yet the news of Stalin's death was like a rebirth for me. I felt a distinct renewal of hope and faith in goodness. Once again, anything was possible. I came home that night in a euphoric state. I was so eager to share the good news with my grandmother and discuss it, in whispers, with Costa.

"Things will be better, for sure," I told them.

As it turned out, I was right. But I could never have imagined the extraordinary events about to happen some 4,800 miles away in New York City and then around the globe, leading to our release and a reunion with our parents.

It was late one afternoon in May 1953, some two months after Stalin's death, when my father received a phone call. He was in his corporate office at Standard Oil Company, where he'd been working for the past seven years. The voice on the line was heavily accented with the typical rolling "r" he remembered from his youth in Romania. Here is how the *New York Times* reported the unfolding events, over the course of more than a year:

### TEXT OF AFFIDAVIT

WASHINGTON, May 26, 1953—Following is the text of the affidavit given by V.C. Georgescu of New York to officials of the State Department concerning the effort of a Rumanian Legation official to barter the release of his two children from Rumania for his "political collaboration" with the Communist regime:

Yesterday morning, May 20, I received a telephone call at my home in New York, 45 East End Avenue, from a stranger. The time was approximately 8:40 a.m. The stranger asked to see me and gave a name on the telephone that sounded like "Costapeter." I said I did not recognize the name. He said it did not matter because he did not know me personally.

I asked him to come and see me at my office . . . he said that he had recently come from Rumania and would like to inform me that my children are well and healthy, and then he added, "Mr. Georgescu, if you want to see your children, this can be arranged, and I am proposing to you the following deal. You may see your children within the year if you will accept to collaborate with us."

I said, "Collaborate with you, what does that mean?" He said, "We want you to collaborate politically with the popular republic." I said, "You want me to collaborate with the present Communist regime?" He replied, "Yes, but it does not make any difference." I said, "It may not make any difference to you, but I have sworn allegiance to the United States Constitution, government and flag, and I mean to maintain it."

He said, "Do you take things that way?"

"I certainly do."

"Well, if you want to see your children, you have got to do something about it," he said.

"I don't intend to sell my conscience, because as I see it, you want to bargain for the release of my children against my conscience," I said. "There is no deal there."

I then escorted Mr. Zambeti to the elevator.

On the same day, the *Times* published another story about my mother:

### WIFE OF GEORGESCU APPEALS FOR SONS

Mrs. V.C. Georgescu made a personal appeal last night to the mothers of Rumania "to see that my children are spared."

Mrs. Georgescu sat beside her husband in their two-room apartment on the ninth floor of 45 East End Avenue, as the oil executive repeated the story he had told Washington officials.

When her husband had finished, Mrs. Georgescu, an attractive woman with reddish-brown hair and sad eyes, added what was in her heart.

"We just pray that they will not be harmed," she said. "Our prayers must be heard. For nine weeks I have made a novena at St. Patrick's Cathedral—I am Greek Orthodox; it makes no difference—to St. Anthony, the patron Saint of children, that they will be released."

Mrs. Georgescu said that she and her husband originally never had wanted to make the detention of their children a "public issue." They had used every recourse in an effort to obtain the children's release . . . but to no avail.

Mr. Georgescu mentioned that they banked on "prayer and world public opinion." His wife took up the theme.

"They are two innocent children," she said. "They have no connection with politics. What crime did they do? They are political in Rumania, but they must be human. No person who is human can keep two innocent children from their parents."

"My wife and I had a very difficult decision to make," Mr. Georgescu said. "But it was the only way; we could have no dealings with a Communist regime. We hope and pray that this will prove the best way to protect our children.

"We hope and pray that they will be spared and maybe, some day, with the help of world opinion, we will be in a position to obtain their release."

Sympathetic Rumanian and American friends remained with the couple. The Rumanians commented that they had long known that the Communists had exploited the best sentiments of people in their "political blackmail," but now "they are caught red-handed."

"If everyone takes a stand like this," one Rumanian exile remarked, "this vicious practice may be stamped out."

In an editorial, "A Father's Choice," published May 28, 1953, the *Times* commented:

How easy, comparatively, for a man of Mr. Georgescu's courage had he only been asked to barter his honor for his own life or safety! But for a man to put principle above any price, even the safety of loved ones, that was something new to First Secretary M. Zambeti of the Rumanian Legation. He was stunned, almost incredulous apparently, at this display of conscience. M. Zambeti will have news for his Communist masters when he gets back to Rumania. There are men in this world who are not for sale. They will be praying, along with the many of us who hope but can't be sure that we would have acquitted

ourselves so well in the bitter test, that the Georgescu boys
will be spared from a vindictive reprisal.

And then things really began to shift.

## U.S. EXPELS DIPLOMAT FOR 'BLACKMAIL'

WASHINGTON, May 26, 1953—A Rumanian diplomat was
ordered expelled from the United States today after a naturalized citizen of Rumanian descent had stoutly refused to barter
his own "political collaboration" with the Communist regime
in return for the promised release within a year of his two
sons, held hostage in their native land.

Gen. Walter Bedell Smith, Acting Secretary of State,
declared Cristache Zambeti . . . "persona non grata" . . . on
the basis of "verified" information provided by Rica Georgescu
of New York, a Standard Oil company official. Mr. Georgescu
described, with tears in his eyes, the deal proposed by M.
Zambeti as the price of freedom for his two boys . . . now in a
"camp" near Botoscani in northern Rumania.

Mr. Zambeti had "engaged in activities incompatible with
his status as an accredited diplomatic official" [said] Lincoln
White, State Department spokesman, who was asked if this
phraseology meant that M. Zambeti had attempted to get Mr.
Georgescu "to spy for Rumania."

## MESSAGE TO BOYS BROADCAST

MUNICH, Germany, May 30, 1953—Twenty transmitters
were used by Radio Free Europe today in a "saturation effort"
to get a message through to the Georgescus' sons in Rumania.

The message over the privately sponsored American

station told why Mr. Georgescu, who lives in New York, refused to be blackmailed into spying for the Communists. The voice broadcasting was that of the boy's mother.

In a recording made in New York yesterday and flown to Munich, Mrs. Georgescu said that giving in to the Communist blackmail would have brought "eternal shame to our family and our name."

Acceptance of the "offer" would have meant freedom for Constantin and Peter from the camp in Botoscani, in northern Rumania.

The broadcast of Mrs. Georgescu's message was preceded by frequent announcements yesterday and today that the "saturation effort"—said to be almost impossible to jam— would be made. Twenty short and medium wave transmitters in West Germany and Portugal were linked for the effort. Regular Radio Free Europe broadcasts to Rumania normally are made by only two short wave transmitters.

**EISENHOWER AID SOUGHT**

WASHINGTON, July 21, 1953—President Eisenhower took under advisement today a resolution adopted by the Catholic War Veterans of America urging him to intervene personally on behalf of the two minor age sons of Mr. and Mrs. V.C. Georgescu of New York, who are in a concentration camp in Rumania.

What followed all of this domestic publicity was a firestorm of negative publicity about Romania throughout the world media. Unknown to us, we had become an international story, the subject of reports virtually wherever newspapers were published. With all of this attention and pressure on Romania from around the world, the American government may have found it easier to apply its own quiet pressure on the Kremlin. After months of maneuvers, working with individuals and groups sympathetic to our plight, our parents were led to believe that a secret exchange had been arranged. In return for our freedom, the United States would free someone, whose identity we've never determined, who had been arrested on charges of espionage for the Soviet Union. The deal, as we learned, was between Eisenhower and Moscow. Romania, as always, simply became the pawn in the negotiations of the superpowers.

Psychologically, I would leave Romania with a firm belief that I'd left evil behind in Europe. Communism was the culprit. America was the land of hope. My simplistic model of the good people versus the bad had served me well. It had given me strength and a system of belief that I was an utter captive and pawn. It kept me alive, defiant and proud. It sustained and protected my spirit, even though it could do nothing to preserve my body. The history of my early years had been divided into these two camps, the black team and the white team, in a game far deadlier than touch football.

Yet, when I escaped Europe, the malignant reality of what I'd experienced started to emerge from my memories. To protect myself from the truth of my helplessness in those years, I convinced myself that I was leaving the plague of Communist-dominated politics behind me and that evil would be quarantined in Europe, unable to infect my generous and caring new home. Soon enough, even in this land of Oz, my old model of good and evil would find itself eroded by behavior I saw all around me.

# CHAPTER 5

# GUARDED BY ANGELS

IT WAS APRIL 13, 1954, THE DAY I FIRST SET FOOT ON AMERICAN soil. I was fifteen years old. I've always called it my second birthday, my American birthday. The three of us—our father, Costa, and I—had boarded the Pan Am Super Constellation at London's Heathrow Airport the day before and headed for New York.

We had said a tearful goodbye to our blessed grandmother, Michie. She had been the foundation of our emotional survival. She had been forced to stay behind and went to live with her family in Bucharest. When we needed courage, she had supplied it. Her strong values were both an inspiration and the constant reminder that good people existed in this world. In a way, she was the first of all the guardian angels in my life. A decade after our liberation, when she was finally allowed to leave the country, she rejoined my parents in England, where they were living then. She passed away peacefully in her mid-eighties in the company of her loving daughter, knowing in the end that her grandsons were on their way to productive futures in their new world.

Everything from then on represented a dramatically different life from what I'd endured in Europe. In many ways, what I experienced during the ten years that followed was an utter reversal of our suffering in Europe: a fairy-tale transformation. Yet, behind and beneath all of it, what I'd endured in Romania kept simmering, the memories patiently waiting to rise up and exact a toll on the happiness I felt in being able to immerse myself productively in the world around me.

I was an ambitious young man full of great enthusiasm and eager to start a normal life in my new home, with lofty aspirations that weren't in the least diminished by what I'd seen and experienced. My hopes were buoyed by the simple fact that America had to be the land of the good people. I believed all the evil ones remained behind me in Europe. My worldview hadn't changed. There were good guys and bad guys, and we'd left the latter behind as the train sped us from Bucharest to Vienna, where we embarked with our father across the Atlantic.

My early years of my American life only reinforced this vision: so many American guardian angels appeared along the way to help me, and each one of them demonstrated to me how goodness becomes an agent of change in the world, through individual human commitment and effort, one person at a time.

————

Our flight from Europe to New York City will be forever memorable. My brother and I were overwhelmed by this radical shift in the quality of our lives. The roar of the powerful props lifted us over the Atlantic as a butler set our table in the first-class cabin. The few other passengers hardly noticed us. Even so, we were a bit self-conscious, young men sporting jackets but without ties. A couple of ladies we'd never seen before, wearing beautiful dresses with jewels, settled in to sip champagne. This was not only an adventure. We were entering a new world, as radical as a shift from black and white to Technicolor. This was a Super Constellation, essentially a ship with wings. The transatlantic flight took almost twenty-four hours in those days before jets, so a first-class ticket bought you a bed as well. The butler announced that our berths for sleeping had been set up; yes, berths. I climbed up into the most comfortable one with plenty of room and delightful, fragrant sheets. It was hours before I could fall asleep, I was so eager to see my parents' new home. I wanted to visualize Manhattan, but I had no way to picture the skyline. It was a complete mystery to me.

I opened my eyes shortly before the plane came to rest at Idlewild Airport. The somnolent drone of the engines fell silent. The boarding stairs docked at the side of the plane, and then, for some reason, we had to wait for everyone else to get off. *Where is our mother?* Finally an affable gentleman appeared and gave Dad a warm embrace. His fedora still on, Jim Crayon (as I learned later, the PR man for Standard Oil) told Dad everything was ready for us to emerge. Standard Oil had paid for all of this and underwritten a lot of the expenses of our release and transport to America, which goes to show that corporations do have a soul. The three of us—Dad flanked by his two boys, each holding one of his hands—slowly stepped out onto the ramp of stairs. I took a quick look at the throng of several hundred people, trying to spot our mother. We were caught in a crossfire of flashbulbs. At the bottom of the stairs, an emotional woman I didn't recognize, with dark glasses and a delicate small hat, reached out and encircled us with her arms. That scent I'd completely forgotten. It was our mother. None of us was quite sure what to do. I felt moved yet self-conscious as the center of attention for all these cameras. "Copii mei" (my children), our mother said, laughing and crying at the same time, tears streaming down her face.

Eventually, we escaped the noise, the hubbub, the photographers, and the press conference by slipping into a huge limo, which sped us toward New York City, our new home and new land, our future.

————

That was how it all looked and felt from my limited, half-comprehending point of view. I didn't know that the world was following along on our journey, through the press, as in this *New York Times* article:

### RUMANIA FREES BOYS HELD AS SPY PAWNS

WASHINGTON, April 12, 1954—Rumania has released two youths whom it used as hostages a year ago in an attempt to make their father, a naturalized United States citizen, spy for his former homeland.

Their release followed President Eisenhower's personal intervention in a letter to the Rumanian government.

Today, after a seven-year separation, the two boys, Constantin and Peter Georgescu, aged 19 and 15, were reunited with their father, Valeriu C. Georgescu, at the airport in Munich, Germany. They telephoned from the airport to their mother in New York.

The State Department announced that "their departure from Rumania came about as a result of a long series of approaches by the department in which President Eisenhower and Secretary Dulles took a personal interest."

The boys . . . left Bucharest for Vienna by train Saturday, accompanied by David Mark, second secretary of the United States Legation. They flew from Vienna to Munich, where their father met them to take them to New York.

During a stopover at Frankfurt, Germany, they stood by smiling while their father answered questions. Since 1951, he said, he had not been able to write or receive letters from his sons. Early this morning, Mrs. Georgescu walked to St. Stephen of Hungary Roman Catholic Church to pray.

"God deserved my thanks," she said. "And then the rest of the world."

And then in the *Times* a few days later, April 16, 1954:

### GEORGESCU FAMILY IS REUNITED HERE

Prayers of thanksgiving were said yesterday by the Georgescu family.

Mrs. Lygia Georgescu was reunited with her two sons who for the last seven years had been held as hostages in Rumania. The boys arrived in New York with their father, who had met them in Munich.

The meeting between mother and sons took place aboard a plane at the New York International Airport, Idlewild, Queens. When all the passengers except Mr. Georgescu and his sons had left the plane, Mrs. Georgescu went aboard.

The family spent the day resting and talking, Mr. and Mrs. Georgescu trying to get acquainted again with their sons.

"We prayed and hoped and God was good to us," said Mr. Georgescu. "The hand of God works in mysterious ways. We give our thanks."

These stories offer a superficial overview of what, for my parents, amounted to years of anguished and expensive efforts to secure our freedom. Ironically, these reports are virtually the only information I have about their seven-year struggle to save us. Whisked to our new residence, on Manhattan's Upper East Side, we had only a few hours, it seemed, to get to know our parents again. And yet on that day and on every day afterward, not a word about the previous seven years was spoken. I don't know if they simply couldn't bear to hear what we had been through, or if they didn't want us to have to relive any of it in the retelling, or if they believed that by focusing only on the future they could help heal the trauma we thought we'd left behind.

It was as if we were all participating in a subconscious effort to repress everything that had been happening to all of us and ignore the uneasiness behind our happiness. We closed our eyes to what we'd been through; we shut our mouths, and we smiled at one another as if we'd only been apart for the duration of a summer vacation. We lived in the moment.

Years later, I had to unearth these old newspaper clippings to gain insight into what had actually happened. We did learn one significant bit of inside knowledge in addition to these reports in print. Though my parents never discussed with us the various ways in which they'd tried to arrange our release, we learned they had borrowed larger and larger sums, as the years went on, paying for one rescue effort after another—all to no avail. By the time we made it into America, they were seven figures into debt. Because they had left Romania without any of our family's wealth, which had been seized by the Communists, it took them years to pay off their creditors. This astonishing dollar figure was virtually our only clue to exactly how they'd tried to save us.

My parents could tell that my brother and I had grown so much that we were, in some sense, new people, strangers, not at all the children they had left with our grandparents. My mother especially found this startling. Emotionally, it threw her off balance, and I'm sure my father felt as if maybe he'd just adopted someone else's kids rather than being reunited with the two little boys he'd left behind.

What followed that week and the next, and well into the rest of the year, was a crash course in American citizenship. We were guests on *The Ed Sullivan Show,* ten years before the Beatles made their American debut on the show. Next came *The Today Show*, which had just begun broadcasting a year earlier, with host Dave Garroway. We were asked to visit the President and Mamie Eisenhower at the White House. We were interviewed, with the help of interpreters, by a long series of reporters and had our photographs in all the major publications: *Life, Time, Saturday Evening Post,* and the *New York Times*. It was an abrupt, extreme transformation. In one of these interviews, I explained that I'd never owned a necktie. A few days later, thousands of ties arrived at my parents' apartment in the mail. Suddenly, as intensely as we'd been hated in Romania, we were beloved. After a few months of learning English, my life assumed the routines of a well-educated upper-middle-class American youngster. Only I wasn't.

---

After about two weeks of our celebrity circus in New York, I noticed the recurring face of an elegant lady with knowing, piercing blue eyes. To say that she was treated with deference by everyone she met would be an understatement. Like royalty, she seemed to part the waters every time she entered a room where we waited for another photo op. I realized I was seeing her at every major event during our first weeks in America. Not only that, when Ed Sullivan was about to introduce the "Georgescu boys," she walked onto the stage first, as an honor for her crucial role in our rescue. *Ladies and gentlemen, Congressman Frances Payne Bolton.* And when we were introduced to President Dwight David Eisenhower at the White House, there she was again at the president's right side receiving the great man's respect and affection. Finally, I brought up the subject with my parents on our return from Washington: who *was* this woman?

"Your guardian angel," my mother said.

It was a designation I've never forgotten, a term I've since adopted for an entire rank of people in my life—soldiers for good—and there have been so many of them. In the weeks that followed, Dad began to elaborate on the story that had already been told in newspapers, magazines, and television. Yet it would be some months before our English would be good enough to grasp the details. For now, Dad summarized the amazing saga of this lady who had more than earned the title of angel.

Shortly after Zambeti and his Romanian and Russian handlers asked my father to spy for them in return for the safety of his children, the press started barking in unison: "American citizens blackmailed by the Soviets." It was a juicy cliffhanger that kept readers buying papers: Every headline trumpeted the next installment of our saga, and the public became so invested in our fate that the name Georgescu had become a household word long before our release. Everyone cared.

But one woman did more than sympathize. She was Congressman (that's what she liked to be called) Frances Payne Bolton. At the other end of the phone, on the day she first called my father, she said, "No one will blackmail American citizens and get away with it." By that date, my parents had become naturalized Americans. "I won't have it," she told Dad in so many words. "I'll get the boys out. Consider it done."

One story in *Time* (May 30, 1953) described her efforts clearly:

> The Georgescus redoubled their efforts. Bolton approached Russia's Andrei Vishinski at the U.N. . . . (who said) "Rumania is not my country." (Then) she took the Georgescus to see Under Secretary of State Bedell Smith. As a result, a personal letter from President Eisenhower was delivered to Rumania's Prime Minister.

Who was this amazing person, and why would she pick up the cause of this strange family caught up in the throes of the Cold War?

Frances Bingham was born into a wealthy and cultured Cleveland family. She eventually became part heir to a fortune from her uncle Oliver, one of the richest men in America, a partner in Standard Oil. Throughout her life, because of the early deaths of her brother and her daughter Elizabeth, she developed an intense spirituality. She saw her wealth, and eventually her calling as a politician, as a way to drive social change. It wasn't a custom for a young woman of her station to attend college. Yet, being a totally driven youngster, she would stay up until 2:00 a.m. reading history and philosophy from her father's extensive private library. She simply needed to understand the world she lived in and how the social and political system worked. In her teens, she wrote in her diary about news stories of women suffragists wanting the right to vote: "I must think deeply about this issue. Are women ready for this immense responsibility?"

After her brother Oliver died, she went on a tour of Europe, to let her father mourn in private, and it turned this solitary, introspective young woman into a leader. She roamed everywhere abroad, feeling her self-confidence increase every day, and when she returned, she enrolled in private school. Europe had transformed her from a solitary thinker to a leader. She became president of her school's glee club, only the start of a series of roles that prepared her for her future national prominence. As an adult, this talent expressed itself first in her involvement with the social reform movement in Cleveland, where she became active in the Visiting Nurse Association, helping people who were too poor to afford medical care. In her early twenties, she married Chester Bolton and, at the age of twenty-four, gave birth to their first son, Charles. A few years later in 1912, a second son, Kenyon, arrived.

In 1917, she inherited part of her uncle Payne's wealth, yet she continued as a housewife and mother, enjoying an idyllic life on a farming estate in Ohio, as her husband became minority whip in Washington, D.C. But her bliss didn't endure. World War I began, as well as a worldwide flu pandemic, which killed more people than the war, including her third newborn child. After her baby's death, she began to believe that death was merely a curtain and that human life was a part of a much larger, unseen reality.

Now thirty-six, still in mourning for her lost baby daughter, she made one of the most significant choices of her life. She moved to Nyack, New York, to study yoga under a self-styled guru—many considered him a charlatan—who appeared to be as interested in money as he was in the secrets of spiritual wisdom. Whatever his motivations, Bolton learned about the mystical religions of the East and never returned to Christian orthodoxy, practicing yoga the rest of her life. She discovered that her *practice* was a way of harmonizing her individual life with the force of good. Her husband opposed all of this. Frances Bolton concluded, "I could live with a man, but find it hard to accept subservience to him."

When her husband, Chester, died prematurely of a heart attack in 1939, Frances Bolton was nominated by the local Republican organization to take his place in Congress. It was wrongly assumed that she could fill his seat for a short year while the party bosses could select the best male candidate to keep the congressional seat in Republican hands. Well, it turned out she'd have none of that. She quickly saw the opportunity to use her talents and experience to do good for tough, diligent, working-class constituents and the nation as a whole. Thus began her three decades of service in Washington, as a congress*man*.

"It is as if some inner force urged me to see that not one thread goes untied. I am not the first woman who has had to be alone and rediscover herself," she said. So, in her mid-fifties, she began a completely new career as a public figure and Washington insider, and in 1940, she won her first election in a landslide. In the critical 1952 election, Frances Bolton was to play a pivotal role in the future of America. During the Republican National Convention held in Chicago, Bolton became an influential leader of the Ohio delegation. Quite remarkably, she convinced her delegation to vote against their "favorite son," Ohio's own Howard Robert Taft, in favor of war hero General Dwight David Eisenhower. It was a pivotal moment in the bitterly fought primary campaign. Her arguments were persuasive. She warned them of the rising specter of Soviet global ambitions, having traveled to Eastern Europe, studied Soviet dominance, and submitted to Congress a brilliant treatise on the threat of the USSR's imperialist plans. She concluded that Taft's views were too soft on the Communist bloc and that the nation needed a tough, mature, and proven leader, experienced in warfare—for a new set of battles that were surely to come. That's why her candidate for America was General Eisenhower.

After hanging up the phone from my father, Congressman Frances Bolton went to work on our behalf. Driven by her sense of fairness, by compassion, by her extraordinary commitment to good—and crucially, by the ordeals of her own parenthood—Frances Bolton found the cause of two young boys irresistible. She went to the UN repeatedly to meet with Molotov, the Russian foreign minister. He dismissed her, saying, "Trust me, Mrs. Bolton, we Russians have nothing to do with the two boys. It's the Romanians." Meanwhile, the Romanians were pointing a finger at the Russians. After months of this unsatisfactory diversionary Ping-Pong, Bolton went to her good friend President Eisenhower and simply said, "Ike, you've got to get the boys out of Romania and reunite them with their parents."

In her camp Frances had another ally—Frank Wisner Sr., the OSS operative who'd collaborated with my father from prison in the early 1940s, and who had become one of the founders of the CIA with Allen Dulles and Walter Bedell Smith. Frank and his wonderful wife, Polly, became close friends with my parents during their early assimilation into the United States. Wisner's kindness and personal involvement were to become invaluable to us. His partnership with Frances Bolton became an irresistible force.

Some forty years later, after years of my seeking to find out how Eisenhower and Frank Wisner Sr. found a way to get us out of Romania, a gentleman appeared in the reception area of Young & Rubicam insisting he had to see me privately. Curious, I ushered him into my office and closed the door. He sat down, refused an offer of coffee or a glass of water, and said, "I work for the government, and I'm here at the request of some important friends you have who have requested I look into your old files from 1953." (Actually, the help came from Frank Wisner

Jr., the son of our benefactor, and the most senior-ranking career diplomat in his day.) The stranger continued, "You can call me Mr. Smith, but that's not my name, and I've never been to your office. I've personally read your files. While there are no specific names recorded, my best guess is that you and your brother were traded for some individuals important to the Soviets who were then in U.S. custody. The pattern of correspondence and memos appear to indicate that's how you got out of Romania. You two kids were traded for some Russian spies."

My relationship with the incredible Frances Bolton was only beginning. Later, over the years, I remember when my father would take me to Washington, D.C., and we'd have dinner with Allen Dulles and Frank Wisner Sr. Sometimes Frances Bolton would join us, and her commitment to our welfare only got stronger. When she learned, in 1961, that I had been accepted at Stanford Business School, she quietly arranged for a partial scholarship, writing a check for my education without hesitation. (She likely contributed to my Exeter and Princeton education as well.)

While I was in California, working on my MBA, she would fly me coast-to-coast to her home in Palm Beach during my spring breaks. It was an enormous estate on the Atlantic Ocean that the Bolton family used to own. We talked during my stays there, and I absorbed so many things from her, not just her goodness but also the leadership strengths she embodied, the ideal combination of toughness and compassion.

In the end, she had nothing to gain in all of this, other than a sense that she was following a higher calling, a way of doing good in the world. In those days, I didn't know what the word *gravitas* meant, but now I know that's exactly what she had, but with a gleam in her eyes, a quick wit, and a talent for dinner party repartee. As polished and gritty and effective in the world as the veteran politician she was, she had the purity of heart and faith of a child. Those pale blue eyes penetrated everything. It was as if we'd known each other all our lives. We were the oldest of friends. There was always the sense of a connection; it was as if she could tell that "I got her." A warm and fuzzy soul burned brightly behind her majestic persona, and I adopted her as my American grandparent.

I've never called her that until just now, but it strikes me that she *was* very much a female counterpart to my grandfather—dignified and politically esteemed, famous and burdened with a role that required a formality in her bearing. She was so respected that she stood before the Republican National Convention and had the honor of nominating the first woman to run for president, Margaret Chase Smith, from Maine.

Bolton's career achievements are legendary. She helped enable the African American Tuskegee Airmen to fight in the Second World War. She opened diplomatic doors to the continent of Africa. She served as the symbol and reality of rights for women and civil rights. Yet behind this lofty role in the world was a loving woman who still mourned her losses, who felt the suffering of others because she suffered so much herself.

———

Within days of my arrival in America, true to its reputation, this new land offered me one opportunity after another. I was aware that I was on something of a hot streak. Whenever I approached another gatekeeper—with none of the usual credentials for admission—I'd be given a pass. Frances Bolton was only the first of many guardian angels, disguised as deans or recruitment scouts or friends, who gave me a chance, when most others would have locked me out. At the time, I realized how fortunate

I was, but in a way I expected no less from my new home. It was consistent with my naïve view of America, the land where the good and deserving people were favored and the evil eventually fell on the slippery rocks. When I should have been paying closer attention to these instances of compassion and generosity, I was taking it for granted as evidence that my view of the world made sense. We'd been delivered from captivity and flown over the Atlantic to the promised land. *How incredible! But I deserve it. I'm wearing a white hat.*

Moved by the publicity about us, William Saltonstall, the headmaster at Phillips Exeter Academy, took an interest in my unique educational situation. He came from a distinguished family in New England, born and bred to be of service to others, as an obligation of his privileges. It was rumored that at one point he was offered the presidency of Harvard and yet declined because he felt he could have a more lasting impact on younger students. Eventually, in retirement, he became head of the Peace Corps.

Having seen all the stories on television and in the *New York Times*, Salty (as his students affectionately called him behind his back) phoned my father within a week of my arrival in New York. The photographs of the Georgescu boys prompted him to offer his help. Meanwhile our father hired an educational consultant, part tutor, part career counselor, to help me and my brother get up to speed in school. That phrase comes so easily now: *get up to speed*. In reality, we're talking about a level of acceleration suited to open-wheel racing; our English was, at that point, almost limited to the word *Coke*.

Let me give you a more concrete notion of the challenge we faced in the first two weeks after our arrival. Some dear friends of my parents decided they wanted to do something nice for the boys. They invited us to have lunch at the New York Yacht Club.

My father showed me how to fashion a Windsor knot, picking a necktie from the thousands that had arrived in the mail. On the face of it, this luncheon was a thoughtful idea, but, on closer inspection, maybe not so much. Neither of us spoke a word of English. We were a pair of curiosities making our appearances, hustled from stage to limousine like rock stars, and then on to our next appointment, unable to exchange a comprehensible sentence with anyone.

At our table, our hosts ordered for us, of course. When a dozen oysters appeared on a plate of ice between knife and fork, Costa and I gave each other a look. Neither of us had ever seen an oyster. You can imagine our expressions, gazing down at the half-shells filled with those shiny, slick, glistening gray orbs. It was an exquisite setting—the meal, the company, our dish presented on beautiful pink tablecloths draped over tapestries that covered each table, with ornate and almost medieval patterns—like a table from a Vermeer interior.

My brother leaned over and whispered in Romanian, "I think these things are alive."

"I think mine moved," I said.

This conversation continued, while the others ate and chatted with the friends who came to our table for a handshake with the famous boys.

"No way I'm going to eat that," I said. "I am not going to swallow one of those things."

My brother mastered his caution and gulped an oyster. I wasn't persuaded by his courage. I slipped one into my mouth, chewed a few times, and then brought the napkin up to my mouth, spat the oyster into it, and dropped it at my feet under our table's tapestry.

So imagine this particular boy, with his anonymously donated necktie, thrown into a class with a group of East Coast teens at your typical prep school, their neckties and collars properly frayed and loosened, oxford shirts unbuttoned at the neck, their chinos and penny loafers looking as if they'd been worn for about a dozen years. Those kids knew how important it was to look like a world-weary rebel even in an old school tie. Here comes Peter Georgescu, with a modicum of education and his belief in how God favors those who make good choices. Bill Saltonstall could see all of this with one simple glance at one of those photographs of us coming off the plane at Idlewild. He put it all together, knowing how unprepared we would be for American culture in the months and years ahead of us. It seemed so similar to the way Frances Bolton had picked up the phone to speak with Ike on our behalf. And now, without thinking twice about it, Saltonstall asked his assistant to get my father on the phone. He had nothing to gain by it; he simply wanted to see if he could help.

"I saw pictures of your younger son, Mr. Georgescu, and I'd like to do something for him," he said.

"Really? That's thoughtful of you."

"Let me explain."

"Peter speaks virtually no English," my father told Exeter's principal. "His last level of formal education stopped after just a few grades."

"He survived Romania. I think he can handle this," the principal replied.

"He'll be going to summer camp in New Hampshire this year where he'll be immersed in English and will pick up quite a bit that way. At least a working knowledge," my father said. "That's what the educational consultant recommended."

"He was thrown into the deep end many years ago. He swam."

"At the end of the summer, I'll bring him to Exeter and you can meet him. If you still feel he's up to it, very well then. We'll do it."

Of course, my father had more than summer camp lined up. In the following weeks, I spent long days being drilled in English at the Latin American Institute in New York City. I also watched television incessantly, trying to decipher what was being said while eating quarts of Howard Johnson coffee ice cream, my newfound dietary staple. The ice cream had little impact; I was still a skinny runt. On schedule, I did my five weeks at summer camp and came back with a practical proficiency in English. Late in August, we took a train to Boston and then drove to Exeter. I remember my impression of the school as overwhelmingly beautiful.

That evening, we had dinner with Dr. Saltonstall. It was a seminal moment in my life. The thing is, I can still see it all, but it's like watching a movie with the sound off. I can't recall what we said, other than our conversation at the end. It was a relaxed and comfortable night, that much I remember. I felt completely at ease with this tall, distinguished, graying gentleman who had to have been in his fifties. You could see gentleness in his rugged face, weathered by years of sailing.

"I think you can handle the academic work here," he said.

So I was welcome to join the Academy.

"However, since it's impossible to test aptitudes, and there's no point in testing to confirm your lack of academic knowledge, I'll offer you a deal. You will simply have to pass—only pass— all your courses at the end of the first year. Just squeak through with a Romanian gentleman's D-minus. We won't handicap the results. You'll have to earn that D. If you can't do that, I'll find the right school for you."

He paused and looked into my eyes.

"Fair enough?"

I nodded and grinned. I didn't have a clue what he was talking about; I nodded because my father looked pleased. We shook hands, and he put his arm around my shoulder and turned me around, and asked something he had probably never asked any other student, before or after: "What grade would you like to be in when you start?"

Again, I had no idea.

"I'd like to be in a class with kids my own age," I said.

He grinned and said, "You'll be a sophomore."

That's how I got into Exeter. Hardly a month goes by now when I don't ask myself what made him pick up the phone and offer this to my father and then to me. My fifteen minutes of fame had come and gone, so it wasn't a play for publicity. It had an indelible effect on my education, as well as on my emotional and social development, and set me on a path that made it relatively easy to become the best person I could be.

I remember Barbara asking me when we were dating how I felt, having just been reunited with my parents, only to be shipped off almost immediately to boarding school. Was I hurt that my parents didn't want to keep me close and dote on me for a while to catch up on all the hovering parenthood they had been unable to provide for us all those years? It might seem odd, but it didn't faze me a bit. It never occurred to me to think twice about heading off to prep school. It felt so totally comfortable being on my own and living my own life, so to speak, that the notion of being separated again from my parents was not unnatural. Compared to what I had been through, heading off to the comforts of the special-looking school I visited with Dad that August seemed like a cakewalk emotionally. I had gotten past the need for hands-on parenting many years earlier and was more or less a premature adult at this point. I was eager for the opportunity, not fearful of separation. My parents, ironically, were the ones who suffered, the ones who sacrificed. They dearly wanted to keep me close, but they knew, by sending me to Exeter, they were launching me on a path that would serve me well when I was fully grown.

This is not to say that the experience of a thorough and

rigorous academic education, at long last, wasn't harrowing at times. It wasn't smooth or easy. I ended the year with two D-minuses and three Ds, yet I felt a deep pride in my accomplishment. My instructors knew that I had the intelligence to get better grades, and they also had observed how arduously I had studied and participated in class. During that first year, I did set a school record I am quite sure will never be matched. I got seven zeros in my first daily quizzes in Algebra II. So my professor pulled me aside and said, "I think we need to explore this." Explore, we did. And very quickly, we both discovered that I didn't know how to divide. I could add, subtract, and multiply, but I'd never learned long division. That can be a slight problem when you're trying to do advanced algebra. So I learned, and I moved forward.

While I was there I learned American history from John Mayer, a tall, imposing gentleman who, unlike Salty, had a stern demeanor, a florid complexion, and reading glasses perched at the tip of his nose. The unique quality of a classroom at Exeter was the Harkness Table, an innovation funded by Edward Stephen Harkness, who gave $5.8 million to Phillips Exeter Academy in 1930 to create this new method of education. The Harkness Table was a place where the teacher was merely a facilitator, and the students would discuss and debate the subject matter, rather than memorizing facts and answering questions to test their understanding of the material. It was mostly self-directed learning, with the teacher acting as moderator, letting the students drive the discussion. Around this oval table sat a dozen students at most, everyone facing everyone else, with no place to hide. You came prepared and were expected to discuss and debate various approaches to the subject, and if you weren't prepared, it would emerge within a few minutes. Before it all began, Mayer always singled me out in class, standing me in front of a map of the United States.

"Peter, would you show us where New York City is? Very good. Okay, where is South Dakota?" he asked.

"Right below North Dakota," I said.

The class broke up, and Mayer smiled.

"True, but I think we'll need you to point it out," he said.

When it was obvious I'd never be able to do it, he put his hand on my shoulder and said, "I know Mr. Georgescu will do better next week."

At that moment, I was flooded with a realization of how far I'd come from the interrogators of Romania. Mayer cared. The class cared. I was being questioned, something I knew all too well, yet no one was here to abuse me or humiliate me. It was all to help me, done with compassion in his tone of voice, facial expressions, and evident understanding of my unique situation.

I graduated in the upper half of my class by the end of my final term. I scored well enough on my SATs to gain admission to Princeton University.

My Exeter chapter never closed, because I have been functionally and emotionally involved in the school ever since. America was a place of endless ice cream and the Harkness Table a place of endless learning. Every time I open a book, I sit at that table again.

---

In many ways, the momentum of this self-directed learning I gained at Exeter carried me through Princeton. My knowledge and understanding deepened, and I developed a greater sense of command, standing before groups of students giving reports. I became a better writer. There was no way to get through Princeton without being able to write. At Princeton, I refined my tendency to cherry-pick ideas and ways of thinking from many different fields, which became a lifelong habit of bricolage. Because I was able to maintain a high enough grade point average, my major in political science allowed me to take almost any course in the university. I dipped into anything that caught my eye: comparative religion, history, literature, and a variety of other disciplines in the liberal arts.

During my college years, my parents had moved to London, so I was able to spend a good part of my summer and holiday vacations visiting England. The first couple of years in England I relaxed and enjoyed my time off, but the second two years, I took jobs—one at a diesel engine factory in the eastern countryside and the other in the oil fields in France, near Bordeaux. Once again, my father threw me into the deep end, unprepared. Waiting until the evening before I crossed the English Channel, my father looked across the table at me and asked, "By the way, how's your French?" I told him I didn't know any French.

"Never mind," he said with a smirk. "You'll pick it up."

I did, sort of, at least enough to survive productively for six weeks in the oil fields.

My voice would rise up over the sounds of work: "Donnez moi la hammer? Donnez moi la wrench?"

My wrench was far better than my French.

In my four years at Princeton, I signed up for NROTC, enrolling in the marine air wing of the navy program. Everyone was dubious about my qualifications as a leatherneck. All the other guys got a kick out of hearing me, with my Romanian accent, get in front of the class and recite the length of time a marine was likely to survive during the first seven waves of an amphibious landing: "Sir, the first lieutenant's life expectancy during the first seven waves of a landing is thirty-two seconds, sir." They were trying to scare me back into the regular navy, where they all believed this lightweight belonged, not in the Marine Corps. I'll never know if they were right, because my ulcers forced me into a 4-F exemption from what could have been a dangerous rotation in Vietnam. (In those days an ulcer was thought to be induced by stress. More recently the cause has been determined to be bacteria.)

Growing up in Romania, where fighting on behalf of the good guys was considered just another way of expressing Georgescu family values, I was outraged when I found I couldn't serve. I began a long series of appeals that did nothing but inspire a thoughtful, curt note handwritten by General Shoup, a hero of WWII, who was then commandant of the Marine Corps. "Mr. Georgescu, we appreciate your interest and admire your eagerness to serve, but the rules are the rules. They cannot be changed. Good luck in your life." It literally brought tears of disappointment to my eyes, but I'm probably alive today because of those rules.

In the spring of my senior year, I realized I was now free to do whatever I wanted with the next four years I'd planned to commit to the Marine Corps. I decided to follow my father's path into the trenches of American business. With an assist from him, I lined up a job at Esso International that was waiting for me if I could get through business school, which I didn't expect to be a slam dunk.

There was a slight problem. My academic performance at Princeton was actually okay. Yet in May, I was tracked down by a call from the dean of Stanford's Graduate School of Business. Enter Ernest Arbuckle, my newest self-appointed guardian angel. Rather naively, I only applied to Stanford because, as a traditional immigrant, I wanted to see and experience the entirety of my new homeland. Dean Arbuckle took ten years off from business to run Stanford's business school, during which he helped establish it as one of the most respected schools in the country, and then he returned to Wells Fargo as its chairman and CEO.

"Mr. Georgescu. This is Dean Arbuckle, at Stanford. I'm interested in your case."

"Seriously? I'm so grateful that you even noticed it," I said.

"Yes, well, how to put this? I couldn't quite make sense of it."

"It's been an interesting four years," I said, stalling for time, at a loss.

"I would think *so*. The admissions office put you on the waiting list, so I read your files. I have to say I'm intrigued. I'm dying to know more. I noticed that you just graduated with honors from Princeton, and you received an extraordinary commendation from the wife of the football coach—that took me by surprise. You didn't even play football, did you?"

"No. No, I didn't. We met and she offered to . . ."

"Fine, fine. I'm more interested in your board scores. You scored close to an 800 on English, and yet you were in the lowest fifth percentile on math. I would have to say math comes into play a bit in the world of business. Wouldn't you?"

"Yes, it certainly does."

"So. Tell me more."

I started at the beginning and told him the whole story, my childhood, my aborted education in Romania, our life in the work camp. I even threw in a comment about how much I wanted to understand electricity as a kid and was unable to because of this weakness in math. Finally I summarized my educational history in America. I'd done my best to catch up, but it had been an attempt to fast-forward through too many levels of advanced mathematics in too little time.

"Well, I suspected something like that had to be the case," he said. "You're going to get in, I'm happy to say. You're a Stanford man, now. But we'll need to provide you with some remedial calculus. It isn't going to be easy. You'll be taking calculus at the regular university and taking economics and business classes here at the business school. Are you up for the challenge?"

"Yes, I am," I said. "I appreciate the chance you're taking on me."

Only problem was, I couldn't afford the full tuition. Yet, once again, Frances Payne Bolton rescued me with a grant from the Payne Foundation to cover a good portion of the costs.

My parents were still struggling to pay off the enormous debts they'd accrued in their various attempts to free us. I wasn't exactly living the life of a trust funder. Observing my roommates, George Clark, Fred Stratton, and Richard Scurry, who all ended up as CEOs or successful entrepreneurs, I began to understand the fundamental rules of American capitalism. They each had a Porsche. I, however, drove an eight-year-old Mercury Monterey. We didn't draw straws for the bedrooms, instead we bid on them. That's why George and Freddie took the two biggest rooms and I slept at the foot of Richard's bed on a cot. We each took turns cooking and washing, but individuals had the right to auction off their obligation for cash. I ended up cooking and cleaning quite a bit, but the cash wasn't enough to get my Mercury repaired. The car had developed a fatal short in its electrical system, which drained the battery in a matter of hours. It would have cost $300 to fix, which was more than I paid for the used car in the first place. I had only enough for jumper cables: $7. Wherever I went, I had to park my car near enough to a car that I could use to jump-start my own, with or without the other driver's permission. In those days, you could open the hood of any car with ease.

So, I ended up at Stanford Business School. With ninety hours of study per week, it was a challenge, but one of the great gifts of having been put through the injustice of a work camp is that, no matter what you face the rest of your life, it seems comparatively easy.

Again, ever since that day, I've asked myself what could have prompted Dean Arbuckle to pick up the phone, the way Saltonstall had done before him. He wasn't the dean of admissions. He had his own pressures and responsibilities and probably treasured his free time as much as any other executive, and yet he spent maybe half an hour on the phone with this young student, someone he didn't know, because he cared enough about the plight of other people to try to make a difference. Personally, he had nothing to gain by letting me get my foot through the door. He simply did it because he could.

My favorite course was in my last year, a class on business ethics. With classic case studies from actual situations faced by various companies, we had great discussions and debates, an extension of what I'd experienced at Exeter's Harkness Table. Rather than focusing on marketing in my studies, which would have been what most people would expect of someone who ended up in advertising, I studied accounting, finance, and computers. Back then, the term *computers* meant mainframes and Fortran code, so I learned how to shuffle a deck of punch cards and do some rudimentary organizing.

The man in charge of placement, Bill Lowe, became a trusted friend. I'd met his daughter, who was an undergraduate, in one of my math classes, and I ended up getting invited now and then to dinner at his house. After dinner, Bill and I would talk casually about life, school, the business world, current events. There were no hidden agendas, because I already had that job waiting for me at Esso. Yet one spring day I ducked into his office to say hi, and he asked me if I would do him a favor. Someone important, a recruiter, had flown from the East Coast to California for the day, but only two students had signed up for interviews. Would I be willing to step in and give the recruiter a chance to do the job he'd come there to do?

"Act interested in his company," he said. "That's all. Doesn't have to lead anywhere. We just need him to keep coming back."

"I don't have any classes until the afternoon," I said. "If I can show up later in the day, no problem." After all, my 90-hour-a-week time was over. It was close to the end of my stay at Stanford and I felt relaxed.

I loved getting up at ten or eleven, the only time in my life I've ever been able to sleep in. When I showed up, I didn't recognize the company's name. Young & Rubicam meant nothing to me. In the interview room, I was surprised to find a man with his arm in a sling, offering me his left hand as he introduced himself, "Peter Langhoff." He was tall and distinguished with graying hair. An imposing businessman, from where I sat. He explained that he'd had a little downhill wipeout on a recent ski trip, slipping and falling on a stretch of corn snow, hence the broken arm.

"What do you want to do in business?" he asked.

"I love people. I'm a people person."

This was about the best I could come up with. I can't believe that he didn't show me to the door, at that point.

"Hm. Let me tell you what we have to offer: It's a training program that lasts three years, in the research department. You learn about the wants and needs of consumers. It's the backbone of what we do. When you know intimately what makes people buy a product, then marketing can actually work. At the end of the three years, you have a choice. You can become a research professional or an account manager. In that latter case, you would be integrating various aspects of our work: creative work, media buying, marketing strategy, and consumer research."

He paused to let this sink in.

"So, if you were to come to Y&R and complete the three years, which direction do you think you would take? Stick with research or move into account services?"

Without hesitation, I said, "Research would be fine training but my interest would be absolutely, undoubtedly account management. I'm better with people than with that kind of dry research."

Clearly, it didn't matter: Simply making a choice with that much conviction showed that I was interested enough; he had me. Whipping out a plane ticket, he tossed it on the table, grinning as if he knew he'd just slipped a fourth ace into my hand.

"It's an open-ended ticket, prepaid to New York City. Just set up a convenient time and fly to New York during the next couple of weeks. You have nothing to lose. I'll arrange for you to meet everyone."

Getting back into Manhattan, my old digs, for three or four days sounded like great fun. Grabbing the ticket, I had no idea that inside that envelope I would discover essentially the rest of my professional life. It would introduce me to the company where I would work until I retired.

A couple of decades later, I happened to attend one of Y&R's special events for senior company alumni. They would come annually to be briefed about the progress at the company, and also meet with top management and have a chance to encounter their old friends and former colleagues. By now I was president of Y&R International, and I'd just finished giving a presentation on our overseas expansion. Afterward I spotted Peter Langhoff, the gentleman who'd interviewed me at Stanford. It was the first time I'd run into him since his retirement in the mid-1960s. Delighted to see him again, I went over and introduced myself, just in case, but of course he knew me. We chatted, and just before I moved on to mingle with others at the gathering, I leaned in closer and said, "Peter, can I ask you something?"

"Yes, of course."

"That day you met me at Stanford, what made you reach into your pocket and hand me that plane ticket? It changed my life. This is the only place I've ever worked. I met my wife here. In a way I have you to thank for everything."

"Exeter. Princeton. Stanford. Clearly you were smart enough. But that wasn't what won me over. It was your personal integrity."

I gave a little laugh.

"Really? Well, thank you. It's nice of you to say that," I said, shaking his hand and walking away, until, at about twenty paces, I stopped and turned around.

Heading back, I could see he was waiting for what he'd said to settle in.

"You saw integrity? How?"

"Easy. You told one of the most important leaders in American business research that you preferred account management over being a boring research professional. That's what I call honesty, Peter."

I shook his hand again.

"Thanks for reacting to that the way you did," I said.

Walking slowly away, I didn't tell him that, at the time, I'd had no idea what he did at Y&R.

---

I'd had so many people looking out for me in my life that, for many years, this green zone of benevolence around me solidified my worldview: everything good in life comes to those who are, themselves, trying to do good. Foremost among all my guardian angels was Barbara herself, and the constancy of her guidance many times became critical for my survival, quite literally. I would have been lost without her quick eye, penetrating judgment, and ability to charm nearly anyone. I wouldn't be sitting here in Chautauqua at my dining room table, pondering all this, without her. She discovered this place and had been coming here for years before she finally convinced me to visit. Without Barbara, I'd never be writing these words. Her continual encouragement over the years convinced me finally to write about my life's search for meaning.

Now that women are steadily gaining an equal footing with men in business and in public service, it's a bit easier to laud the virtues of a woman who decided to quit her career in order to raise our son and help guide me through the social and professional labyrinth of our corporate life, literally around the world. Many women, after years of facing the frustrations of professional life, now realize how rewarding and challenging it can be to assume a role as wife, mother, homemaker, and volunteer for worthy causes. It's turning out that this role can indeed be one half of an equal partnership. In our case, that's exactly what it was.

For example, in Amsterdam, when Barbara learned how to make rice taffle—those thirty, small Indonesian dishes—she made it possible for us, as a couple, to form personal bonds with dozens of people I would otherwise have known only in a professional setting. Establishing a personal connection to clients and fellow workers is absolutely crucial in any profession, but especially in a service industry that centers on persuasion and selling ideas. Barbara could play Katharine Hepburn to my Spencer Tracy, creating an aura of warmth and vivacity around this obsessive fellow who didn't think he was doing his job if he didn't go to the office seven days a week. Her charm and hard work followed us wherever I worked, rounding out my personality and giving me the assist I needed at all levels of the organizational chart.

Our clients welcomed us into their homes because of Barbara, not because of me. We got to know them and their families as people, and their ordinary human issues strengthened the quality of communication and trust with our key clients around the world. She was my diplomat. I would not have broken through their personal side without her. Barbara increased the level of intimacy and loyalty far beyond what I could have achieved in business meetings or on trips with clients. Without her along, I would have lived out of my hotel room, and you could have drawn a parallelogram of lines on the hotel's floor plan to show the confines of my path: from my room to the conference hall to the bar and restaurant and then back to my room. Quite simply, my success would have been impossible without Barbara's crucial influence in all areas of my life. In fact, in my twenties, I reached a point when, without her help, I might not have survived. Under the accumulated stress of everything I'd experienced in my life, both bad and good, I nearly came apart.

Throughout my life, I had met the good people, those who not only influenced the events of my life but also helped shape me into the person I've become. They did it altruistically because they could and simply wanted to do it. It was not about them, their needs, or their egos. It was all about me: my needs, my well-being, my happiness. I came to realize these people represented the anthropomorphic God I thought I'd lost, intervening in my life, making sure that I had the help I needed to succeed. God was there all the time, acting through the compassion of these wonderful people, watching me through their eyes. Yet the tests ahead were to become even more subtle and trying. I found myself, early in my career, at a moment of genuine despair and collapse, needing something more than the help of God through the agency of other people. I needed to find God within myself as well.

# CHAPTER 6

# THE CONSTANT CHOICE

WHEN I FINALLY JOINED YOUNG & RUBICAM, DIRECTLY OUT of Stanford, I joined the workforce full of hope, confidence, and thriving ambition. All of my extraordinary good fortune, as a result of some key people who gave me breaks, simply proved to me that I'd been drawn into the fold of the good, at last. I may have even begun to take for granted the amazingly fortunate sequence of events that paved my way. Yet it didn't take long, now that I was immersed in the world of business, before clouds of doubt began to shadow my euphoric fantasy.

Little by little, in the corporate office, the darker side of human nature emerged in the behavior of good people—people I liked, trusted, and admired. Compared to what I'd endured in Romania, my first disillusionment will sound absurdly run-of-the-mill. A close friend, I will call him Art, was passed over for promotion. That's all. But I was discerning enough to see the prejudice behind what he suffered and realize, at least subconsciously, how Art's misfortune threatened my entire vision of the world. This worldview had sustained me through seven years of captivity and child labor and illness, but one faint breath of this unfamiliar evil darkened my view and shook me in ways I'd never felt.

Ginger-haired and friendly as an older brother, Art was competent and kind and a crucial mentor for me. He taught me fundamental lessons about business: how to work in an office, how to interact with others at meetings, how to behave in a professional setting.

His boss, Charlie Geffroy, moved on. Charlie had become another good friend and mentor to me, but he was promoted to run Y&R in Canada. His position was crucial, so someone had to move into the spot he'd vacated, and Art was, by far, the most qualified for it. We all, down to the last employee, simply assumed Art would be promoted into that role. He'd earned and deserved the promotion. He had the right age, tremendous experience, and a superb track record. Yet more important than all these factors, he wasn't Ivy League. He wasn't part of the elite club that ran Y&R. Art came from a modest background and made it through public schools and state college on the merits of his intelligence and work ethic. That made him even more admirable in many eyes. But that, it seemed, would also be his Achilles' heel. His promotion was not to be. He wasn't one of the boys.

Our new supervisor, Richard, entered the picture, and he fit in perfectly with the privileged crew who promoted him. He wore dapper blue suits, white shirts, and a colored kerchief in his breast pocket. He was an Ivy League alum who smoked a pipe. Unlike Art, who would work late into the night with the rest of us, Richard almost never missed the 5:08 train to Connecticut. He was a nice enough man, well-bred and easy to serve, but he didn't have half of Art's grasp of the business in specific terms, or of the advertising business in general.

Ironically, it all turned out well for everybody. Art's work became the foundation for one of the most famous campaigns in the history of advertising: the Excedrin headache. Art went on to a successful career elsewhere in the agency. Yet, even knowing that Art had emerged from that episode without much harm, it still turns my stomach. My wife, Barbara, and I knew Art's wife and his children. He was a wonderful father and a fanatical worker. To me, he was the ultimate role model—good to his people, supportive, an educator, a mentor, and a man who drove the client's business forward. To have a person like that not simply ignored but almost *put down* raised some of the most fundamental questions about life. I recognized it as a personal threat. And behind my reaction lurked all my suppressed experiences in Romania.

Until I saw this happen to Art, I believed I could apply myself, do my homework, come in on weekends, and all would be well. Now, none of this held up. Art was good, America was good, but he didn't prevail. So a hairline crack appeared in my protective shell, in my deepest beliefs about how evil worked. My experience of it in Europe was heroic and cinematic. The sort of evil I faced there seemed nowhere in evidence here in my new home. The darker side of human nature in America slipped into my awareness the way it does in a stage play: a quiet entrance from the left, as light falling on a drawing room dims almost imperceptibly. A few words are spoken, and although someone's life has been diminished, no one is dying. Something has taken place, and it doesn't seem quite right, and yet everyone keeps smiling.

I remember coming home that day to our little apartment,

choked up, and emotional. Barbara consoled me by saying that this happens all the time in business: "I know about this sort of thing from stories my father has told me throughout his career." It wasn't personal. Her words meant nothing to me because my world, my whole ability to motivate myself as a human being, depended on my basic faith that hard work gets rewarded and good people win.

For much too long, I didn't realize how, in America, every blow I felt at work contained within it a hidden, Romanian fist. Buried under my anxieties about Art, I realize now, was the sense of being cast aside when I had earned the right to represent my class in Romania but was unable to fulfill it because of my family's political and economic heritage. To someone else, this little setback, like the blockage in Art's career, might seem slight; but psychologically, I desperately needed the world to operate in a certain way. This faith in moral cause and effect was, spiritually, the root of my survival in Romania, and I had believed it would serve me the same way in America. I had expected rewards for hard work, advancement for the good guys, and a God who intervened on my behalf. To be told that I couldn't represent my class, or to see Art passed over for a new job, shook the deepest foundations of my beliefs and perceptions, as well as my own sense of self. The way evil erupted as repugnant behavior in the lives of otherwise good people made no sense to me, as a Christian.

———

Art's situation was only the beginning. I remember an important meeting with one of our überclients, a man named Kennedy. He had a reputation for being very smart but extraordinarily impatient and intolerant. So we prepared with complete thoroughness for the business review with this tyrant. For a relatively young account executive, I was allowed to play a significant part in the presentation. At one point I launched into a passionate argument for how much he should spend on television commercials.

There was just a slight problem: I used the wrong possessive pronoun.

I insisted that *our* money would be particularly well spent. As soon as the words crossed my lips, Kennedy slammed his fist on the table. With his face red with anger and neck muscles bulging, he pointed at me and said, "Young man, let me remind you, this is not your money, this is our money." There was total silence in the room. No one dared to stand up for me. Certainly not my new supervisor Richard, although he may have slipped that kerchief out of his pocket to dab his forehead before he relit his pipe.

I was back in the interrogation session with the uniformed bullies in their jackboots. It took a long time for the adrenaline and fear to subside. What did I do wrong? *Did* I do wrong? What motivated this man to attack me from his position of power—a position I couldn't possibly have threatened—with such cruelty? My distraught reaction to his anger was entirely out of proportion to the offense.

As the years passed, I found myself in one situation after another that added cracks to my protective shell. With each new incident, I knew my vision of evil couldn't explain what was happening, but I had no other explanation, so I clung to my belief in God, but it was a troubled faith. In some cases, I was the offender. I watched myself engaging in behavior I would have despised in someone else. Values are easy when there's little, or nothing, to lose by acting in an honorable fashion, but when it's a matter of a significant loss, you can easily ignore your own behavior if it serves a selfish purpose.

I am in the middle of my morning run around the periphery of Chautauqua. I follow a path I've jogged hundreds of times before, through our narrow little residential streets, then down along the lake, then back uphill toward home, past the Institution's gated entry, for a final, cool-down stroll to our front porch. I'm good about this daily run. I rarely skip it, because it has become an integral part of my physical and emotional well-being. I began this discipline at a time in my life when all the stress of my childhood and early adulthood nearly destroyed me. Looking back, I realize I was probably suffering from post-traumatic stress disorder, but at the time I had no name for it. I knew I was falling apart, and I had no idea how to handle it.

In Europe, my enemy was outside. In America, he moved in. At first, I didn't notice. I was too busy tackling one challenge after another with such alacrity that I'm sure I thought of myself as one of God's favored few. Compared to what I'd suffered in Romania, no matter how many hours I worked, it seemed easy. I couldn't speak English when I stepped onto the tarmac at Idlewild, yet over the course of the next ten years, so many doors opened at the sound of my approaching step, I lost track of my luck and the gestures of goodwill that made my new life possible. It was so continuous: Exeter, Princeton, Stanford, Young & Rubicam, my marriage to Barbara, my residence in what was then the most advanced and privileged society the world had ever known. My path in life appeared, at each turn, clearly marked, and I simply took the next step forward, as if my happiness had been mapped out from the start. Yet, as my good fortune assumed its own sort of magical momentum—all the more miraculous in its contrast to my life in Romania—my inner world was crumbling. My own mind and heart were taking me down.

I'd worked for three years in Y&R's research department

until mid 1965 and then moved into account management for the next decade. The pressures of this new role, and the way it required a whole new skill set, were something I hadn't anticipated. I woke up in the night, my mind racing. I worked Saturdays, and then Sundays. Terrified of failure, I had no strategies for coping with an unfamiliar anxiety that was almost entirely internal; the demands I faced weren't out in the world, where I could face them, as they'd been in my childhood. This time I worried more about whether I could trust *myself*, my own mind and body. I was fighting to survive, but I couldn't see what was working against me.

Barbara's pregnancy with Andrew compounded the stress when she took a leave of absence from the Y&R research department where we'd met, leaving me as the only wage earner for what would soon be three of us. At about the same time, my parents retired to Italy. I had almost no support system, no extended family, no circle of trusted friends, because I hadn't had enough leisure time to build that kind of safety net. Emotionally, I felt like a skiff rising up the slope of a perfect storm. What was I really doing here? How would I survive if I failed? I'd brought with me to America the Old World's view of a man's responsibility: A husband and father provided for his family. Others would suffer if I didn't measure up.

I'd begun to develop a number of nervous ailments: claustrophobia, panic attacks, and hypochondria. My blood pressure was spiking. Riding the subway became an exercise in controlling my panic and dread of being boxed in by the lightless tunnels and the lack of elbow room. I was just as terrified of flying. I avoided routine business trips that required even a short airborne commute. Mark Vexler, our general practitioner in New York, a friend of my parents, took note of all this. He could see it in my face when I brought Barbara in for her checkups.

One day, as he brought Barbara back to the waiting room, he said quietly to her, "I'd like to see you every three weeks."

"Really? Is something wrong?" she asked. "Is it the baby?"

"No," he said. "It's Peter. I'm worried about him."

He could tell, just by glancing at me sitting in his waiting room when I accompanied Barbara on her visits.

I began to suffer from frequent stomachaches. Not until 1980, over a decade later, did I find out that I had gallstones and had probably had them from childhood.

On top of that, I'd been eating food seasoned with MSG. We would eat a lot of Chinese food, and MSG was almost always an ingredient. I didn't know it at the time, but I was allergic to it. It was the cause of my stomach distress. Soon, an ulcer I'd developed while at Princeton began to perforate again. I'd wake up in the night, my pulse pounding. It was partly the stress of the job and partly these psychosomatic afflictions. I was determined to tough it out, as I'd learned to do so well in Romania.

Essentially, I was on edge every minute of the day and much of the night.

One day, on a street in New York, I suddenly felt an acute sense of desperation and terror. I had this weird sense that I was channeling the emotions of someone else. I looked around at the sidewalk full of the usual Manhattan foot traffic—tourists, executives, couriers, and shoppers—all laughing, chatting, or just walking along. No one that I could see was in a state of anguish, until someone yelled, "Hey, look!" High above us, on a window ledge of an office building, a would-be suicide was perched, one step away from free-falling.

I can't tell you what happened to that poor soul, because I didn't stick around to find out. As soon as I saw him, I fled down Madison Avenue. Somehow, I'd internalized that man's suffering. My own skin couldn't protect me from the horrors around me anymore. I had no defenses left. I was either on the verge of a nervous breakdown or in the early stages of one already. Or else I was beginning to change in ways I had no way of comprehending.

In retrospect, I know part of what was turning me inside out was my growing recognition that evil had not been quarantined in Germany, Russia, or Romania. It had found fertile soil here in the new world and was waiting for its opportunities to emerge in the behavior of even the most civilized people around me. I saw what had happened to my wonderful boss, Art, and it precipitated the crisis that led to my quest for a new way to understand evil.

During my early years of success in America, my faith got put on hold. So much good had happened that I was mentally free from the sources of evil. I was in full flight. No, I did not deny God. I just stopped thinking about God or a role for God in my life. Perhaps I no longer thought I had a need for God.

Yet, as the crisis intensified, the lack of God's presence became palpable. In my old model, God or Christ would be there to help protect me. But now He seemed to have forsaken me. I had stopped praying with any regularity, and I felt terribly alone, scared, and empty. Of course, Barbara could see all the manifestations as clearly as our doctor did.

————

The bleakest and most painful year of my professional life started happily enough. The drama about to unfold caused me to question the definition of evil. The word *evil* is easy to apply to my experience in Romania. Yet events that could be passed off as "just office politics" or "hard-nosed management style" don't justify certain kinds of organizational behavior. Evil should be defined by the degree of suffering inflicted on others. No act that causes deep, serious emotional pain can be justified either at home or at work.

It all began with my promotion to a regional vice presidency at the Young & Rubicam agency. I was now in charge of Y&R's advertising, direct marketing, design, and public relations businesses in several countries. This was a big promotion for me and maybe even a stepping-stone to greater future responsibilities. In my years as a manager, I'd learned to trust and depend on my colleagues. I was a smart enough advertising executive but far from the smartest at Y&R. My success had come from helping and encouraging others more talented than I—writers, artists, marketing strategists—in creating brand-building ideas for our clients. In my new assignment, I knew that an important factor in my success would be the efforts of one of my direct reports, a fellow I'll call Mike.

Both Mike and I were Y&R lifers. We'd started about the same time, in the early 1960s, and our career paths had often crossed. In fact, Mike had been a strong candidate for the regional job I'd won. Mike was an outstanding revenue producer for the company and a gregarious Irishman with an abundance of wit and charm. As general manager, he also had great rapport with the writers and artists in the creative department. When they clashed with clients or with other departments at Y&R, Mike battled staunchly on their behalf. In return, they worshipped him.

In the past, Mike and I had always worked well together. I'd once been his direct report, and our relationship then had been congenial and mutually supportive. I assumed Mike would give me the same kind of loyalty. But within weeks of my promotion, disturbing bits of gossip began to surface. People were whispering that Mike was trying to undermine me. They said he

was putting together a team committed to following him personally—a sort of mutiny.

The rumors troubled me. I shared my worries with my wife.
Having had her own career in advertising (remember, we first
met as junior executives at Y&R), Barbara is a savvy judge
of corporate politics. She's also an unusually reliable judge of
character. She refused to believe the rumors. "Mike's a good
guy. He's your friend," she said. "You're probably exaggerat-
ing the problem, this time. And I just don't believe that what
you're describing could happen at Y&R."

On that point, I agreed with her. In my years at Y&R, I'd
always found it to be one of the least political companies in
the advertising business. "I guess you're right," I told her, and I
tried to shake off my concerns. Still, the rumors persisted. People said that Mike had been trashing my policies in meetings
with key lieutenants, saying, "I am your leader. Let me deal with
Georgescu. I'm the one you listen to. I haven't let you down in
the past, have I?"

So I called Mike to my office and asked him about the stories. Mike dismissed them. "Peter," he assured me, "you and I
go back too far together for you to believe such silliness. There
must be some misunderstanding. Believe me, I'll clear it up right
away." I went home to Barbara feeling reassured. "Mike's on the
team," I told her. "I've got nothing to worry about from him.
These must be rumors meant to hurt him, not me."

But in the weeks that followed, the undercurrent of tension
throughout the business deepened and spread. People began to
talk about the "philosophical differences" between Mike and me,
differences that Mike and his followers were at pains to exagger-
ate. They accused me of being shallow, a technocrat, and, worst
of all, "anti-creative." That stung. We'd finally pulled together
a team that thought first about the effectiveness of our creative

work on behalf of a client's bottom line, which was the only ethical way to operate. We did not produce work we thought had artistic merit but did nothing to sell a product.

In a business like advertising, where the only real product is creativity, to accuse someone of being anti-creative is to suggest the individual is a power-hungry careerist who will give the client anything in order to build business, regardless of quality. It ignores the subtle distinctions between "great creative," considered as original works of human imagination, and "strategic creative," where original ideas build the client's business. I desperately wanted to help build an agency that generated brilliant, hardworking creative ideas. It was an all-important distinction: I wanted great creative, aligned with the right strategies for our client's businesses to achieve the best possible results.

In the process, Mike portrayed himself as a heroic defender of the human imagination. "I'll commit any atrocity," he once declared, "in the service of great creative work." It rallied a large portion of the creative staff against me, which is all it was meant to do. Mike understood and even respected the distinction between great creative in a vacuum and great creative that builds business, but he was working to build support for his own career, at the expense of mine. It was such a radical, unsettling example of duplicity and denial on Mike's part that, once again, it shook my assumptions about good people.

Mike promised his followers they'd soon have free rein to run the business when he took over my job. Some people at Y&R believed Mike, while many of those who knew the truth did nothing to challenge him—whether out of timidity or because they assumed that Mike would eventually win our duel and supplant me as the head of our regional business.

Most bizarre of all, and in some ways the most painful part of this whole crisis, was Mike's personal behavior toward me.

Face to face, he acted as if we were the same old pals as ever. Jokes and family news filled our conversations. When I tried to bring the conversation around to the core issues that Mike was using against me, the distinction between great creative and strategic creative, Mike would nod enthusiastically: "Peter, I completely agree with your position on that. I'm sorry I gave anyone a different impression. I really can't understand it. I'd never say such a thing." And so on. Arguing with him was like trying to box with a huge soap bubble.

Eventually, I had to quit making excuses for him. The stories about Mike's war against me became too persistent and too thoroughly corroborated to be disbelieved. Even Barbara was convinced. I had no choice but to accept the truth. But how should I respond? One option, of course, was simply to fire Mike. But, I couldn't bring myself to fire him. Mike was a tremendous asset to the team. He was a skilled leader and manager, good with clients and gifted with superb creative judgment. Getting rid of him would mean sacrificing a powerful business asset. He just wasn't himself anymore. It had to be my last resort.

I decided to pointedly ignore Mike's campaign, and I hoped my willingness to avoid a fight would eventually disarm Mike and his insurgency. But the less I responded, the more Mike attacked. Things continued to get worse. Mike told his people to avoid me completely. I wasn't invited to meetings I would normally have attended. When I decided to crash these little parties, Mike manipulated the agenda to keep substantive issues off the table. Worse, because Mike directly or indirectly controlled most sources of business revenue in our region, I was utterly dependent on him. Although I was supposed to be Mike's manager, Mike was instead managing me, and very skillfully. In time, everyone in the organization became focused on our battle. Work began to take a backseat to the political warfare. People spent entire afternoons clustered in twos and three behind closed doors, whispering about the latest twists in our combat. The flow of new business slowed down to a trickle, and a few long-time clients departed in disgust.

Worst of all, the quality of our creative work began to slip. As the months passed, I felt a deepening sense of pain, humiliation, and frustration. I was no longer sure whose side my boss would take in a final showdown. I felt everything I'd achieved in my life beginning to slip away. Barbara was worried about me. I couldn't stop thinking about Mike, even when Barbara dragged me to a movie or to a dinner party with our best friends. I lay awake at night; I spent days feeling listless and enervated; I was plagued with sudden, throbbing headaches and wrenching stomach pains.

And through it all, a deep-seated feeling of resentment, even rage, was slowly building inside me. This year of torment was made even worse by the fact that nothing in my experience had prepared me for an assault like Mike's. He wasn't wearing jack-boots; he was one of the *good* guys. I'd spent my entire career at Young & Rubicam. For most of that time, Y&R's leaders had somehow made the company a humane and caring place to work, marked by a surprising degree of openness and honesty that enabled creativity to thrive.

Finally, after a long year, I couldn't let it go on. I had to have a direct and final confrontation with Mike. He must have known he would have a bright future at Y&R, without having to unseat me. Nonetheless he had mounted a deliberate, cunningly conceived plan to destroy me and pursued that plan methodically, day after day. Ironically, it was hard for me to see Mike's behavior as evil. But it was. Yet Mike wasn't an evil man. I kept holding out hope that Mike could evolve. I hoped he could wake up to the reality of his actions and change, as a person. But, finally, after a year of watching this contest eat away at both morale and the quality of our work, I couldn't stand it. I couldn't wait any longer. My health had deteriorated, my nerves were scraped raw, and I began to feel a sense of hopelessness, as if the world itself had turned against me.

My boss, Alex Kroll, who had been watching all of this from afar wondering who would win this battle and who would emerge as the man he would keep, decided he couldn't stand it any longer. "You have to fire him," he said.

*Now* he tells me, I was thinking. I felt relief. And yet, as soon as he said it, suddenly I realized I didn't need to fire Mike. I saw another way to handle him.

"Let me do it my way. I don't want to fire him. He's too good."

"Knock yourself out, Peter. But I would have fired him long ago if I'd been in your position," he said.

I called Mike in. I told him, in detail, what he'd been doing and why it could no longer be tolerated. I went through it with the sort of precision he couldn't simply shrug off. I didn't yell. I didn't strike back emotionally. I didn't treat him as if he were a different person from whom he'd been in the past. But I made it clear there was no way out for him now. No way to deny to himself, or to me, what he'd been doing. My only focus was to get to the truth and go from there. It changed everything, and Mike astonished me with his honesty and courage.

"You're right," he said. "That's exactly what I've been doing. I thought it was the only way I could survive in this place. It was unfair. I thought I deserved the job you got, and I couldn't see how maybe you deserved it too. Some things can't be changed. I didn't want to face that."

And then he went on. "You have every right to fire me. I deserve that. But before you do, let me ask you to consider something. I've spent so many good years in this company. For most of that time, I've given Y&R my best. I cared for our clients. I got results for them. Then I went crazy and did all this. I can't tell you how sorry I am. So here's what I can offer. Give me the ugliest problem in the company, anywhere in the world, and I'll fix it. Then I can leave this place with my head high. Last, let me tell you this, Peter. You'll never have to watch your back. Never. Not only that, I'll be your most loyal and trusted advocate and supporter."

I looked Mike in the eye and I told him, "If you really mean it, you've got a deal." We shook hands; we hugged.

In the end, Mike got a job worthy of his talents and ability, a tough and demanding job, a challenge critical to the company's success. Mike took to the assignment with enthusiasm and relish. He did a great job. He got results. He, indeed, became my most loyal and ardent supporter. He just kept doing his jobs well, until the time he thought it was right to retire.

Unlikely as it may seem, Mike became one of the colleagues I admired most. He changed. He demonstrated that he could be trusted. It turned out that Mike was a big man, the good man he'd always been. He became one of our go-to players. He achieved a new kind of humility and evolved as a person. So why could he have changed so dramatically during that year of betrayal? The question demanded an answer. I had no way to understand the out-of-nowhere emergence of this sort of darkness when it rose up in the life of a good man, as it had in Mike.

What matters most to me now from this episode is that I was able to respond to Mike with empathy, to understand and deflect what he was doing without retaliation, and as a result, he was able to see the reality of his own behavior. It enabled him to make good choices, releasing him from the destructive patterns he'd been locked into for so many months. The ultimate outcome of Mike's behavior was that he woke up to the nature of what he'd done and chose goodness instead.

———

It's my favorite hour of the day again. In a quarter hour, at 10:45 a.m., the amphitheater will fill with Chautauquans, who will have assembled to hear Elie Wiesel, Nobel Prize winner and Holocaust survivor, speak on the subject of good and evil. I want to hear his words more than those of any other speaker scheduled this summer. Barbara and I walk briskly through the village and arrive to see a crowd of people filling the amphitheater seats. By the time Wiesel steps up to the podium, it's standing room only.

We're seated near the back, and even from that distance he has a venerable, benevolent aura, with his shock of white hair combed back from his high brow and his craggy, aged face, in which you can discern both strength and suffering. There's just a bit of the Old Testament prophet in that visage, at least seen from this distance. This is not surprising since he had been raised in a strictly observant Jewish household in Romania, in the same town my grandfather was killed. He speaks quite a bit about stories from the Bible. He ranges throughout the Old Testament, drawing wisdom about the nature of morality from the various books, moving from the Garden of Eden and on to Cain and Abel, and then King David. His take on all of his readings offers a startling and fresh perspective.

When he speaks about the myth of the Serpent in the Garden, about the Fall, he suggests that Adam and Eve's failure had more to do with their *lack* of curiosity about consequences, rather than the reverse, which is the usual interpretation. Most would see them as too curious, too eager to taste the fruit and know its flavor, yet Wiesel tells us they failed to ask God *why* they shouldn't eat from the Tree of Knowledge. They should have been more skilled in conversation and dialectic. In essence, they should have grilled their Creator about the rules until they understood the game.

I like this. This is exactly the way I would have looked at this myth: It's their fault for breaking the rules without understanding the implications. It wasn't a matter of too much curiosity, but too *little*. If they'd understood the nature of their choice, they never would have made it. Of course, this isn't quite the lesson I recall from church. Traditionally, God isn't required to tell them why the bite of an apple would lead them into a world of suffering, a knowledge of good and evil, and a lifetime of ambiguous choices where consequences can be hard to fathom. He simply told them not to do it and required obedience. Probably, God would have known that nothing but the taste of that apple would have satisfied their curiosity, yet Wiesel likes to use the story to awaken his listener to the importance of careful, cautious choices. His is a thoughtful interpretation; Adam and Eve weren't skeptical enough about how they were inclined to exercise their freedom. Then Wiesel went on to ponder not what happened to this human couple, but how all of this affected the Serpent who was cursed with an inability to feel human pain. Again, an odd but thought-provoking interpretation:

> When the Serpent seduced Adam and Eve, he had a human form, but after their Fall, he was condemned to squirm across the ground and eat dust. He was no longer hungry for food. That was his curse: not to be hungry. He could not understand hunger in another creature. Not to feel another person's hunger is immoral. When you see someone hungry and don't feel an obligation to feed him, that's immoral. More than a billion people are hungry today, but most of us don't think about them. Yet people are hungry for more than food: for liberty, happiness, love or humanity.

In other words, the opposite of evil isn't obedience, but compassion. Our problem is not that we're like Adam and Eve. It's the cold-blooded Serpent within us that causes havoc in the world.

Nobel laureate Wiesel fascinates me because of his ambivalent relationship with God. Having survived the Holocaust, it seemed at first that he had lost his faith, but he talks now to us about his relationship with God as a "wounded" faith. When he was awarded the coveted Nobel Peace Prize, the committee said he was a man who delivers a message of "peace, atonement, and human dignity."

"There are two things that trouble me about America," he says, from the lectern today. "I'm constantly told to relax and, secondly, to move on. I don't want to relax. There are a lot of serious issues to deal with. Secondly, I can't move on until I'm ready to move on. I have to understand what is."

Apparently, this would have been his message to Adam and Eve and anyone else contemplating a choice that might involve harm: understand the apple before you take a bite of it. Be acutely aware of the implications of your actions at all times. It's a surprisingly subtle, and seemingly modest, admonition from someone who has been through one of the greatest human catastrophes in history, where the most dramatic and diabolical evil led to millions of deaths. On the surface, the Holocaust would seem to confirm my childhood vision of good and evil: The bad ones murdered countless innocent people while the good ones descended on Europe and liberated it. Either you were on the bad team or the good team. Yet millions of innocent people died before the Allies defeated this particular evil.

Wiesel doesn't speak in broad terms about such epic malevolence. He talks about ordinary people looking, without flinching, at their own everyday behavior. Do you feel the pain of a hungry child in Africa or an injured woman in Haiti? If not, what does that say? He knows the Holocaust was an accumulation of professional, managerial decisions—how to transport entire populations into camps, how to keep the victims moving into the death chambers, what chemical to use, how to dispose of the bodies effectively. It was all efficiently industrial, and all done by people who couldn't feel the pain of their victims. Most of the people involved in this vast effort could do their work without ever seeing someone killed, even though their work made countless murders possible. Thousands of people had their small roles in this vast factory of death and all of them strived to do their best, given the rules of the system they needed to serve to stay alive, before going home to their family at night. Most of them undoubtedly lived in denial about what they were actually doing, and those who knew failed to examine the ultimate reality of their actions.

As he talks, I remember my lunch with him in Davos, Switzerland, where I was giving a talk at the World Economic Forum. I was on a panel with Steve Case, the only other American in a forum dominated by Europeans, and we were all speaking about the impact of technology on communications.

I was invited by the organizer to have lunch with a few leading speakers. So there were eight of us at the table in a private room, warm and well-lit, though outside it was bitterly cold, but sunny. With so much ice and snow, it was hard to simply walk from one place to another at the conference. Wiesel had just spoken, and some had not heard him because we were on another panel. We were trying to get his perspective on the source of evil. Was it really isolated more to the German nation in some special way? Could the Holocaust have happened outside Germany? Could such horrific evil possibly exist in other places in the world?

Gingerly, Wiesel said he didn't think that one particular nation or race was evil. In his travels around the world he had come to believe it's an integral part of human nature. Having lived through the atrocities, he was tortured by this question: Was forgiveness for this crime really possible? He talked about how he'd been very religious before the camp. His faith had suffered as a result, and his renewed faith, a "wounded" faith, was still a work in progress.

None of this surprised me, but then he said something completely unexpected: "History is valueless. There is nothing to learn from human history." At these words, I put my fork down. This went against everything I believed, with my assumptions that by learning and studying human behavior we can succeed in trying to make better choices in the future.

"Look at the last five million years if you want to know what we're going to do tomorrow," he said. "That legacy is more likely to have an influence on us than the past two thousand."

People nodded, without really probing for more, probably thinking about what they were going to say on their next panel, but those words startled me. I couldn't shake what he'd said. They had the sound of truth. Yet I didn't quite know how to apply them to my own life. He seemed to suggest we are condemned to behave the way we did on the African savanna, when our struggle to survive as upright creatures walking on the ground—rather than living in trees—encouraged us to become a skillfully predatory, violent species.

I didn't know what to do with these insights from Wiesel at Davos, but they felt like a turning point. After decades of feeling mystified by humanity's darker impulses, while I struggled to live a moral life, Wiesel's words somehow suggested a path toward understanding and resonated deeply with my own European memories. In his own life, Wiesel had confronted an evil more murderous than what my brother and I had experienced in Romania, yet the result was the same for both of us: the traditional view of a God who intervenes on behalf of good people simply didn't hold up. He'd lost his idea of a traditional God and of a comforting moralism that most people profess—we both had—and yet he believed in the supreme importance of compassion. I had to work through all of this, somehow, and make it fit with my own view.

All my life, and especially during the most fruitful years of my career, when I was blessed with the generous rewards of corporate success, I worked as hard as a human being can work. I did so partly because, psychologically, I'd never left the sewers of Romania. Inside, I remained an eleven-year-old boy, proving my worth to people who could either reward me or kick me into the street to die. I'd never forgotten how capricious people can be. A boy who seemed like a decent, ordinary chap can decide one evening to betray his own parents. A low-level bureaucrat, who loves his own family, smiles as he tells you to sweat blood. Another orders you to reach into a transformer buzzing with a high-voltage current and waits for you to electrocute yourself on your rounds.

Now in my work, my life wasn't immediately at stake, but my career was just as vulnerable, and ultimately, my life in this chapter depended on my career. So it was a high-stakes game either way. This had nothing to do with culture. It was the human condition. I was running hard from the truth of human nature. I believed in God. I believed in goodness. But every year, they seemed more remote, more indifferent to the problems I faced. My faith seemed to be founded on illusion, and I kept hiding from my inner knowledge of this. I could no longer visualize God. So I worked harder and harder, trying to succeed to the point where none of this would matter anymore. I would be invulnerable, with or without God. The motto assigned to me, behind my back, was: "If you aren't working on Saturday, don't bother to come in on Sunday." Though it soon became a public joke, it accurately reflected the sense of discipline I created first for myself and then demanded from others.

I was also still that curious boy in Romania's work camp poring over a textbook on electricity, desperate to understand how the world worked. If I could just figure it out, then I would know my life had the kind of meaning it had when I lifted my wooden sword as a child in the woods and swung it at phantom opponents only God could help me dispel. Why did people behave the way they did? I no longer understood any of it.

Year after year, I flew around the world, met with CEOs, plotted marketing strategies and breakout advertising campaigns. As if this weren't a burden enough, I was also staying up late, delving into obscure books, trying to make sense of this strange universe I inhabited now. I craved something far more elusive than my success: wisdom. My brain simply wouldn't rest until I put the puzzle together.

I'd never let go of my faith, and yet I felt I was subconsciously defending myself against doubt at every turn; the persistent darkness in human nature, even here in America, land of the free and home of the brave, made no sense to me. Why would God create us in such a way that we could surrender to our destructive impulses so easily, so readily—sometimes with a feeling of finally, honestly, doing what we *really* want, even when it's destructive, harmful, counterproductive, and narcissistic? None of my reading explained how this could be the case. In fact, the drumbeat questioning "why people do evil" was going to become intolerably loud. Soon enough, I simply had to come up with an answer.

# CHAPTER 7

# FROM DESPAIR TO DISCOVERY

THE INCIDENTS AROUND ART AND MIKE WERE TROUBLING but, certainly, less threatening than what I had endured in Romania. Careers were hobbled, families would suffer, all as collateral damage. Though I was removed from them, I was troubled by the dramatic tribulations that filled the evening news where evil showed its face in a more recognizable way. Yet, without a personal connection to a school shooting or gang violence, the news stories seemed to be about other people who lived in some other realm, not quite the same human beings who resided in my apartment building or down the street. Inevitably, the violence of my childhood rose up within me disguised as anxiety, despair, and panic, years later, when I was starting to feel the pleasures of early success in business.

One Sunday morning, Barbara opened the *New York Times*

and spotted an advertisement for something called Silva Mind Control. The moment she pointed it out to me, my life began to change and put me on a footing where I could begin to piece together a new vision of my own spiritual nature. At the time, she was thinking it was simply something that would help me calm down and get centered. In reality, once again, Barbara saved me.

Everything that followed from that moment essentially rescued me from the siege of an unfamiliar enemy: myself. I remember my turning point quite clearly. When Barbara showed me the *Times* article, the advertisement said: *Lower your pulse rate and blood pressure—learn your way to better health. —Free Seminar.*

"Looks interesting," she said.

I called the number and reserved a seat for the following Sunday. September 25, 1966, turned out to be a chilly, drizzly day, and combating my usual case of nerves, I forced myself to step onto the subway, getting off at Lexington and 51st Street. A few blocks away, on the second floor of a building on Lexington, I found a gathering of 30 or 40 curious people, all of them probably feeling as self-conscious as I did. They represented what turned out to be a cross-section of New York life: lawyers and doctors, police officers and garbage collectors, schoolteachers and store owners—men and women of every age from young adulthood to white-haired retirees.

It's humbling to talk about all this. It's so obvious how desperate I'd become. I was an easy mark. But I went up to that floor and stepped into that room like someone joining a recovery group, full of misgivings and hesitations, taking one small step at a time, with no other way to turn. The lecturer was young, confident, and articulate, with a friendly baritone voice. He described the program's founder, José Silva, as "an average man who discovered an extraordinary truth about human life."

Well, this was more or less the premise of nearly every Hitchcock movie I'd ever seen, so my jitters weren't getting any better.

"The mind," this young man said, "operates in certain unusual ways that few people understand. Silva Mind Control is simply a method for helping an individual control his own state of mind and thereby perform at will things that ordinary people can only do occasionally and at random."

*Mind control?* Anyone else in my corporate position, with my education and my life under Communism, would have bolted. You could have measured my despair by the seconds that passed as I let those words slide. He talked about different lengths of brain waves. I didn't have a clue what he meant. He mentioned beta waves, the ones that produce an ordinary waking consciousness, and alpha, the half-awake state that most people experience just before falling asleep, that zone between waking and sleep that poets like Keats and Coleridge celebrated as a wellspring of creativity. He said it could be induced at will, with training. Children under the ages of 7 or 8, he said, are almost always in an alpha state. Many religious disciplines around the world, he suggested, would induce it through meditation, chanting, fasting, or contemplative prayer. It could also be attained through music, dance, drugs, and drink. He indicated that theta and delta waves had even lower frequencies, holding richer spiritual rewards, and were much more difficult to induce. These were the states, people claimed, of the great teachers such as Christ and Buddha.

After a talk lasting an hour and a half, he said we would be shown some mental exercises, and if we were interested in knowing more, we could sign up for a four-day, twelve-hour-per-day seminar. In some ways, Silva was a bit ahead of his time. This was all less than a decade before the human potential movement sprang up on the West Coast with its various retreats in which people participated in marathon sessions to achieve some kind of mental awakening. This movement generated, in many quarters, the same kind of skepticism I was feeling as I listened to this talk. But then shortly thereafter, the medical profession introduced biofeedback technology, which gave some scientific respectability to many of the things Silva taught.

At this point, it all sounded strange and dubious to me. Throughout the lecture, my curiosity and discomfort grew in equal measure. I wanted to know more, and I was certainly eager to see how this sort of training could help me, but it just seemed too offbeat. The term "mind control" worried me. It sounded like something out of *1984*, *Brave New World*, or communist Romania. It all smacked of charlatanism, or worse, the brainwashing of a cult. If he'd only talked about lowering my pulse and blood pressure, calming my mind and emotions. But he went much further than that, and what he was saying made me so uneasy that I would get to the point where I was ready to stand up and go, and then he would say something I found reassuring: "José Silva has developed a special technique of meditation to control one's own mind and allow one to operate in an alpha state. That's all we mean by mind control. You're learning here how to control your own mind."

I wanted to believe all this. It was exactly what I needed at this crisis in my life, but much of it smacked of pseudoscience. It just sounded too weird:

"Together, we will perform a series of exercises in which we'll mentally explore the world. We'll go into a leaf with our minds. You'll be able to visualize the capillaries and see the nutrients flowing through them. You'll gain insight into other living beings and inanimate objects. The alpha state will enable you to connect with other people's minds. You'll be able to sense their problems or worries. In the future, having absorbed these lessons, whenever you come across a problem some other human being is struggling with, it will be your responsibility to try to help solve it. You'll be able to intuitively know what's wrong with another person's health."

He was talking about compassion. But it was in such bizarre terms, approaching my mental image of witchcraft, that I couldn't take another word of it. Fortunately, he stopped talking and announced a fifteen-minute break. Most people congregated together in small groups discussing what the man had said. In less than a minute, however, I was out of that room and heading down the street toward the subway station and home. I wanted no part of this. They were duping a couple dozen people into parting with more money than they could afford to spend on a comforting fantasy. Isn't that how religion itself is viewed by the hardcore skeptics? Satisfied that I'd seen through the whole thing and would have to find some other way to cope, I got a couple of steps down the subway station and came to a halt. My panic was back, the ache just under my lungs throbbing again, no doubt a tumor, and only the abyss of my life ahead of me, a void without any sense of inner direction or mastery. I knew I had no choice. I had nowhere else to turn. I had no usable faith, no practical allegiance to anything except myself and my compulsion to work hard. I had no source of energy larger than my scrappy little ego and what felt like a mountain of new obligations to handle. I'd become a sputtering survival machine, and it was turning me into an emotional puppet to everything around and within me.

I thought to myself, *If you run from this, you'll be running for the rest of your life.* It took all the courage I could muster to take the first steps and look my fears squarely in the face.

Back in Silva's seminar, just in time for the first introductory exercises, I took off my raincoat and sat down. Thus began my lifelong exploration of the true meaning of goodness in human life.

---

So I signed up. I had to resort to some maneuvering to free my time from work. I had to find a way to get time off on a Friday and Monday from my understanding boss, Jim Cameron, no relation, of course, to the director of *Titanic* and *Avatar*. I spent four days, 12 hours a day, learning and practicing the concentration exercises.

First, we learned how to relax. I would have gotten the full value of my fee if I'd simply absorbed that much and left. I visualized all of my muscles relaxing, moving downward in my imagination, during the course of half an hour, from my scalp to my toes. By the end, my pulse had dropped, my mind was calm, and I felt at peace. Everything else followed from this establishing exercise, which increased my mind's sensitivity to its surrounding and its powers of concentration. Over the course of 12 months, I went on to more advanced classes, and eventually Barbara joined me. We met Silva himself, a cherubic Texan of Mexican ancestry, and he took a liking to me.

What I hadn't foreseen was how a practical course on meditation—hardly more exotic than a yoga workout—would open up new vistas for me emotionally and spiritually. I developed a practice of meditating an hour every day, which I continued to follow for years. (I meditate much less frequently now.) I began to realize I was tapping into a power that worked through me when I was in the alpha state, and it was as if I were aligning myself with something that gave me back my life, and life's meaning. It was something I'd always felt within me, at random intervals, this higher energy that carried me along. I'd just never had a way of organizing myself, inwardly, around it; I'd had no way of seeing myself as, in a sense, a servant of it.

The most fundamental imperative I brought with me from Romania was a pledge to myself that I would live a life entirely different from the lives of my interrogators, the Communists. My mission in life would be to avoid becoming those people. I would make every decision, every action, in accord with this aspiration. I had vowed to live for the good. That resolve flooded back during meditation, and I thought, *That's who I was. That was my vow. I need to recover that sense of mission.* It was an underlying, only partly conscious sense of purpose—to be good—and now these exercises made me feel as if I could actually put it into practice with greater frequency. They gave me the power to do what I chose to do, and they showed me there was something more to life.

I recognized that the content of our conscious minds is only the tip of a much more interesting and far less apparent iceberg of awareness, an interconnectedness of life on the planet we can't access in our normal, waking state. I began to realize that what I saw and heard in my daily experience was only a fragment of what was actually operating in me and throughout the world. All of my physical and emotional complaints began to slowly diminish, except for the gallstones, of course, which were eventually diagnosed and removed.

In large part the Silva techniques are, as I mentioned earlier, a system of biofeedback, enabling a veteran of the exercises to become aware of his body's autonomic processes and influence them at will. The program, as I'd feared, also claimed to do things traditional science would dismiss with a chuckle. It claimed to enable its practitioners to connect with other minds across distances, or diagnose and heal others simply through the power of the mind. Though similar claims are commonplace in many Eastern religious traditions and "faith healing" continues in a few Western traditions, such matter-of-fact assertions at first, sounded ridiculous to me. In time, I began to be less skeptical of these claims, although this sort of thing has never played a significant role in my life.

What was crucial here, though, was that I didn't dismiss any of this out of hand. I suspended disbelief and proceeded with the practice, not needing to have a rational certainty about any of it. I simply adopted the mental discipline and watched to see what happened. If anything, this ability to tolerate uncertainty without needing to make quick conclusions about phenomena you can't explain seems to be something woefully lacking in our culture now. We live in a world of extreme certitude. The atheist and the religious right seem to cling to their certainties with a fanatical zeal that is essentially dishonest. They claim certainty in circumstances where no certainty is possible, which breeds animosity, conflict, and a general kind of wrongheadedness.

I'm more than willing to admit that psychic phenomena are manifestations of actual properties of the physical universe that we haven't learned to detect or measure or predict, but I don't insist on it, because I don't *know* this to be the case. I am willing to admit it *might* be. This willingness to resist an easy, reassuring skepticism, or—by the same token—a fanatical, reassuring faith in what is inexplicable, seems to be a kind of intellectual humility we've lost as a culture. It's a humility that serves a person well in all walks of life. The ability to live with uncertainty can be enhanced considerably through spiritual practices like meditation.

Ultimately, the Silva program gave me a new sense of the possibility of God. I hadn't gone into it expecting anything like that, and it wasn't a part of Silva's teaching. My new relationship to God had become something that grew out of a practice, a discipline of the mind. I began to realize God, the force for good, resided within *me*. The closer I got to the "still point of the turning world," as T. S. Eliot called it, at the root of my perceptions, the nearer I got to this God. It was the God of the mystics, not the God of conventional dogma.

At the time, I didn't see this happening. Silva's meditation was my way to achieve emotional and mental stability and strength; it was a sort of spring training to be a happier and more productive player in the summer of my life. It wasn't as if I understood God. I would use the word *understanding*, but a little differently. It was as if God and I had come *to an understanding*, a working relationship. It led me to a new vision of God, but for many years it was a vision I found difficult to fully take in.

---

Looking back at events that occurred nearly forty years ago now, my memory may have magnified things in ways unclear to me, but I know that, after intense practice of the Silva exercises, I was able to come up with some insights that astounded others. I can't explain them. When I recall them, I try to maintain that attitude of intellectual humility I was speaking about. My boss, Jim Cameron, asked me about this odd program I'd been attending, and I gave him the executive summary: "Relaxation. Meditation. Mind reading. Routine stuff."

"You're putting me on, right?" he said.

"Not really."

"Well, whatever it is, it's working. Take whatever time off you need. Your performance continues to be excellent."

When I was finally done with the course, he asked me, "How'd it go?"

"Why don't I demonstrate," I said.

"You going to walk through a wall for me?"

"Almost. We do remote physicals," I said.

"Oh boy. Here it comes."

"Bear with me, my friend. It means you give me the name of someone I don't know, and I will tell you what's wrong with him."

"No, thanks. As long as you feel better, that's what counts."

"I'm serious. Give me a name."

"Sam Green. Tell me all about him," he said.

I had no idea who he meant.

"On the days I meditate, I'll focus on the name. I'll come back with a full report," I said.

He shook his head and rolled his eyes.

"Oooooh kaaaaay."

The results were disappointing. Instead of seeing a fellow named Sam Green, I saw a grass-covered hill with a huge oak at the top. Maybe Sam was buried there, I thought, but I had no image of a gravestone or other marker. In the following weeks, I forgot about the whole thing, probably because I'd failed. But about four months later, Jim and I were talking about a client over lunch when he said, "Hey! I keep meaning to ask you, what about Sam Green? Did you diagnose any of his problems?"

"Well, I guess I failed. All I came up with was a very green hill under a huge oak tree," I said. And then I gave him a detailed description of the hill, the tree, and its surroundings. "No sign of Sam anywhere."

A bit of color drained from his face, but he said nothing for a moment.

"That's the *other* Sam Green," he said. "That isn't who I meant."

"What?"

"I meant my neighbor in Westchester. He hurt his arm a couple of months ago, tennis elbow or something. I figured I'd give you somebody you could actually look up. A little research and you could've saved face and had an answer for me. There's no way you could know about the other Sam."

"Who was he?"

"We served together in the war; in fact, he was my best friend. In France, there were five men in our company. Sam was sleeping on a hill next to an oak tree. We were a few yards away from the German line. A grenade landed next to him and he dived onto it to save the rest of us. We buried him right there on that hill. We had nothing to mark the grave. I'd completely put that out of my mind. Until you mentioned that oak tree."

Jim never teased me about Silva again. I still don't know what to make of this ability, if that's what it was. It doesn't play a role in my life now. I'm an agnostic with an open mind when it comes to psychic phenomena, leaning toward a willingness to believe there's something to it. I did find that I could sense, much more easily than ever before, how people were feeling, what was on their minds, and when they were lying to me. It heightened my intuition, my awareness. So much of this could be explained as a magnification of my ability to read body language. But how I could have translated any of that into an insight about the fate of Sam Green is beyond me. Like anything else, the more I practiced the Silva methods, the more my own abilities surprised me.

Episodes like this have recurred throughout my life—so often that I find it hard to dismiss them as random happenstance.

When I was attending Stanford, I spotted a class in the course catalog called Human Potentialities, a term borrowed from Aldous Huxley and then applied to an entire movement for self-actualization rooted mostly in California. At this point, it was an extremely popular elective offered by—of all things—an electrical engineering professor. I bit, and in the first few weeks discovered a warm-up for what was to become the human potential movement, which encompassed est, the Esalen Institute, Gestalt therapy, and many other practices that came to characterize the New Age culture in later years. In the class, we studied the writings of Abraham Maslow, Carl Jung, and other sociological and psychological thinkers and held many debates about how to expand the limits of human consciousness.

One day, the professor divided the class into two groups. "We're going to conduct some firsthand experiments," he announced. "Half of you will attend a service at a well-known 'spiritualist church' in San Francisco. The other half will observe experiments, conducted under medical supervision, into the hallucinatory effects of a new drug called LSD."

I was assigned to the first group.

On the appointed day, a group of us piled into a Porsche convertible belonging to one of my roommates (because we needed a car that, unlike my rather tempermental Mercury, would actually start on its own). We drove to the San Francisco Spiritualist Church, where the Reverend Florence was the pastor. There were the usual rows of pews, nearly filled with people; I would guess between two and three hundred. But there was no altar or any other furniture at the front of the church except for a single chair.

In the foyer, cards, envelopes, and pencils had been offered to us and to the others who'd arrived for the service. The ushers who handed out these materials had instructed us, "Write a number on a piece of paper, seal it in an envelope, and put the envelope in this basket." Now we saw that the basket, filled with envelopes, had been placed by the empty chair in the sanctuary.

Our group settled down in one of the back pews, and the minister walked in. "Big Flo" (as we, the antic row of skeptics in the cheap seats, far in the back, dubbed her) blindfolded herself and went into an ostensible trance. Then, supposedly in her altered state of consciousness, she began the "service." Big Flo would choose an envelope from the basket, hold it between her hands, and call out a number. The person whose number had been called would stand, and she would discuss his or her problems—and judging by the reactions of the participants, she got most of it right. She didn't pull any punches.

"Stop cheating on your wife," she might say. "She knows you're fooling around. Do you understand?"

"Yes, Mother," was always the response.

"Okay, sit down," Big Flo would say and pick up another envelope. "Number 59."

"Yes, Mother."

"I want you to quit that job. That place is no good for you. Take the job your cousin just offered you instead. Is that clear?"

"Yes, Mother." And so it went. She spoke to each person in turn, offering very specific advice: "Buy that hotel." "Sell that factory." "Get married." "Don't drop out of school." "Quit eating cheese puffs."

Through it all, those of us in the back row were whispering to one another, "This is a sham." But then Big Flo called out, "Number 182," which was the number chosen by one of my friends, a fellow I'll call Henry. He stood up and responded, "Yes, Mother," as everyone else had done, trying not to laugh.

Big Flo looked at Henry and said, "I want you not to worry about your dad. He's on an island, where he's resting and recovering. He'll be just fine. So don't worry about him."

"Yes, Mother," Henry dutifully replied, and sat down.

The service soon concluded, and we left, as skeptical as ever. As we drove back to school, Henry commented, "Dad is playing golf in a tournament at his club outside L.A. today. I spoke to a friend of mine yesterday morning and she said he was just fine.

I'll call him later and tell him what Big Flo had to say. Boy, that was a bust."

Later that evening, back at school, a couple of us were studying in our room when Henry walked in. "I just called home," he said. "The butler answered the phone. You know what he said? 'Oh, Henry, I'm glad you called. You must have been so worried. But it's all right, the doctor says your father will be fine.'"

"What are you talking about?" I asked. "Yesterday, you said he was fine."

"Well, apparently he had a heart attack some days ago—not a serious one, thankfully. The family was trying not to worry me until Dad was doing better."

My roommate let out a low whistle.

"But what about that part about your dad being on an island?" I asked.

"That's the really weird thing," Henry replied. "The doctors said it would be okay for Dad to travel, so he arranged to be flown to his favorite resort to rest and recuperate—in Hawaii."

The next weekend, three of us piled back into the Porsche and drove down to San Francisco for another visit. The drill was the same—papers, pencils, envelopes, and the basket. This time, after speaking to a number of other people, Big Flo called out my number.

"Yes, Mother," I said.

"You're going out with a young woman," Flo began.

That was true—Polly.

"She's a lovely person," Flo continued, "but she'll just be a good friend to you—nothing serious will happen with her. Do you understand?"

"Yes, Mother." I thought Flo was finished with me, and I began to sit down. But she didn't call out a new number. "By the way," she remarked, "tell me about your older brother."

"He's in grad school," I replied. Costa was studying Middle Eastern politics and languages at Harvard at the time.

"No, no," Flo said impatiently, "I mean your other older brother—the one who died when he was just four days old."

I was stunned. It was true—there had been another child in the Georgescu family, a boy born a month prematurely who was baptized and then died after just four days of life. But we rarely spoke about him, and only a handful of people in the world even knew he'd ever existed.

"Well," I responded, "I know there was another older brother, but I don't know much about him."

Big Flo pondered a moment. "I can tell you this," she finally remarked, "one of his missions in the other world is to be your guardian angel."

"Yes, Mother," I answered, and sat down, rather shaken.

This story has an even more startling sequel. Some twenty years later, in the mid-1980s, Barbara and I were visiting the Brazilian province of Bahia where Young & Rubicam was about to open a new office in the capital city of Salvador. There were the usual meetings and celebratory get-togethers and one unusual suggestion. One of our Brazilian partners took me aside and said, "Peter, there's a Brazilian custom you ought to follow. Whenever we're about to begin any new venture, we consult the bouzio."

"The bouzio? What's that?"

"It's a holy man who tells your fortune and gives you advice. He throws shells and stones onto the floor and then reads them. All of us here will feel better about the new office if you go to see him. It's important to many Brazilians."

Following the directions they gave us, Barbara and I drove to a little house on the outskirts of Salvador, where a small, elderly white-bearded, white-robed man greeted us in a room whose walls were lined with brightly painted religious statues of all kinds. Sure enough, he tossed a handful of shells and stones on the table between us, and from the pattern they formed he gleaned some glimpses of our future.

First, he made a few remarks about Barbara's life, and he advised her to buy a statue of the Madonna. Ordinarily, this might have given us a start. Did we need some extra protection? No, we were told beforehand that the only way to pay a bouzio is to buy a statue at his recommendation. So this was a routine transaction.

"The Virgin Mother is your guardian angel," he explained.

When it was my turn, the old man tossed the shells and though I don't recall exactly what he said, he made a comment I haven't forgotten.

"Curious," he remarked, "I see here who your guardian angel is. It's a very unusual one—a guardian angel I've never seen before."

"Who?"

"It's St. Sebastian. Here is his statue."

The old man stood up and rummaged on a high shelf in the corner of the room, bringing down a rare, old, dusty statue of St. Sebastian, in his traditional pose, his body pierced by many arrows, which was how St. Sebastian was martyred back in the fourth century AD. I'd thought maybe the bouzio would need to backorder one, but no, he was well provisioned even with saints he'd never encountered in the guardian role.

All the while, Barbara had been checking my face for a reaction and not quite being able to decipher the astonishment she saw there.

"What is it?"

"Sebastian was the name of my older brother—the one who lived only four days. That's how they christened him just before he died."

"Ah. Your guardian angel," Barbara said softly. "According to Florence."

"I guess she had it right."

On another occasion, when I had a chance to retire from Y&R but couldn't decide whether it was a good idea, Barbara drew a line in the sand. I was fifty-eight, and I could have continued as CEO, I'd been running things for about six years. She said she'd loved being my travel companion, but she wasn't sure she could keep up the same pace anymore.

"You keep doing what you're doing for as long as you like, but I don't think I'll be traveling with you most of the time," she said.

I'd surrounded myself with a talented team of younger executives. I could go to the board and say it's time to turn this place over to the next generation. Or I could sign up for one more tour of duty, another five years, give or take. The timing was right for either a transition or a re-up. I asked her to suspend final judgment for a few weeks to give me time to think about it. My instinct was that I had spent thirty-five years at Y&R and if I retired at sixty, it would be a pretty good run. It was probably time to do something else. I promised myself not to worry about the next step but focus on the business of the next two years.

When I'd decided, I told Barbara, "Hang with me for two more years, and we'll retire."

Around that time I was having lunch with a good friend, Tom Shortledge, who was a great art director in Chicago and one of the originators of the brand identity for Crate & Barrel. Tom had just retired from Y&R, and in our conversation, he told me about an encounter he'd had with a medium. Her name was America Martinez, and she lived in the outskirts of Chicago. He gave me her telephone number. Knowing I would be in Chicago a few days later, I was fortunate to get an appointment. I met with this youngish woman. She was mid-thirties, dark-haired, with no visible evidence of having a sense of humor. The sun was going down when I arrived because I'd begged her for an appointment late in the afternoon. She proceeded to tell me she had done "a reading on me" already and was prepared. I assume she meant she had gone into some kind of trance and had pulled up some ethereal files on my future. With my exposure to the Silva experience, I just nodded. Anything was possible, as far as I was concerned.

Yet she said, with this fierce expression, which looked a lot like disapproval to me, "Why are you here?"

I told her I didn't know whether to retire or continue as CEO. Again, she gave me a stern look and she said, "I know all that. You already know the answer. Why are you here?"

"I think I know the answer, but I'm not so sure," I said.

She began to share with me her observations about my past and current situation and she was accurate in every detail. She knew everything: my parents, my brother, my professional experiences. My pal Tom Shortledge knew nothing of the details of my past. This was long before Google. You would find none of this information with a Google search even now. There was no way she could have gathered this information through any physical process. So her insistence that I already knew how to proceed helped confirm what I'd told Barbara, and her inexplicable awareness of so many details of my life bolstered my confidence that I was, in fact, proceeding on the right path.

———

At the risk of coming across as a bit of a kook, I'm telling you about these episodes simply because events like these meant something to me. Being specific and clear about exactly *what* it and other experiences like it have meant, though, is difficult. In a letter to his brothers, poet Keats spoke about *negative capability*, "when man is capable of being in uncertainties, mysteries, doubts without any irritable reaching after fact and reason." Maybe I'm an odd duck in this regard. I can certainly suspend disbelief, but I also compulsively reach after "fact and reason," although not in an irritable, skeptical spirit. I tend to expect a good explanation will be forthcoming, at some point, and have the ability to live with this assumption in the absence of any rational defense for it. The episode in my childhood with the Gypsy fortune-teller and his amazing predictions about my father's prison release and my parents' trip to America may strike some people as nothing more than an incredible coincidence, one of those events that seem to defy the laws of probability without daunting a statistician. After all, the lottery is virtually impossible to win, and yet *somebody* always does, eventually, without divine intervention. The world works by statistical rules, and usually someone can do the math to show that even the least likely coincidence is just another accident.

Yet a moment such as this can open up the imagination to the possibility that your solitary life fits into a larger fabric, whose pattern will never be entirely visible to you. It suggests there is more to the world than we understand—maybe more than we *can* understand. I'm comfortable with that, but only up to a point, since it's in my character to try to figure out how things work. In fact, I'm not happy unless I'm convinced I understand, at least in layman's terms, how *everything* works. Talk about "reaching after fact and reason."

What I felt was only somewhat connected to the Orthodox faith I'd inherited from my parents and, more important, from my grandparents; the Bible doesn't exactly authorize the predictions of psychic Gypsies. My reaction was closer to an immediate sense of the human spirit's connection to a reality it can't access through the senses, except in moments of heightened awareness. It was a small awakening for me, an early epiphany of a spiritual quest that would continue all through my life. Over time, I began to rely on these experiences to gain a more enlightened understanding of the essence of Jesus.

Just how wild is it to maintain an open mind about phenomena like this? How impossible is it to believe that some people, like this Gypsy, can intuit a level of reality inaccessible to the senses and impossible to measure with technology? Even distinguished scientists, working at the most obscure frontiers of research, speculate about relationships between the future and the present that hardly jibe with common sense. Over the past century, science has become more and more divorced from common sense, willing to entertain and sometimes prove theories that at first sound wild. As Dennis Overbye put it in the *New York Times*:

> Craziness has a fine history in a physics that talks routinely about cats being dead and alive at the same time and about anti-gravity puffing out the universe. As Niels Bohr, Dr. Nielsen's late countryman and one of the founders of quantum theory, once told a colleague: "We are all agreed that your theory is crazy. The question that divides us is whether it is crazy enough to have a chance of being correct."

More recently, scientists have been speculating that our universe is not alone. In *Warped Passages*, Lisa Randall, a brilliant physicist, addresses the possibility of multiple parallel universes. The string theory, supported by some mathematicians and scientists, contends that there are some nine to twelve dimensions in the universe while our human senses and consciousness operate in a four-dimensional world. Isn't it possible that we (or some select, naturally gifted humans) could be able to connect occasionally with these other dimensions that scientists insist exist?

We've entered an age when some people feel the obligation to explain away everything that perplexes an ordinary observer, and they aren't satisfied until they can make confident assertions about the nature of the entire universe. We seem eager to overlook how the human mind is a tiny pinprick of light in a vastly unilluminated realm. We have our supercolliders and microchips and genetic engineering, all of which are wonders of science and technology, as was the Da Vinci device that may have saved my life, and these marvels have given some people an assurance of reason's omniscience. Still, the effort to render the totality of the world in rational terms seems a bit like trying to pack the entire planet into a carry-on bag. Is the individual human mind really big enough to understand everything, including itself? There's a recursiveness in this effort that seems to set a limit on how much understanding is actually possible, by definition.

By whatever means, the Gypsy gave me hope. I've chosen to accept that my life matters because it's a part of something greater than me and my individual understanding. It is something good. This ability to tolerate the possibility of realities that can't be explained enables me to find meaning in what others might dismiss as superstition. This acceptance allows me to say I have no way of knowing the Gypsy wasn't tapping into something as real as the things I can touch and see and hear, the things I do understand. Partly as a result of these intimations that reality works in ways I can't fully comprehend and in ways that are fundamentally benevolent, I have lived with a sense of hope and faith that has blessed me in countless ways. Yet this hope and faith have not prevented me from deepening my comprehension of the unknown, and I keep asking questions with an open mind and with hope of greater understanding. That, too, is my karma and the pattern of my life's journey.

---

I'll never forget my father's reaction when I called to tell him that I had turned down the Esso International job and would join Young & Rubicam. He panicked. "An advertising agency?" The inaccuracy of his three words perfectly encapsulated the common misunderstandings that surround this industry. We did far more than advertising. My father understood very well that I was an adult with a mind of my own. Let's be honest. I became an adult a decade earlier, when I weighed 100 pounds, working in Romania. I was emotionally independent, canny and determined to survive labor that might have defeated many grown men. Here, nine years later, at age twenty-four, with an MBA, was a man who surely had the right and perhaps the wisdom to decide how he wanted to make his living.

That wasn't how Rica Georgescu looked at it. We didn't belabor the subject in person, but our terse and strained conversation led him to write a six-page letter, virtually a manifesto, on why I would never make a good Madison Avenue man. First, he listed my ulcer. It was as if my 4-F military status had come back to haunt me yet again. A man with an ulcer would never survive on the front lines of account services. In his view, alcohol was the *elixir vitae* of Madison Avenue. My ulcer wouldn't tolerate it. It would keep me from putting in the requisite three-martini lunches with clients. The second problem, according to him, was that I didn't have the stomach, in another sense, to provide the sex our clients would demand as a perk. My resume was light on pimping. In his vision, in order to hang on to our clients, we needed to keep them drunk and sexually sated. Whatever we did beyond that would be puffery.

I knew he wasn't talking about me, but about how our industry was disparaged by those who didn't work in it. Our business was sordid! We were all future Willy Lomans, relying on a shoeshine and a smile, a bottle of gin and an escort to con our clients and the American consumers into spending money they didn't need to spend. Remember, this was the male-dominated 1960s, but seen through the boozy, sexed-up fantasy depicted so stereotypically in television's *Mad Men*. It had nothing to do with my qualifications. He was simply spelling out for me how much he disapproved of the filthy business of selling.

But the people I met at Young & Rubicam, when I accepted Peter Langhoff's offer to visit the agency's New York office in the spring of my second year at Stanford, were smart, professional, and studied. This was a lab, not a bordello. These were the practitioners of an art that had all the precision of a science. The talk was about how to probe into the lives of actual consumers, discover ways to satisfy their needs, and then help companies link their services and products to those needs. I heard comments about business strategies, about the need to work with clients on product improvements and innovation. I was exposed to mathematical modeling techniques that are still being used in marketing. These are algorithms used to predict certain behavioral patterns based on unrelated activities of a consumer. Sometimes these predictions made sense, sometimes not—but they worked. With these calculations, we might discover that, if you were to buy a Marantz amplifier and additionally take a vacation to Trinidad, you were more likely to want an import car. We called this *laddering*, the relation between product attributes and benefits and the ultimate value of these qualities in the mind of the consumer. Our communications built around the product had to relate to all three levels of this ladder. This was a far cry from getting clients drunk and laid. It wasn't simply advertising. It was marketing, something more sophisticated and complex. Advertising was only one of the many ways in which an understanding of customers could be used to communicate with them about product benefits and values. It was all business, specifically how marketing could impact a profit-and-loss statement.

At Y&R, I worked directly for one of its most legendary employees, Dr. W. Edwards Deming, who eventually left our agency, went to Japan, and originated the entire Total Quality Management movement, which revolutionized Japanese industry and then began sweeping through American business in the late 1980s and 1990s. Though he has since died, he's regarded as a national hero in Japan and his principles are taught in virtually all business schools. His theories have transformed the way corporations operate around the world. The research department I entered as a newbie was created for Y&R in the 1930s by a brilliant young man named George Gallup, our first research director, who went on to found the famous Gallup polling organization.

My career in advertising, actually in marketing, to correct my father, proved to be exactly what I expected. During my first few years in the research department, the notion that you couldn't market to a group of people unless you knew in great detail how they thought and felt and behaved—in other words, until you got to know their hearts and minds—became second nature. It meant we were in the business of serving the actual, genuine needs of people, not figuring out clever ways to sell them things they wouldn't ordinarily have bought. We were doing the disciplined handiwork that geniuses like Steve Jobs apparently did intuitively. Our task was certainly to produce great, entertaining, and emotionally persuasive words, images, and stories, but behind it had to be a confidence that we were doing something for the benefit of the end user, not simply our client. What we did had to be honest and truthful, without false or inflated or tricky claims. People were smart. Once they realized you'd fooled them, if what you sold them didn't live up to your promises, you were dead.

So how did my spiritual orientation figure in all of this? Obviously, these early years weren't entirely a joy. They brought me to the edge of a nervous breakdown. Yet the Silva methods of meditation gave me a new spiritual aplomb and vitality—a new source of serenity to bolster the confidence I needed to compete in what was essentially a brutal sporting environment. It was and probably still remains one of the most competitive industries in all of business. This was not work for the delicate and frail, but it wasn't debasing. We did our jobs with integrity and creativity, both of which were strengthened by my new grounding in goodness.

Yet my Silva training did more than give me the emotional stamina to survive the ordeals of Madison Avenue. It also instilled in me a model of behavior and awareness that ran in parallel to the way we did business, believe it or not. The intellectual humility I mentioned earlier found its way into our methods of dealing with clients: We didn't force solutions or campaigns on them in a rush to reach closure with an account. We watched and listened and studied the way they operated, how they dealt with customers, and we dissected how their products and services had a competitive advantage. We became servants, in a sense, gathering as much knowledge as we could and then working long and hard to find exactly the right solution. Anyone who has ever brainstormed knows how arduous and painful it can be: hours of thinking up words, slogans, tactics. Then listing them on a white board, looking at the list in despair, trying to find connections between one group of ideas and another, trying to see how one idea would convey exactly the message the client needed to get across. It requires hours, days, weeks of living with uncertainty, resisting every impulse to come to a quick conclusion, and then selling an idea with charm and showmanship. A great idea will sell itself, but being able to live with the anxiety of not having that great idea, waiting for it to arrive—that's the task. It was exactly what I was learning in my personal life as well: how to endure uncertainty and anxiety and focus on what it was that gave me clarity and peace, while I lived through all of it.

This new spirituality I was discovering didn't exist in a vacuum, or in some kind of subjective hour of bliss. While I worked on getting my brain into an alpha state, it was something that lived within me every minute of the day and had direct expression in the way I related to other people and did my work. The first serious test of my new spirituality was when I was sent to work for three years in Amsterdam. On my own, I had to organize, motivate, and lead a hundred headstrong Dutch employees of an agency Young & Rubicam had just purchased. The previous owner, Rudie Koster, had an office directly adjacent to mine and had the fun of watching my struggles on a daily basis. As it turned out, our record was fine during those years, bringing the group's revenues from the red back up into the black, although I wouldn't consider my tenure there as anything exceptional. It was good training, a test I passed, before coming back to the United States for a far more intense trial.

Near the end of my third year in Amsterdam, I attended a retreat in Spain, where Alex Kroll approached me and said, "It's time we bring you back. I want you to spearhead our efforts in bringing in new business."

"You must be joking," I said.

The Manhattan operation brought in about half of the entire

company's revenue. It was the taproot of the whole tree. To put me in charge of what kept the entire operation humming struck me as a bit insane.

"No. I'm not joking. We need you. In the past three years, we haven't brought in a single large new account. And we can't hold on to every single existing account forever. There's constant attrition. To stay profitable, we have to constantly win new business. I think you're the man to turn this losing streak around, Peter."

As it turned out, the next three years back in New York heading up new business were the most challenging years of my adult professional life and what probably enabled me to succeed for the rest of my life. They forged my personality as a businessman, refined my values, shaped me as a person, and showed me how this new spiritual center I'd discovered through the Silva meditation, which I continued to practice, could steady me.

What I did not consciously realize at that critical turning point in my career was that concern for the "other," in this case the consumer, was the key to any business success. My instincts, observations, spirituality, and training in consumer research led me to act on this path of caring for the consumer with deep empathy and genuine compassion. Only after years of practice and reflection did I realize that this same emotion was the key that helped me eventually turn the business around. It was the same caring a loving parent or spouse or friend showers on the objects of their affection. Today, I see company after company fail as a result of their total lack of caring for their customers or for their employees. In fact, I believe that is the primary reason why companies fail, and why, before they do, they so negatively impact the communities around them.

And yet, at first I failed. And then I failed again. And then again. (Repeat until thoroughly shaken.) Most of the personal strengths I needed grew from my Silva practice. The meditation deepened all these characteristics: resiliency, confidence, commitment to hard work, creativity, and a pinch of good luck. This new assignment was really the ultimate test of my emotional recovery, my new applied spirituality. If I could survive, let alone succeed, in this new job, I'd be ready for anything. Romania had certainly taught me to work under pressure and ignore outcomes that struck me as unfair, but now I had a new instinct about God's presence in my life that enabled me to look beyond the anxieties and pressures and see what was fun, innovative, surprising, and nourishing in situations that would have caused many others in my position to change careers.

It was brutal. Often our competitors would spread false rumors about us to the press regarding our current clients. Their attempts to divide and conquer, suggesting that we had secret sweetheart deals, left us distracted and unfocused in our approach to new business. Other times, we suspected them of doing unethical things to bribe clients for whom we'd spent long hours doing research for a more intelligently targeted marketing campaign. It was, at times, as my father has suggested, a dirty business. But largely the pressures were all internal and rose up simply from the effort to find the right approach and present it effectively.

Avon was our first pitch, and I thought the meeting went quite well. We put together an impressive history of Y&R and showed some of our best work. It was a showcase for our pride and confidence. *Enough about Avon! Let's talk about us!* I remember Barbara Pasin, head of Avon's marketing, calling me shortly after the meeting to say we weren't going to make it to the finals.

"How close did we come to making the cut?" I asked.

"You came in seventh."

"Seventh? There were seven agencies? I thought there were only six."

"That's right, six," she said and hung up.

I dragged my tail into Alex Kroll's office. He smiled.

"Get used to it, my friend. This is only the start. You're here to learn the ropes. Remember, Peter, we haven't won a major account in three years. We need to find a new approach. Get back in and figure it out."

So we got into a nice predictable rhythm of hard work followed by abject failure, and I became familiar with the taste of humiliation. Yet I took it all with the attitude of a golfer, say, who looks at the ball tailing hard to the right and then stands at the tee once more while focusing on tempo or stance or grip. Swing, observe, analyze, adjust, and swing again. It was our own little continuous improvement cycle, which Dr. Deming himself would have admired. Another pitch, another rejection, retrenchment, adjustment, creative improvements, a good honest look in the mirror, and then back into the next pitch. All along, I kept grounding myself with meditation, reaching down into that still, calm center, reminding myself that none of this mattered nearly as much as my connection to this force, this mysterious sense of deity. Without this wellspring of renewal, I doubt that I would have lasted through even four or five of these failures.

After our ninth failure—nine in a row—I began to realize this was getting old indeed. I couldn't bring myself to walk through the office and look anyone in the eye. But there was little chance of that anyway. As soon as they heard me coming, everyone looked the other way, feeling my discomfort, not wanting the curse to rub off. I was jinxed. My bosses, Chairman Ed Ney and President Alex Kroll, never wavered; they just kept the faith, said a few encouraging words, and helped me realize how much closer we were getting to a new model for bringing in new business with every pitch. Can you imagine this sort of paternal apprenticeship happening now, in the cutthroat world of short-term results that reigns throughout so much of the business world today?

Young & Rubicam's CEO from 1970 to 1986, Ed Ney, was a statesman for the company and the industry. He was also my mentor, friend, and supporter throughout the formative years of my career. The culture of superior excellence, with fairness and humanity, that Ed and Alex championed contributed to the enduring success of this extraordinary organization to this very day.

And we were getting *very* close to success. We were slowly inventing a completely new way to win business that was different from every other agency's approach at that time. We were doing what I'd learned to do in the research department, where the spirit of Mr. Gallup brooded over our thinking. We were learning how to focus entirely on our potential client's business and completely ignore our own credentials as an agency: In our proposals, we talked about the specific challenges the client faced, in their product development, their market penetration, their brand image, and most important, in understanding their customers in a deep, caring, and compassionate way. All of this came from intensive research on our part, a kind of research no one else was doing. In other words, our presentations became the diametrical opposite of our first one to Avon, touting our wonderful accomplishments, with nary a word about Avon's predicament. Now our philosophy was "We're all about you. You'll have to ask someone else if you want to know about us." In the late 1970s, this approach was indeed completely revolutionary.

In that ninth pitch, which was lost for political reasons, we didn't utter a word about ourselves. It was all about the client. We had gotten to know their consumers better than they knew themselves. We were trying to be different, and we ended up being unique, in our approach. On top of everything else, all the other agencies would bring in several different advertising ideas, yet we would present only one: we were super-confident, but not boastful nor arrogant.

On our tenth pitch, we won the business. In the twenty-five new business pitches that followed, we won all but one of them. That's a championship season, and it had to do with our original approach, this new understanding of how marketing had to work: not as clever or tricky advertising, but as a multipronged campaign of communication that grew out of the deepest possible understanding of what consumers actually wanted from a client's products or services. It was a translation, into business terms, of the Golden Rule. Put the other one first. Put yourself last.

The most radical way we put this into practice was before we pitched Kentucky Fried Chicken. I actually took a job cooking chicken in one of their franchises, learning exactly how to do it, watching and listening to customers, knowing the business from the ground up. When we pitched KFC, I knew precisely why their batter, their secret recipe, clung to the chicken, and I proved my understanding during our presentation, demonstrating that we knew KFC from the inside out. There was a quality of humility built into all of this completely unlike the way other agencies were crowing about their capabilities and presenting their dazzling work without speaking very much about the client's customers. We'd put on an apron and cooked chicken and served it to actual customers. This was humility in action.

In this winning streak, we landed what would become the largest and most profitable account in the history of our agency: a huge allocation of Ford Motor Co.'s annual marketing budget. But while I was learning to succeed in the business world,

I had to discover new insights and grow in my personal life as well. I needed new tools to be a better husband and father. As a father, I carried quite a burden of memories from my own childhood that often came between me and a full understanding of my son's challenges as a boy and young man. I continued to hear the reverberations of evil from my childhood, throughout most of my life, and it occasionally deafened me to the call of goodness. My spiritual practice took me only so far. There is no way to disarm evil other than to choose constantly against it every day, and sometimes you aren't going to make the right choice. I discovered the truth of this, to my dismay, not as a young executive but as a parent.

---

In parenting, I have to say, the application of my reborn spirituality was more difficult. Like most parents, we loved our son Andrew from the start. No surprise there. It can be a bit of a shock, though, to find you love someone before you've even met him.

What I've just said is true, but I should reverse the tape and point out that my relationship with Andrew actually began in terror. I had no confidence in my abilities as a father, and it was part of what led to my breakdown, the discovery of meditation, my recovery, and my tentative sense that I could hold myself together enough to provide for this child.

I remember pacing in agitation outside the hospital, waiting for Andrew's birth. I'd left Barbara at the door into the delivery room, in those days fathers were unceremoniously dismissed from the drama of an actual delivery. So on that evening of March 23, 1967, I walked in circles around a little park across the street, baffled to find myself unexpectedly suffused with joy. This was a completely unanticipated reaction, considering I'd nearly fallen apart half a year earlier thinking about what was unfolding now.

My daily meditation had begun to enhance my ability to see into the reality of my life at that moment and fully apprehend the great gift of it. They say a parent bonds with a child soon after birth, and it's this subconscious, physical, and at least partly chemical fusion of hearts and souls that enables a parent to endure years of servitude, of arranging his or her life and hopes around the well-being of an enormously selfish, demanding baby. Yet for me, the bonding began before Andrew was even born, at a distance, in that little park, and all I could feel was anticipation and gratitude, and this had far less to do with my own workaholic character than with this force of goodness I had discovered through my spiritual practice.

When I built up the nerve to ask about Barbara at the front desk around 6:30 p.m., I was told: "She's just fine. Your son was born at 6:09, and all is well."

Despite a string of sleepless nights (his crying prompted us to take him to the doctor who discovered he had a hernia, which was quickly treated with minor surgery), our early days with Andrew were wonderful. He was full of joy, a genuinely benevolent child who, as he grew older, developed an imagination constantly in overdrive. He was able to play with a few random objects and invent stories and games to occupy himself for hours.

In school, he was thoughtful about others to a fault. I know I sound like a parent blind to his offspring's faults, but these observations have been confirmed by others many times in our lives. For example, he tried out for wrestling but immediately begged to be excused because, being taller and stronger than almost any of the others, he was worried about accidentally hurting them. He'd inherited my grandfather's build; neither of us, his parents, is as tall as Andrew. If he'd ever been snared in a military draft, I'm sure Andrew would have filed as a conscientious objector.

Yet, as easy as he was to parent, as Andrew began to grow into a teen, I backed off and began to fail in my role as a father. This is where my experience in Romania became something of a deficit for me, a hindrance. The evil I'd suffered took root in my own behavior and began to work against me in a number of different ways. I'd survived in Romania, essentially fabricating a defensive illusion in order to feel in control of my environment, by becoming the hardest worker in the captivity town of Botoscani. My work ethic and my traditional Greek Orthodox faith in God kept me alive and whole. It was my way of proving my worth and making myself indispensable. This ability to work ceaselessly as a child became an enormous advantage for an adult executive. Most people enjoyed having the weekend and evenings off, while I thrived whenever I was pushing myself to the limit. There was a certain pathology in all this that I refused to acknowledge, and Andrew suffered because of it. I saw much less of Andrew than he would have liked, and I know how my shortcomings grew from a fanatical work ethic forged in Romania, a childhood strength which had become a weakness in my role as a father. *Some* evil I was unable to overcome through adaptation.

I wasn't just missing as a father. I appeared to be in hiding.

The more Andrew came home with the perfectly understandable problems of childhood (his teacher was ignoring his requests for help after school, or some friend had snubbed him at a party and he couldn't understand why), the more I turned a deaf ear to his complaints. If he came to me with another plaintive account of what, to me, sounded like a trivial moment of frustration, I felt nothing other than the urge to tell him to man up. Anguish over trivia like this made no sense to me. It wasn't that I judged him at fault or as lacking in some way;

it was that I literally couldn't imagine why he felt the way he did. The luxury of his problems! My memories were forged in circumstances that still felt so dire to me that the emotional reverberations of my life in Romania drowned out the more subtle and common American noises of sadness, disappointment, insecurity, and pain, even when they issued from a boy I loved. At his age, I'd been facing my grandfather's likely death in the Romanian gulag and dodging hungry rats in the sewers of Botoscani.

In a sense, the repercussions of the evil inflicted on me in Romania rose up again and stood between me and Andrew, and I didn't see it for what it was. Fleeing my own inadequacy as a father, I retreated into my work. The evil of Romania was both creating the crisis and offering me a way to avoid it. I found myself unable to feel Andrew's pain, unable to honestly sympathize, so I pulled back, which only compounded the problem itself. He was forced to seek support from only his mother, while wrestling with his troubles, and he did, successfully. But it left him wounded in ways I could have prevented, had I been a better father.

None of this is to say I felt anything but total devotion to Andrew; it's simply that during this period, if what he faced didn't remind me of what I'd faced as a child, I couldn't respond. Something in me froze up. But it didn't last forever. It ended the moment I was, at last, able to identify with his anguish.

During our stay in Amsterdam, when we sent Andrew to a boarding school near Eastbourne in England, I finally became a real father to him again. We'd hoped to put him in the International School in Amsterdam, where the curriculum was taught in English. Unfortunately, we discovered that fifty Japanese students were enrolled, kids around Andrew's age who didn't speak a word of English. We worried that the classes would turn out to be largely a matter of teaching English as a second language, regardless of the ostensible subject. So we made the decision to send Andrew to England with four other American youngsters in the same predicament.

Now, father and son were to be separated by a large body of water, and this was a growing pain I *fully* understood. It was our family tradition, acting itself out once again. The school asked us not to visit our children on the weekends between their first day on the grounds and their first "home leave" six weeks later. By the third weekend, though, we said to hell with the prohibition and got into our Fiat, took the ferry across the channel, and drove to the school. It wasn't because Andrew had called for help. It was because I missed him too much. It was a fabulous weekend, fun for all of us, but as we were about to leave, Andrew came up, tugged on my jacket and said, "Can we talk?"

We walked to a private spot and sat on a bench, and he said, "Please, Dad. Take me with you."

I was stunned, feeling more and more helpless as the precious minutes ticked away. But I kept my game face, told him it wouldn't be long before he could come back for a week, and he had to be strong. It would get better. He would get used to it. And we'd be reunited in a few weeks.

We drove away, and I was in tears within minutes of getting into the car. It wasn't just Andrew's plight that tore me apart, it was all the emotions I'd had to control and suppress in order to survive, when I'd been separated from my own parents. Now, finally, it was safe to feel that loss, along with what Andrew was going through. We were at a distance from one another for weeks, but after this day, we were in reality closer together than we'd ever been before.

He adjusted to the life of boarding school, and he matured as a result of the challenge. From that point on, I began to find myself able to identify with the challenges he faced: boarding school, college, his first job, a career, and finally, parenthood. Yet those years when I withdrew, both emotionally and physically, had a lasting effect on him, and ironically my challenges as a father inspired him to make difficult but outstanding choices in his life.

When he was about fifteen years old, we were taking a long walk beside a river, the location escapes me now, probably because what he said startled and unsettled me and made everything else about the incident fade in my mind. We had just finished playing tennis, and it was the first time he'd been able to take a set from me. His big forehand and bullet serve were too much for his aging father, so maybe the win represented a Freudian milestone for him in more than the game of tennis.

What occurs to me now is that maybe losing that set undermined a competitive sense of superiority I'd always harbored, subliminally. I viewed my son's ordeals growing up as lesser than mine; I had struggled more. My superiority was momentarily proven to be an illusion, by my loss on the court, so what Andrew was about to say shocked and hurt me even more than it might have, otherwise.

It certainly felt that way when he said, out of nowhere, "Dad, when I grow up, I don't want to be like you."

There were a number of ways to interpret this, none of them flattering, and since I'd never heard anything quite this assertive from him, it actually took me a moment to work up the nerve to continue talking. Finally, I asked, "What do you mean?"

"I don't want my whole life to be about getting ahead in the world of business."

"Oh," I said. "Well, I can understand that. I know what you're saying."

I did. He wanted to be a more attentive father and have more control over the time he spent with his family, and he was kind enough to phrase it the way he did.

"What would you like to do?" I asked.

"I want to be a teacher."

Relieved, I told him that was a great ambition and that we'd certainly be supportive. His work as a summer camp counselor showed he had a talent for offering guidance to younger people. In fact, years later, when I visited an investment fund to discuss how it would sell shares in Young & Rubicam after we went public, a youngish partner came up to me and asked if I were Andy Georgescu's father. I said yes, and he said, "Andy was my camp counselor. He changed my life for the better in many ways. I've never forgotten how much he helped me." This seemed utterly remarkable to me at the time, and still does.

The discussion with Andrew, beside that river, wasn't quite over. He continued to circle around the subject of parenthood, which is clearly what had its hook in him. He asked how much a father and mother owed their children. Do parents have an obligation to love and support their children, no matter what? I must have sensed that he was getting closer and closer to the subject of how remote I'd been, emotionally, during those years when I couldn't identify with his experiences. He was boxing me into a corner.

So I said something that makes no sense to me now because it isn't what I believed, nor do I believe it now. I said, "A parent is obligated to support and nurture and protect his children."

"And love?" he asked.

"A child has to earn love," I said, without any hesitation.

I'm still stunned at my own words. The complexity of my motivations in this baffles me a bit, even now. He said nothing in response to this chilling assertion. I know I was defending myself without thinking about the full significance of what I'd said. Andrew realized I was shutting the door on the possibility of admitting that I'd come up short as a father during those years when he came to me probing for advice, comfort, and sympathy. I offered less comfort than I should have because I was unable to feel or respect what he was suffering.

We finished our walk, and he never raised the subject again. But my own words continued to haunt me, and with each passing year I find it harder and harder to believe that I spoke them. The only way to explain it as a reasonable response is to believe that I meant to say "respect," rather than "love." A child has to earn the respect of his parents, and I couldn't respect his pain because I couldn't understand it. He felt it in response to what were, for me, trivial annoyances. But love? You earn a parent's love? I didn't believe this. Unconditional love is what makes you a parent, and if parents can't offer this, they shouldn't have children. I've seen enough people who don't offer it to know that they aren't fit to be parents. But I believe I said those words in self-defense, hiding behind them, the way I'd conveniently hidden at the office. Though Andrew knew that we loved him, he spent years trying to decide whether these words were true.

Looking back now, I see the evil embedded in my competitive judgments about Andrew's ordeals. I was taking pride in my own harrowing experiences, the way I had suffered and prevailed. Looking at the comparatively easy problems he faced in his own privileged life, I essentially gave his suffering a failing grade. It was cold, a nearly heartless way to look at my own child. I loved him dearly and yet couldn't tell him so. It was as if by holding back my affection, I would make him tougher, or force him to live up to my standards for endurance. And I wonder if my defeat on the tennis court that day wounded my competitive stance toward Andrew and made me say something that turned me, in a twisted way, into the winner. It is terrible to think so, but I have to honestly say it's possible. And that is evil. It's an evil that rose out of my pride in my own toughness, which itself grew out of the evil done to me. It reminds me a bit of how abused children became abusers themselves as adults. My attitude, even if subliminal, toward Andrew was, "Show me how much you can endure and then I'll respect you." And that was precisely what I wanted my own childhood tormentors to say to me, so that I could prove to them how worthy I was, through my torturous labor.

In his own life, Andrew has loved his three daughters unconditionally, never asking them to earn anything from him, emotionally. Working as an executive in Detroit for Ford Motor Co. in product development, he has driven a minimum of six hours each way to visit his girls in Barrington, outside Chicago, where they have lived with their mother. He has done this every other weekend over the past six years following his divorce. I certainly can't take all that much credit for teaching Andrew this kind of compassion.

But it's possible Barbara's and my convictions about God and choosing goodness may have set an example that has reverberated throughout his life and behavior, so that he has the wisdom to be *able* to make choices like this. He attends church, even though I don't with regularity. In so many ways I'm not going to recount, Andrew follows in the footsteps of a certain carpenter who continues to be one of my greatest heroes, although the equivalent of my wooden sword in childhood has become my open, inquisitive mind trying to separate what's true from what isn't. And now I feel I have many things to learn from Andrew, simply because he's been able to take the better parts of my personality and put them into action, without being hindered by the experiences that have held me back for a long part of my life. I'd also like to think the simple practice of meditation, during those crucial years of my crisis before he was born, enabled me to demonstrate at least some of the values that motivate him to make that drive from Detroit to Barrington and back again every other week. He's proving to me that it really is possible to get better and better at something as crucial as parenthood. His actions are testimony to the power of a parent's love. How much I admire and respect Andrew for being not only my son but also a special human being!

# CHAPTER 8

# THE REAL ORIGIN OF EVIL

IT WAS A CRISP SATURDAY IN DECEMBER, NOT TOO COLD BUT not warm either, and Barbara and I had just returned from a big shopping excursion to prepare a holiday dinner party for the Y&R executive committee. By then, I had been promoted to CEO of Y&R. Thirteen members of the company's top management and their spouses would gather in our apartment. It was our way of celebrating the end of a productive year and looking ahead with positive energy to the future we could create for ourselves, for our families, and for the agency's 15,000 employees around the globe.

I was in the process of moving chairs from the living room to a guest bedroom, to make space for the gathering on the following day. I heard the phone ring, but I was wrestling with a large easy chair, huffing and puffing. I thought surely Barbara would get it, so I continued with my labor. A few minutes later, Barbara found me and said, "I think I just got a crank call."

"About what?"

"The person on the line said he was with the police. He asked whether we had received any packages lately and, if we had, he told me not to open them. Before he hung up, he said they were sending someone right over."

I wanted to ask whether she got the man's name so we could confirm that he was actually with the police, but I was in the middle of moving the easy chair and so I said, "Probably right, a crank call."

Yet, a quarter hour later, the doorbell rang and we let in two uniformed officers with badges in hand, as well as a tall civilian in a suit and tie. Inside, they asked to see any unopened packages. It struck me as odd that they said they would take any unopened gifts with them to be X-rayed. As Barbara, shaken up by all these odd developments, pointed out packages we hadn't yet unwrapped, the tall civilian pulled me aside and spoke to me quietly. He told me that there might be a plot against our company's top management. He asked for a list of the very people who were to come to the holiday dinner a day later. Would I go with him to my office and give him contact information for my colleagues so they could be warned? It wasn't until we got into his car and were halfway to our Madison Avenue office building that he quietly said, "We're doing all this because a colleague of yours was killed. Tom Mosser. Not killed, murdered. Earlier today at his home."

"At his home? What about his wife? His children?"

"They're okay."

In the Mosser home, a few miles away across the Hudson River in New Jersey, Tom and his wife, Susan, had finished breakfast early. They were anxious to head out to buy a Christmas tree and decorate it with their daughter Kelly, who was eighteen months old. Their thirteen-year-old daughter, Kim, was upstairs asleep. Tom had just returned from a weeklong business trip and was eagerly looking forward to the ritual effort of finding the perfect Christmas tree. Almost at the front door, Tom noticed a package on the table where the car keys were placed. It was Susan's habit to leave Tom's letters there and anything else addressed to him. The brown paper package caught his eye, partly because there was no indication of who'd sent it. It was small, about the size of a brick, secured crudely with a length of string. He picked it up and turned into the kitchen, just as his little girl squirmed out of her mother's arms and led her on a playful chase into the living room, out of range. Only seconds later, the kitchen exploded, shaking the entire house and taking Tom's life. No one else was killed.

As it turned out, there was no conspiracy against Y&R's management. It was a premeditated, carefully planned terrorist act by one individual specifically against Tom. Some months earlier, Tom had been on a business trip to Burson-Marsteller's San Francisco office. BM was the leading international public relations firm, part of Y&R's group of companies. Before becoming Y&R's general manager, Tom had been COO at Burson-Marsteller, and the company represented the local Exxon offices. The top local TV station wanted to do a piece on the Exxon-Valdez oil spill along the northern coast of Alaska. The local Burson manager begged their experienced leader, Tom Mosser, to appear on air and explain Exxon's cleanup action plan. Tom agreed to do it and he handled the interview well.

Among the many people who saw this interview was a man named Ted Kaczynski, the Unabomber. For his kindness in helping out his friends at Burson and an old client, Exxon, Tom became Kaczynski's target. He was the victim of a terrorist most people consider deranged. I'll never forget our horror and shock and grief at Tom's death. Yet, over the years, as I've gained distance from the event, I've come to see this incident as belonging to a continuum that stretches back to my childhood. Like the Communists who were true believers in their political creed and like the terrorists who brought down the World Trade Center, who considered their own suicides an act of sacrifice to something larger than themselves, Kaczynski believed and likely still believes that his cause was just.

The struggle to avoid evil, both in the world and in ourselves, depends on the ability to see our own dark potential to convince ourselves that doing something we know is wrong can somehow be okay in special circumstances. It never is, and yet people often persuade themselves that what they face is an exception, an instance where breaking the moral code is necessary. There is no justification for actions that cause evil. The ends never justify the means.

The question of evil, which had been such a constant element of my childhood, stirred in me again and again as an adult, but it was nowhere more poignant and agonizing than when I witnessed its naked brutality in the lost life of my friend and colleague. No other experience in my life brought home to me how evil works its way into behavior meant to be idealistic, beneficial, for the good of humanity as a whole. The ugliness, the waste, the cruelty of this killing only brought back so many memories of my childhood and only intensified my questioning about the nature of evil. In the last decade of my life, in my retirement, I began to seek out places in my travels where this kind of horrific behavior took an enormous toll, as a way of trying to grope toward a deeper understanding of it.

———

It was a gray, damp, unseasonably chilly day in Krakow. Along with half a dozen fellow patrons, as a member of the board of the New York Philharmonic Orchestra, I rode a tourist bus into the misty countryside until we reached the grim site, now preserved by the Polish government as a museum. As our bus pulled up, we saw the stern, gray buildings looming above the lush, manicured grass and groves of trees surrounding the compound.

The parking lot contained just a few other buses; it was a quiet day at Auschwitz. We disembarked and walked in through the towering main gate, surmounted with the cynical inscription, "*ARBEIT MACHT FREI.*" It was uncanny seeing those words in this context. That motto explains quite a bit of my life and career. I trusted in those words and still do, up to a point, but they were most important to me when I was forced by the Communists into labor, for the same reasons that the most capable people in the Nazi camps were made to work. I was cheap, and I was skillful, so it would have been a waste to let me die without extracting some man-hours from me. The false hope I invested in that simple phrase—*work will set you free*—enabled me not only to survive, but it also held me together, as an individual. It was a delusional faith, but it gave meaning to my imprisonment and suffering in Romania. Displayed here, it was an obscene lie, the blackest of jokes, and yet this lie is precisely what had kept me whole as a child. These words preserved me. Life can be exceedingly strange.

Much of the camp remains as it was during the war years; prisoners' barracks, sentry watch towers, barbed wire fences, the crematoria, and the death chambers are all intact, some having been rebuilt after the Nazis tried to destroy the evidence of their atrocities. Scattered through the compound were tourists from around the world, including a few children. I wanted to cover their eyes, but then I reminded myself that some children can endure horrible things and not only survive but prevail, as adults.

My group was led by a young Polish woman in a gray tour guide's uniform. The tour took three hours. I remember most vividly the seemingly insignificant details, not the familiar litany of horrors surrounding them. I knew the story of how a million and a half men, women, and children were murdered with scientific, technological precision at Auschwitz. These were mostly Jews but also Gypsies, homosexuals, and others shipped in cattle cars from Poland, France, Belgium, Holland, Norway, and elsewhere in occupied Europe, including Romania. The tour included, of course, the gas chambers, large enough to hold two thousand victims, with spigots that looked like shower nozzles, through which Nazis filled the room with Zyklon B.

What touched me more profoundly than these horrific scenes were the hundreds of artifacts and photographs on display in glass cases. Small, ordinary things that once held meaning for a unique, individual soul: a toothbrush, a suitcase labeled with a name and address in an assiduous hand, a treasured prayer shawl, a pair of eyeglasses. Quick little fingers had clung to these simple things, until the fingers were forced to let go. To see these possessions, last links to home and a recognizable world, in this context was inexpressibly tragic and moving. It was all the more powerful to view the faded black-and-white photos showing newly arrived inmates being "processed" by the guards: stripped, sprayed with disinfectant, bathed in a cold shower, photographed, and tattooed with identification numbers. The poignancy of those pale, bewildered, anxious faces of the long dead, were still hoping for freedom. Maybe they were still wanting to believe the lies they'd been told until the very last moment: that Auschwitz was merely a holding facility where they'd be kept briefly before being resettled.

As I listened to our tour guide and reflected on the motives and methods of the Nazis, I realized the Communists in Romania had studied the Germans. The Romanian and Russian Communists imitated Hitler's treatment of their enemies, demonizing them politically, isolating them legally, and ultimately seeking to exterminate or exile them. As we rode back to Warsaw on the tour bus, our group was silent, brooding over what we'd seen. I found myself wrestling with a riddle: Which would be worse at Auschwitz—to wake up and find yourself a prisoner or a guard? In a way, was it a blessing to be the victim, rather than the dutiful killer?

Having seen, firsthand, the evidence of what happened in this death camp, I was even more amazed that Elie Wiesel has been able to maintain his wounded faith. In the aftermath of my trip to Poland, I read Viktor Frankl's classic, *Man's Search for Meaning*, which helped me gain a deeper understanding of how I survived my own experiences and eventually thrived in America. Frankl observed that those who survived Auschwitz were those with enough of a spiritual center to hold fast to life simply because it had a value that transcended all circumstances. They believed in life itself, and this alone was enough to buttress their emotional and psychological integrity against the oppression they faced every day. It gave them hope: even if it was only the hope to honor and marvel at life simply by living another day. Those who saw no purpose or meaning in their suffering soon died. As Nietzsche put it—ironically, since he was a nineteenth-century philosopher celebrated by the Nazis: "He who has a *why* to live for can bear with almost any *how*."

As I've mentioned, though, my sense of meaning during my own captivity derived from my faith in that motto over the entrance to Auschwitz. The course of my life had shown me that hard work might be effective as a way of achieving material success, but it wasn't enough to give me a lasting sense of life's meaning.

My confrontations with the past didn't stop in Poland. While I continued to wrestle with Wiesel's thoughts about history, I found myself gravitating, in my travels around the world, to other scenes of unimaginable evil from the past. So in Phnom Penh, I wandered through a museum showing pictures and artifacts from the Khmer Rouge. The building had been a prison during the regime of Pol Pot, where enemies of the state were confined and tortured. We'd joined a group of bright, chattering children, all of us filing slowly into the building. It was fitting to be among school kids in that place, since I was obeying my travel compulsion to be a student rather than simply a tourist, and also because I felt myself going back in age to my own youth as I began to imagine the horrors this country had endured.

This visit to Cambodia was typical for me. Until only recently, I haven't felt right if I haven't come away from a leisure activity without a sense that I'm a little more enlightened. I feel compelled to learn something during any vacation or getaway. On this trip, I'd flown across the Pacific with Barbara and a few close friends in order to see Angkor Wat, the remains of a magnificent Hindu temple built a millennium ago to honor the god Vishnu, the Preserver. I say *built*, yet "sculpted" might be a better term. This temple drew me here, thanks to Barbara. If I weren't married to such a curious, wonderful woman, I wouldn't have found myself on so many instructive detours into humid back alleys and obscure outposts and tidy village homes. Barbara has been my guru in these matters; the way we explore the world is largely a result of her inspiration—and she hardly needs me along. She's in her seventies now, yet recently she flew to South America by herself, not yet fully recovered from an illness, simply to hike off into the jungle to see Machu Picchu. She has trained me to venture out into the thick of a culture, more as an explorer than a tourist. Our plan was to stand in the contemplative silence of Angkor Wat and feel, or at least imagine, the devotional chants that once echoed through its chambers.

We arrive in Phnom Penh and what happens? I was immediately and powerfully drawn to its history of evil. The spiritual beauties of Angkor Wat could wait. I decided to urge our group to confront the horrors of the Khmer Rouge, the Communist regime whose genocidal campaign against its enemies in the 1970s put its leader, Pol Pot, in the company of Hitler and Stalin. What I thought I could learn from yet another exposure to such extreme evil I'm not sure, but I felt obligated to surrender myself to it, to face it yet again, still hoping for an insight that seemed to recede further beyond reach every time I tried to achieve it.

As at Auschwitz, walking through the museum, none of us speaks a word—adults and children both—as we see pictures of electrodes clipped to genitals of the outcast intellectuals. Anyone who wore glasses, along with other "misfits," was arrested. The louder the victim screamed, the higher the voltage would go. When a victim was exhausted, he or she would be murdered. Skulls were punctured with bamboo spears, to save bullets. An appalling silence falls over this group of happy, young students as each exhibit seems more gruesome than the last.

When we are done, I whisper, "How far are we from one of the killing fields?"

"About forty-five minutes," our friend and host, Charlie Todd, says.

"We're going."

When we arrive, the field looks beautiful, serene, and sunlit, the wind blowing gently through the green stalks of grass and bamboo and rushes. It's hard to believe this was one of the places where the Khmer Rouge murdered hundreds of thousands of those it considered enemies of the Communist revolution. To use the word *execute* doesn't convey the deranged evil that flourished here. Children and teenagers were recruited and forced to hold a baby by its feet and swing it in an arc to crush its head against a tree. The idyllic beauty of the scene, which looks almost like a playground now, seems ages apart from the madness that raged here only decades earlier. Near the field is a huge glass case, to memorialize the innocent dead, filled with hundreds of skulls, each one with a hole left by the deathblow.

In Battambang, we make our way through a maze of streets and arrive at a small school where Arn Chorn-Pond, with the help of his American friend Charlie Todd, has devoted what remains of his life to reviving and preserving the traditional music of Cambodia—music nearly destroyed by the Communists, when they attempted to purge the country of its reactionary culture. On the second floor of his school, we found Arn, a handsome, youthful-looking man with a rugged face and intelligent eyes. He's clearly Asian but, having lived many years in America, speaking before various groups about his experiences as a child in Cambodia, he has developed an ease and fluency conversing with Westerners. With glasses of wine or beer, we surround him as he tells us about his life.

At first I think we are going to hear stories of what events Arn had seen as an adolescent bystander: the depravity of the Khmer Rouge, the atrocities of history through the eyes of a witness. But his predicament is more complex, dreadful and disturbing. He was more than an onlooker. Though he was barely into his teens at the time, he had been compelled to become a murderer himself.

"I was fifteen years old when they captured me," he tells us. "I was talented. I played the flute. They taught me to play songs about the new social order, to support the Communist regime. I was given special treatment in many ways."

But though he was singled out, he was also indoctrinated into the regime in the way gangs or mobsters forge loyalty. Murder became the price of admission. He was forced, along with other teens, to kill prisoners, other children, *small* children. It's unspeakably hard, even after decades, for Arn to say these things. But he has felt, and continues to feel, compelled to honestly recount how he became a part of the Khmer Rouge, in order to survive. If he hadn't done what he was ordered to do, he would have been killed too. None of us could hold him responsible. We say, "*He had no choice.*" Eventually, he escaped and lived in the jungle until he found a refugee camp, where American visitors discovered him. He was adopted and brought to the United States, where he studied and then began to travel, speaking to groups about his life. Now, having returned to Cambodia, he conserves the traditional musical arts of his land, as a way of healing both himself and his nation.

At the time, I find my encounter with Arn both disturbing and intensely inspirational. He is a man who had suffered the worst a human being can suffer, at the hands of evil, being forced to commit acts of evil, and he had survived it, overcome himself and his past, to devote himself to others. He was both a victim and a culprit. In the predicament of one young life was the conundrum of human survival down through all of history: To live we have had to kill. To win, we have to defeat. Few would condemn Arn for what he did. Yet, though his collaboration is perfectly understandable, he suffers every day, even now, for having done what he did under coercion.

His story *seems* extraordinary. It has an enormously tragic quality that sets it apart from the mundane decisions most people make in their daily lives, the hundred choices during an average workday. But his dilemma was fundamentally no different from the moral dilemma everyone faces, to a greater or lesser degree. Those who do evil, of any kind, usually feel *compelled* to do it. The compulsion to do evil can originate externally, but even so, the real pressure is always internal and emotional: the desire to avoid loss or pain or death.

For many years now, Arn has chosen to do good. Having been through horror that would destroy many people, both physically and spiritually, he continues to forge a meaning for his life, choosing every day to rededicate himself to it. He may have grown beyond a need to atone for what he did, but the pain of his past won't ever leave him. It's a pain you can see in his eyes, always there behind the kindness, intelligence, and love.

---

In the final decade of my business career, everything inside me was about to culminate in a long-overdue crisis. In my world travel, I avoided the sunny beaches and typical tourist attractions and forced myself to confront these scenes of extreme malevolence. Essentially, I was ramping up my strenuous inner questioning, asking, *Why this evil?* This incredibly destructive, violent tribalism, as Thatcher had put it to me, *How did it arise?* It didn't make sense to me: what happened in Nazi Germany, in Cambodia under Pol Pot, and to my family in Romania, under Communism. It's still with us, in all of us, and if, armed with nuclear weapons, we could give in to this murderous, tribal behavior, we would exterminate our own species and many others in the bargain. Why has this mismatch happened with the imperative to survive that has brought us so far? Why are we equipped with this potential to destroy ourselves so easily, if our most primal impulse is to stay alive? I was so close to an answer that would satisfy me, but it wouldn't come together for me.

Though I have always believed in God, I have never questioned the scientific method or the way in which it made our contemporary world possible. I find no conflict between the notion of a transcendent, spiritual force for good, a deity that had worked actively in the souls of those who rescued my brother and me from our exile in Romania, and the well-established fact that we've arisen through a process of natural selection, over millions of years, evolving from what we so imperiously call the "lower" life-forms.

If I am biased in my vision of the world, it's with a prejudice in favor of science. Though Karen Armstrong brilliantly argues for the incomprehensibility of God in her book *The Case for God*, I can't keep myself from suspecting that the process that began during the Enlightenment in Europe will culminate some day in a rational illumination of everything, including God. Undoubtedly, I'm wrong, but something within me keeps expecting we will understand what all of this has meant, not through a mystical revelation, but through observation and reasoning. The greatest mysteries might eventually become a matter of common sense. This is my heritage as a European and American, a Westerner, and I'm helpless to shed it. It's simply something I both hope and believe may happen in the future. Maybe that means a distant future: hundreds or thousands of years from now. Meanwhile, as my own internal struggle illustrates so clearly, most of us see, as the Bible (1 Corinthians 13:12) puts it, through a glass darkly.

Struggling with what I'd seen in Europe and Southeast Asia, still thinking of what Elie Wiesel had said about the priority of our prehistoric heritage, I came across a small book by Robert Ornstein and Paul Ehrlich called *New World, New Mind*. It's a

book with many passages that still strike me as powerfully inci-
sive and longer sections that read a bit like a cranky op-ed letter.
As I made my way through this book, it was as if all the pieces of
the puzzle fell into place. The book's examples of human perception—the way our brains are genetically wired to see and hear
only certain things because they threaten or advance our immediate survival—resonated in a way that allowed me to extrapo-
late them to the issues that had preoccupied me all my life.

As an evolutionary biologist, Ehrlich knew that human
beings had evolved to thrive in a particular kind of environment,
full of quickly moving prey and predators. Our sensory skills
enable us to focus on fast emerging phenomena, especially at the
start and end of a given sequence of events, and so we tend to
ignore all the gradually emerging trends that, now, have become
a much larger threat than a tiger leaping at us from the bush.
Global warming, AIDS, environmental degradation, population
growth, nuclear weapons—these alone threaten our survival as
a species. Yet our media, and our attention span, fix on the most
trivial, emerging events, rather than being watchful over these
absolutely crucial issues. He points out that terrorist attacks, sta-
tistically, are a tiny and inconsequential threat compared with
chronically underinflated tires on automobiles. It's a reality that
most people drive on underinflated tires, which lead to accidents
that kill far more people every year than terrorists, still no one
reports on it. Few people are aware of the danger, even fewer
keep their tires inflated properly, and so on.

Granted, it's funny to imagine a news channel devoted to
issues like this—the flossing channel, the tire inflation network,
the melting–ice cap cam. But his point is that terrorism—an
unsuccessful attempt to blow up a jet over Detroit, for example—strikes our old brains in a perceptual and emotional way
that used to enable us to survive but now is no longer a priority.

We still have to act quickly to rapidly emerging physical threats: an oncoming car in the wrong lane, say. A reflexive swerve into the breakdown lane will still save our lives. But as a species, these instincts no longer do the work they once did: We need a new mind, acutely alert to gradual, statistical changes in our world. With a retooled educational system, built on this awareness of how our inherited mental tendencies are helpless to recognize and act on the greatest threats to our survival, we might be able to meet the challenges that face us now and in the future.

Though it was published two decades ago, some of Ehrlich's passages are especially pertinent and powerful right now:

Investigators measured what the frog's eye tells the frog's brain by using microelectrodes to detect electrical impulses sent to the brain by the eye . . . Only four kinds of messages were sent to the brain. These four . . . contained information related directly to the two most important aspects of a frog's survival: obtaining food and escaping danger . . .

The frog's brain is "wired" to ignore all but extremely limited types of information. Higher animals, ourselves included, are not as restricted in sensory experience . . . (yet) the visual system of most animals, including the visual cortex, is designed to select information about only some kinds of changes in the environment, to transmit and analyze that information, and ignore the rest.

Among the default (settings) of the human mind are a tendency to analyze everything as an immediate, personal phenomenon: what does this mean to me? . . . Whatever gets close to us in space and time is immediately overemphasized. Viewers of violent movies believe there is more violence in the world than do people who do not see such films.

Americans since WWII have changed attitudes to fit new

phenomena such as TV, jet aircraft, computers, terrorism, AIDS, and thermonuclear war. Other adjustments have been even more rapid. Most people do not realize that schooling also changes the structure of children's minds significantly. Reading, writing and arithmetic, so commonly taught, are not natural acts of the mind, but are radical transformations of the way the nervous system operates. The mind's default positions are for talking and listening, but new mental routines are developed in the child's brain by their schooling, creating a new mind capable of reading and writing.

We have to shift our understanding of ourselves as separate individuals, each seeking our own welfare, to an understanding of how we fit into social, biological, and physical environments. It is not that increasing scientific knowledge makes morals obsolete, but that a new world we've created makes the nature of moral choices unprecedented.

Instead of pondering the local problems of our own life, we need to think about the collective life of our species. If, instead of thinking in terms of decades, centuries, or even the millennia of recorded history, we contemplated our history for many millions of years, then the problems we now face would take on a vastly different perspective.

We need to make available to students in a straightforward way the conclusion by all the world's great religions (and some social scientists) that people can be best seen as "one animal" or all as brothers and sisters . . . and we need to do much more than that; we need to produce a new kind of synthesis between the modern scientific understanding . . . and the essence of religious and esoteric traditions, which . . . (are) different from that offered by many of the "religions."

All of this made perfect sense to me, and it enabled me to

think about evil in a new way, something I'd been struggling to do for decades. I simply took Ehrlich's thinking one step further. Everything he said about human perception seemed to apply equally well to reflexive human behavior in a moral realm. Everything we shun as evil at one time served our interests as a species. To protect the welfare of ourselves, our family, and tribe, we were forced to become an inherently violent people. The urge to do harm to others represents our primal drive to stay alive, and at one time, what we considered evil was a form of brutally necessary and beneficial behavior. It assured that the strongest survived, so that our species could continue to grow and refine itself. The strongest did just that, through self-interested behavior, including violence.

Millions of years ago, it's likely some calamity defoliated the trees in Africa and prompted the most advanced primates to descend, tentatively, to the ground as a new home. It was a radical change from the safety and privacy of those leafy heights to a dangerous, tricky world of fight or flight. There had been few predators to worry about up above. Now the jungle cats hid in the brush and death leaped out in an instant. No watering hole was safe. A genetic journey of millions of years began as the most evasive, cunning, and violent of the primates survived in this environment, while the trusting peace lovers perished. These repugnant, and absolutely necessary, traits became ingrained into our DNA.

A little more than 150,000 years ago (the recent past, really, when you consider the length of time required for us to evolve into human beings) in a small village in eastern Tanzania, our current genetic type, as *Homo sapiens*, emerged. Our pigmentation was black, being so close to the equator. This has been determined by examining the mitochondria in fossilized bone cells that can be dated and traced to their geographic origin.

Using these tests, we can retrace the migration of the human race away from Tanzania to various points on the globe.

We lived at first in small bands and then tribes. We guarded our territories ferociously. We learned agriculture. Slowly, new forms of behavior emerged—loyalty, trust, and devotion to family—as essential to our individual survival. The history of civilization in the past three thousand years, a blink of the eye, has been the ascendancy of these values and their struggle against the far deeper and sometimes far more compelling forms of behavior that now threaten our planet. In the past these behaviors were exactly what enabled the species to survive.

But our world, specifically our capacities and our power and our brains, has grown so rapidly, these instincts that worked in a far more primitive setting now threaten our survival. The bow and arrow, the slingshot, have been replaced by the suitcase nuke and greenhouse gas. When our ability to destroy was limited to another human being or another tribe, our future as a species didn't hang in the balance. But now, self-interested behaviors, still lurking as reflexes in our cortex, if set loose in the wrong context, can ruin the future of our planet.

Our genome keeps imprinting on our cells and behavior those instinctive reactions that were so crucially useful for us over the past millions of years: fight, flight, deceit, treachery, tribalism. The challenge now is to be able to contain those instincts, suppress them, particularly when under stress, and change those negative instincts to a set of behaviors that will actually enable us to survive in the contemporary world. As I mentioned earlier in this book, the advent of epigenetics has demonstrated that if we choose to do this with consistency, we can gradually eliminate the negative side of our evolutionary heritage.

———

Whether this realization of mine strikes others as an acceptable view of evil, it has worked for me. I know in many ways it probably isn't theologically pure, from almost any doctrinal angle. It relies on the theory of evolution so it won't please those who advocate the traditional version of intelligent design. Yet it gave me permission to believe again and offered me a path to follow so that I could have a picture of the world I could accept intellectually. If it strikes others as a crutch, so be it. I'm walking boldly forward, as an individual, because of it. In many ways, this is my metaphorical version of the biblical Genesis story. In this context, the devil is indeed in each of us. He is the dark side of the traits that enabled us to survive for millions of years. He is our unchecked capacity for evil.

This explanation of evil eliminated my craving for an answer. It was exactly what I'd been missing: the beginning of a glimpse of a rational perspective on what otherwise seemed totally inexplicable or is treated as a theological mystery. So, as my life began to unfold, I discovered that the more we know, the more we realize there's still more left to uncover. Over time, I came to be at peace with this realization. It occurred to me that faith is the bridge between what's knowable and the untold mysteries we may be destined to understand in the millennia ahead.

Ironically, my delighted response to all of this was a bit more emotional than rational. I must have seemed like a bit of a stalker to poor Mr. Ehrlich, because I started to pester him, without pause, for a meeting, determined to tell him my views and see what he thought of them.

This was no easy feat. After what must have been a dozen calls to his office, I was able to get an appointment. On one of my trips to the West Coast, I arrived at his Palo Alto office on a beautiful sunny day in late May. I managed to get him to sit down for a few minutes. After thanking him for his time, I told him I was searching for insight into evil. I was hoping that, by understanding it, I might better know how to respond to the prevalence of it in human behavior.

Ehrlich said, "I've just published a new book. *Human Natures.* Why don't you come to New York and listen to my presentation. It's only a few weeks away."

All that effort and all those miles, and that ended up being about all we said. I flew home once my business in the city was finished and showed up for his talk a few weeks later at the Museum of Natural History. I listened and took a few notes. After his presentation, Dr. Ehrlich and I greeted one another and adjourned to a nearby coffee bar to drink tea and talk about the future of the human species.

"*New World, New Mind* meant a great deal to me personally. It helped me make sense of what has happened in my life," I said.

He nodded and said, "Actually, my thinking has evolved. So many people seem to think we humans are somehow hardwired to be aggressive, selfish, brutal. Have you heard about *Rape?* It's a recent book that claims that men are genetically programmed to commit violence against women—as if there's nothing that can be done about it, as if we're doomed to act out what our genes dictate. It's nonsense! No good scientist believes it. Yet the public doesn't understand. And people who have political or philosophical reasons for wanting to defend destructive behaviors like to spread these ideas as if they provide a scientific basis for their propaganda. It's a shame."

"I'm not sure I follow you," I replied. "Don't you write about how human behavior is influenced by our genetic inheritance?"

"Our genes are only a small part of what determines our behavior. Something else has to be the major controlling factor."

"Such as . . ."

"The environment, and especially culture. We have control over our culture. We can change the way we choose to think, behave, and interact. We'd *better* make some changes, and soon, if we want to survive on this planet."

This was a breakthrough moment for me.

What he'd just said allowed me to think that if DNA governs a great deal of our behavior, our behavior might also ultimately influence our DNA—and this seemed urgently important as a way of making our long-term residency on this planet more likely. Change culture, change behavior, and somewhere down the line the DNA will follow: An idea at the heart of *Human Natures* took root in me at this moment. Culture influences behavior. Behavior influences DNA, and then back in the other direction, the chain of cause and effect runs as well: from genetic structure to individual behavior and then to cultural change. Ehrlich didn't actually spell this out, and I didn't have any studies at this point to confirm this notion, but I felt it had to be true.

Now Ehrlich was getting warmed up, and I was warming up, as well, to his elaborations on what I'd read. Examples and stories began to flow quickly between his sips of tea. "You've seen pictures of Easter Island with those mysterious statues of huge heads staring at the Pacific? No one knows who made them. The people of Easter Island vanished so quickly because of the decay of their natural environment that they even left many of those statues unfinished, half-buried in the ground. We're on the verge of becoming those Easter Islanders. Biological evolution just isn't fast enough. We need to change our behavior a lot faster than that. If we don't, we'll probably get done in by pollution, environmental degradation, global warming, or nuclear war. So you see, it's not just violence and hatred and selfishness that endanger our species. It's also simple stupidity and shortsightedness. Our thinking hasn't evolved fast

enough to keep up with our technology. We humans are capable of remarkable changes if only we want to change.

"You've heard of Jane Goodall? She worked with primates
in Africa for many years and discovered a lot about how they
behave and interact—fascinating stuff. Apparently one time a
bunch of young male chimps went a little nuts. They killed an
infant chimp, carried its body up into a tree and started eating
it. Gruesome.

"But here's the thing. These animals were aware of this. They
had grown used to Goodall's company and her observation.
They knew she was watching them. They apparently started to
feel guilty. They stopped eating the baby and looked upset and
ashamed. And then one of the chimps took the remains and carried them through the forest two miles to Jane Goodall's lab. He
left the body right there on her doorstep—as if to say, 'We're
sorry,' and to propitiate Jane, who in some sense had become
their spiritual guide and leader. It was an amazing thing for a
chimp to do. It shows you the power of culture to alter behavior,
the influence of social forces. Aggression is everywhere, but so is
tenderness, generosity, cooperation, love. If chimps can do that,
why not humans?"

At the time when I spoke with Ehrlich, the subject of epigenetics wasn't even on the table. We now know that good
behavior makes human beings more likely in the future to
behave in the same way and eventually do exactly what Ehrlich
predicted: confirm that we can affect our genetic code through
cultural change and individual choice. This has been confirmed
most recently through the understanding of epigenetics.

———

But where in all this is the notion or reality of God? I was still
struggling to reconcile my new understanding of evil with my

faith. When you are brought up to believe in an anthropomorphic, interventionist God, a benevolent being who watches over us and acts on our prayers, your faith is sorely tested by the indifference of a world where survival represents the clash of brutal forces. I still believed, yet I had to put my faith to the test and come to some kind of evolved understanding of God, the way I had found a new understanding of evil.

It had to start where my quest began: the place where I was born. I had to go back and face the memories of my persecution and try to understand how God could have been with me during that time. In the Romanian travel guide I still keep on my desk—the only one I've ever been able to find devoted to my birth land—there's no mention of the town where my life changed so dramatically. There's nothing about Lipova, although it does comment about the nearest city, Arad, saying, "There's not much to see here." So, of course, Arad is where I began my first journey back to Romania as an adult, forty-five years later.

My wife and I arrived and stayed the night in Arad, and in the morning our group began a drive to Lipova, about an hour away. It was a Sunday. The warm spring weather of the previous day had become a gray mist and drizzle, and the closer we got to my old village, there on the banks of the Mures River, the more I could feel my heart constrict.

It was a lovely scene, lush green hills and valley farmlands and villages. None of it was familiar until we crossed an old iron bridge, just barely wide enough for two opposing lanes, and this I remembered distinctly from my youth. It all began to come back, how we played on the banks of the river, fishing and swimming. I remembered more and more, and yet all of it seemed small, so much less substantial than what I recalled and, surprisingly, wonderful to revisit. Looking around at the village, from the center of town, not far from my grandparents' home, which was still standing, I wasn't haunted by anguished memories at all. It was almost uplifting.

We met the town's mayor and other city officials, as well as several of my classmates from first grade. "You haven't changed at all," they said, which made me laugh, partly because I hardly remembered them. We talked about our lives as adults and discovered we'd all become successful in different ways. We visited the house where I'd stayed with my grandparents before the Communists sent us to Botoscani. A portion of it had been turned into a museum of regional art and culture from the Banat region of Transylvania.

Little had changed. Even the cobblestones paving the streets hadn't been replaced. The buildings were pleasantly weathered, in need of repair, but full of character, with windows battened down by heavy wooden shutters—still mostly closed at this hour—painted in a variety of beautiful muted colors, gray, green, brown. Little homes and small shops, whose windows were filmed with dust, seemed packed together in rows along the narrow sidewalks. The town seemed tiny and old, but as comfortable and perfectly fitted to the lives of its people as a worn-out pair of shoes.

My grandparents' home was just as I remembered, a two-story building with a white plaster façade and a gigantic wooden front doorway that led into a long walkway to the center of the property. The house seems to surround you, with wings on left and right, as you stroll into a central courtyard garden. The roses were all gone, the ones my brother and I had watered every day. The walnuts that would fall from the tree were also gone, apparently because the tree had blown over in a storm. The whole place looked sadly unloved now. Inside the house, we were startled and amused to find an elderly couple, a local artist and his wife too poor to afford a home of their own, sleeping in my grandmother's bedroom. We were pleased someone had made this grand old place their home, essentially in an act of kindness from the town.

"What happened to my grandfather's library?" I asked.

The mayor shook his head.

"All burned," he said.

For the first time, I felt angry at what had happened to my family.

One of the older officials said, "I remember it. The secret police built a bonfire in the garden. It took days to burn all of them."

As a group, we drove out of the town to a high field where Barbara and I simply stood and absorbed the beauty of the view. The rain had paused, and in peace and silence we drank it all in as the sun emerged.

"I'd forgotten how beautiful it is," I admitted.

"I have something to show you," our guide said.

We followed him up and over the slope. There, in the very middle of a large, flat, open hilltop, was a tower of rough-hewn stone, a tapered, cut-off obelisk surmounted by a cross, about ten feet wide at its base and rising some thirty-five feet into the sky. Gradually, our little group gathered around this tower, and the mayor pointed toward the inscription on a brass plaque mounted on its base:

100 ANI

DE LA MISCAREA MEMORANDISTA

DIN LIPOVA CONDUSA DE

SEVER BOCU

28 JUN 1992

The peasantry had never stopped looking upon Sever Bocu, my grandfather, as their representative, their hero, even after he'd died. It was a monument, not a grave. It commemorated the one hundredth anniversary of the birth of my grandfather, in Lipova.

It stood as homage to his enduring spiritual legacy, and a salute to the liberation movement he'd spearheaded, but gave no indication that he'd ever died. Though all the books in the world can be burned, some memories can't be erased. I didn't want my memories, no matter how painful, to disappear either.

Later I realized my emotion at the burning of grandfather's books was the only moment of anger in my visit to Romania. My reaction rose up from adult considerations, reflections on much larger issues—the way Communism imposed its power on a population, the illiteracy it tried to induce, imposing its own kind of imperialistic ambitions. I remembered a German poet who in the 1820s once wrote, "Those who are capable of burning books will someday be able to burn people too." My anger had little connection to my own remembered pain. The suffering of my past couldn't threaten my faith anymore. In my own probably imperfect way I understood what had happened. I now understood the behavioral origin of the evil that had changed my life and this eliminated any potential for anger, for recrimination, for an urge to avenge what had been done.

I had no animosity at all toward the people who'd made me suffer. I saw them as puppets of their own atavistic impulses, struggling to survive in their own way, surrendering to behavior that once might have been necessary but now simply destroyed lives. This view of human nature, which I'd struggled to achieve for so many years as an adult, now made it impossible for me to hate these people who had once threatened my life. A word for this attitude might be forgiveness, but it was less a choice and more simply a reflection of my *inability* to hate and feel a rage I might have felt earlier in my life. As Joan Brown Campbell suggested, love had overcome animosity in my own life. At last, it seemed, I'd found the reconciliation to evil I'd longed for all my life.

Ultimately, once I understood the source of evil within me, I also had the potential power to control it. I grasped that those negative, all too human instincts to attack or do harm when under pressure were all part of basic human instincts that had served us well in prehistoric times. But now, when those instincts came forth, I could recognize them for what they were and not only suppress them in the short term but also potentially eliminate them in the long term. Their power over me could be eradicated. It was a choice, a possibility.

Yet where was God when I needed him back then? The nature of goodness, and of God, represented just as big a mystery to me as evil when I looked back on my childhood. In giving up my faith in a personal, interventionist God, the figure who would answer prayers and save me from my enemies, I found myself struggling to find a new way to believe. I needed to understand this love that I was learning how to live by and discover a new path toward faith. How was I to find this good? How could I accept the reality of that embrace? That, too, was part of the journey, part of the path to becoming a better human being.

The notion of a Godless world and the horrors it can evoke pressed in upon me not long ago when Barbara and I were seated on our porch in Chautauqua with Keith and Rose-Lee Reinhard. Keith had been a highly successful leader of a rival advertising agency, back when I was at Y&R, while Rose-Lee was an equally accomplished colleague of mine during our years in Chicago.

This time, our porch conversation took an unexpected turn. We were having a most animated debate about the city of Berlin. We had just heard an outstanding lecture on modern architecture. Featured in the session was the work of the brilliant Polish-American architect Daniel Libeskind, and among his most famous creations was his spectacular Jewish Museum, one of Berlin's most recognizable landmarks. As it happened, the four of us had recently been in Berlin together and had visited the museum. Rose-Lee was having nothing to do with the lecturer's praise for it. "I just can't stand that museum. It's ugly. It feels like a prison. There's no compassion in it."

It was an astute observation, because in a way that museum is meant to show the reality of a Godless universe, where no one and nothing intervenes to save human beings unjustly condemned to die. I can see how that would offend a believer; it would seem to be the embodiment of the atheist's complaint that a world where innocent children suffer and die cannot be a universe created by a benevolent god. Or at least it's a universe in which God does not intervene to save the innocent. That does, indeed, seem to be the nature of the world as a whole, not just the world of Nazi Germany. Behind the horror of this museum seems to lurk the question of "the problem of evil": How could a benevolent Creator have fashioned a world where evil exists?

Later that evening, I reflected on the conversation, making our Berlin trip come alive in my mind. I had found it to be a beautiful city. I'd traveled to Germany dozens of times during my active business career, but Berlin is not a business city and so it never made it onto my itinerary. The more I got to know this remarkable place, the more I saw it as the quintessential metaphor for evil and good.

Observing the Jewish Museum from the outside, I felt the forces of evil in a very visceral way. This work has been described as belonging to the school of "emotional" architecture. It's a very fitting description. Rose-Lee was right. From the very first glance at its lines, the museum's stern look of steel and cement expressed a cold, foreboding quality. The tiny windows gave it the look of a mysterious fortress. It looked as if it held a hoard of dark secrets and possessions. There wasn't a trace of warmth or compassion emanating from its soul. Inside, the mood was darker still. The light is somber, subdued. The corridors make you feel unbalanced, as the floors tilt in a subtle way to one side. Unconsciously, you feel the need to fight this tendency and try to climb against the pull of gravity. I felt disturbed, uncomfortable. Then I entered the open-air Garden of Exile. For the first time in my life I felt literally oppressed entering an architectural space. Now the ground's tilt became aggressive and the columns of concrete appeared ready to fall and crush you. I felt light-headed. I could hardly move forward. Panic began to take over my senses. I wanted to move ahead so I could escape, get out. But there is no out up ahead. The path leads to a blank cement wall. There's only one way out; the way you came in. I felt shaken, lost.

In the Holocaust Chamber, it only got worse. As the heavy steel door closed behind me, a sense of loneliness set in. I moved toward a shadowy end, but again there was no exit. A ladder showed itself tantalizingly. It's about halfway up the approximately 60-foot high cement wall, clearly out of reach. It seems, for a moment, impossible to get out. Claustrophobia sets in. I double back to the heavy steel door, almost afraid to pull on it and find it locked. But it wasn't.

Our guide awaits us outside. He sees my mood. All comfort is now gone. Gently, he asks me if I can handle one more experience. "I'll try" is the best I can answer. Some corridors later, we approach another unusual space. Only the name of the artist, Menashe Kadishman, identifies the gallery. This time the light streaming through one of the few windows brings more visual clarity. Circular metallic objects lie on the floor. They are round disks made out of what looks like dark, gray iron. They are carved with two round holes at the top, and a horizontal slit in the middle. The diameters of the disks vary. Some are around 4 to 5 inches, some bigger, maybe 8 or 9 inches. I look more closely. Now I get it. Slits were carved in the iron rounds for eyes, noses, and mouths. They are faces, of adults and children, humorless, stern faces. You begin to see faces in pain. I see horror in their eyes. My imagination is now in overdrive. I see many faces, I'm told more than ten thousand of them, stacked on top of each other in many, many layers. I don't see the bottom, there's no visible floor. "Go walk on them," our guide says softly. I force myself to take a step. Then another. The noise is horrendous: iron against iron, the sound of screams. A few steps are all I can muster, enough so that I see the room is closed at the darker end. Again, there's no exit.

Yes, Rose-Lee, there is, indeed, no compassion in Daniel Libeskind's house of horrors. There's only the face of evil. That's what this means. I'm overwhelmed, tortured, and desolate. In this museum, the notion of a benevolent God seems entirely implausible.

Once we emerge from the museum and begin our tour of Berlin itself, I start to get an inkling of something else. We see the other side of Berlin—the new Berlin, born from the rubble of the war, then mired in the despair, failure, and collective guilt of a nation that knew it should have done more to stop these horrors. They needed to move on. They believed in the possibility of a better future. They began to hope. But it surely wasn't easy. The city was carved into four parts, with the Soviets gobbling up more than half of the entire area. The Americans, British, and French shared the western half of the city. Then the Wall went up, a fresher face of evil, separating the two halves.

Still, faith in a better life took hold. When John Fitzgerald Kennedy flew into Berlin in 1964, 300,000-plus Berliners gathered in the Town Hall of Schöneberg to hear his message of hope. "Ich bin ein Berliner" meant to them not only his identification with their city but that they too would one day live in freedom, like the Americans they were ready to embrace. It offered them hope, a yearning for the good, a reinvention of the human spirit. When the Wall came down, inch by inch, many years later, that dream took on an encouraging mantle of reality.

For the past two decades, the city has reinvented itself—literally. The greatest collection of architects in the world conspired to create beauty and inspiration. Helmut Jahn, Daniel Libeskind, Frank Gehry, Mies van der Rohe, and more, caught the fever. From the ashes of the war, despair, and a crumbled wall, a new city took flight. The contorted face of evil was replaced by hope in the promise of good. At the very least, Berliners would have the ability to choose the nature of their future destiny. Something else, something good, was evident everywhere in the way this city has recovered and been reborn.

---

The following morning, I woke up early in Chautauqua. I strolled downstairs to the porch. It's my favorite spot to think, to let my mind wander. I made myself a cup of Earl Grey tea. The sun appeared over the treetops. As I reflected about the city of Berlin, I thought about how my own life has a similar history. The aftermath of a horrible war, the evil communist force that could take my respected, venerable, almost 80-year-old grandfather from his wife and grandchildren, and the interrogations that followed, all took a heavy toll. I allowed a loss of control over my life to affect me. Sure, I fought the evildoers. I had a model of an otherworldly anthropomorphic God, who though he was above and beyond our world, would somehow step in from time to time to protect the good and punish the evil. That simple model gave me the faith and strength to survive. I'd lost my faith in this all-powerful, incorporeal God. There was little evidence he'd paid much attention to the people being herded into the gas chambers. And yet, he hadn't disappeared altogether.

Like the city of Berlin, my transition to freedom started fast. But like the city's journey to recovery, my own rehabilitation would take decades to take hold. In the early days of my new world, life took on a very positive façade. Hard work in the sewers was replaced by long hours of study. My mind caught fire. Questions were answered. More questions were raised. The learning process became addictive, obsessive, and very satisfying in and of itself. In many ways, it was almost euphoric. Far more significant, though, all of my rebirth depended on the action of what I called guardian angels, extraordinary people who reached out and became enablers of my good life—the very opposite of my ordeal on the other side of the ocean. For a while, taking all of this goodness for granted, I no longer thought about God or sought deeper meaning in my existence. Many of the social evils of my era did not reach my consciousness. I was oblivious to the history around me: the Freedom Riders' bus rides and terrors of Birmingham and Montgomery. I was too self-absorbed, in love with my new, rewarding life.

Reality finally caught up with me. With time, the harsh challenges of everyday life intruded on my idyllic existence. I began to see good people doing harm to others. The deserving were not getting their just rewards. The anthropomorphic God of my childhood model, a God who would intervene to protect good people, once again had withdrawn, seemingly indifferent. So what did this mean to me? I became more and more isolated and afraid. My life and my beliefs were in crisis mode. But my life's experiences in childhood also made me tough and resilient. I began to fight back. My questioning skills took over. I'd been interrogated as a child. Now I began to interrogate life itself: I wanted more answers. Still, the journey of full recovery took a long time. Just as in Berlin after the war, it took hard work and the commitment and love of many guardian angels to bring beauty and meaning back into my life. My spiritual growth was jump-started by wonderful people who reached out to give me a helping hand, and there were remarkably many of these people along the way. For me, this turned out to be the cornerstone, years after the fact, of a new understanding of God.

# CHAPTER 9

# BE ALWAYS GOOD

AT NIGHT, WALKING BACK WITH BARBARA FROM A MOVIE AT our little theater, making our way home through Chautauqua's quiet backstreets, I glance up at the sky—that vast expanse of stars—amazed at their beauty, but also just slightly uneasy about the immensity overhead. I used to have a policy about the night sky: just don't look up. To be honest, I used to find those vast reaches a little disturbing. The ancient Hebrews considered that vault the "firmament" of their world. They believed the sky was a dome God had used to create a space for life, parting the primordial sea, making way for the earth and everything on it. In their view, that dome of stars and the earth were surrounded by water, a reservoir beyond the sky and beneath the earth. While this cosmology seems both primitive and poetic, I actually find it somewhat comforting and almost wish it were the case. When I try to imagine the infinite scope of our universe, knowing what science has proven about its dimensions, I realize I can't even picture its immensity; my mind can't grasp the scope of this world, which can make an individual human life seem infinitesimal.

I know most people don't react to the beauty of the constellations in this way. In the eighteenth century, David Hume, the celebrated Scottish philosopher, found them inspiring, despite himself. He hated organized religion in ways that made him a proponent of the antireligious sentiment of high-profile atheists like Richard Dawkins and the now deceased Christopher Hitchens: "Examine the religious principles, which have, in fact, prevailed in the world. You will scarcely be persuaded, that they are anything but sick men's dreams." Yet in *The Life and Correspondence of David Hume*, John Hill Burton quotes Hume in a much different mood. As Hume was on a hike one evening with his companion, in a highly uncharacteristic moment he reportedly stopped and gazed up with amazement at the stars and said, "Can anyone contemplate the wonders of that firmament and not believe that there is a God?"

I don't have a personal stake in whether Mr. Hume believed in God. He certainly didn't have any use for religion: On his deathbed there were no confessions, no conversions. So he has remained a poster boy for many hard-nosed agnostics and atheists. What I find interesting, though, is his instinctive reaction to the firmament, because the starry sky had exactly the opposite effect on me. One night, here in Chautauqua, when I looked up at that same sky, a couple of centuries after Hume did, I realized I could no longer believe in a personal God who consciously governed all the natural world, a God who had his eye on every sparrow and human being and star. It was unimaginable to me. Yet I felt God's presence as a power, an influence, in my life. I had never ceased to believe in this Power. I realized that I had to find a way to harmonize my new faith with what I knew about the universe, thanks to modern science.

This new personal spirit of doubt began, more or less, on the night when I looked through my friend Ted Wolfe's telescope, here in Chautauqua, into an unimaginably vast galaxy above our heads. As fellow village residents during the summer, Ted and Nancy Wolfe had become friends. Ted's a tall, slender, handsome gentleman with a passion for astrophotography. After showing me some of his marvelous photographs, Ted asked if I wanted to take a look at the sky through his telescope. I asked if I could bring along my granddaughter Ali, who was fascinated by any trip to a planetarium.

Ali was especially eager to get a look at the sky. Ted had been preparing for a presentation on astrophotography in Miami, so he went through some of his talk for Ali, and she listened, fascinated, but eager to gaze through the lens. I watched her face as he talked about the vastness of the universe, suspecting that she was wondering where her star was located. Her father had gone to the star registry on the Web and had paid a fee to name a star Ali G—her name, and at the same time a humorous reference to a character played by Sacha Baron Cohen. Ali was wondering where Ali G might be found up there. Yet when she finally looked through Ted's telescope, she was so awed by the sky she didn't seem to care whether she was looking at the star named after her.

When I looked up at the stars through his telescope, I found the immensity of the universe unsettling—not just from what I saw, but also from what Ted had told us in his little rehearsal of his presentation. For the first time in my life, I was able to envision myself proportionally as this little mote called Peter Georgescu, among the constellation of stars, thick as dust, that constitute our galaxy. Our sun, I began to realize, was just another star among billions and our little earth, a grain of sand in the Sahara.

And that was simply our own galaxy. Ted would move the telescope a bit and reveal more and more galaxies, endlessly stretching away, dimensions and numbers I couldn't begin to visualize or comprehend. I wondered how an interventionist God could possibly be "running" this vast, infinite show. Of course, this is primarily an emotional response, a way of reacting to my own mind's inability to grasp the totality of what exists—a grasping effort that seems to be an innate human drive, if you consider the compulsions of science to explain how everything began and where it's going and how it will end.

My conversations with Ted here in Chautauqua clarified how astrophysicists can detect radioactive traces, echoes if you will, of the Big Bang, getting measurements of these reverberations back to within seconds of that original explosion. Yet scientists have no credible way of describing the nature of what existed "before" the Big Bang. Using words in this way is paradoxical, because there was no "before," since time and space and matter had emerged at that "moment." As with faith in God, science reaches a point where traditional categories of thinking end, and our minds find themselves at a dead end, unable to imagine or picture what's being postulated. Ted liked to point out to me that our sun has a limited life—a mere 4.5 billion years, at which point it will implode and become a black hole—and our solar system will quit circling the drain, so to speak, and be drawn down into it. This is more than enough time to pay off your mortgage, but it does set a limit on how long the human race will be around on this earth, even if we figure out how to inhabit this planet without destroying ourselves. We're here, and then we're gone. What's true individually for each of us is true for our species, unless we move to another home in the universe, but you'll notice how none of this reflects the beginning and end described in the Bible.

The notion of God as a human being, except in the figure of Jesus Christ, often bothered me. It seemed that if humanity is created in the literal image of God, with arms and legs and a brain, then God would also be like us, including our flawed tendencies. The God of the Old Testament could also behave like a jealous, peevish, anger-prone individual, and I'd never felt this was consistent with a God whose essence is love and goodness. Now, seeing the universe through Ted Wolfe's telescope, it became completely impossible to imagine a God in this way. A human being can hardly remember more than a list of seven things at once, let alone grasp the size and scope of the galaxies. A personal, sentient God, a giant watchmaker who sets everything in motion and then keeps tinkering at all levels to make things better, seemed less imaginable to me, except as a Being beyond our mind's ability to visualize or conceptualize Him as an object of belief. Faith, for me, more and more became a cooperative relationship with a living presence implanted deep inside our souls, beyond the scope of my imagination.

This kind of faith has felt more consistent with the sort of faith science itself now demands from the average layperson. The truths of quantum physics defy common sense; it's impossible to understand, except mathematically, how light can be, or behave, as both a particle and a wavelength. The realities of string theory are even more unimaginable. Our minds think in four dimensions, width, height, length and duration, not in eight or nine different ones as necessitated by the new physics. So, we're perfectly willing to accept assertions about realities we can't imagine, and I had begun to think of God in this way. I couldn't visualize the exact nature of God, since God isn't a creature of our world, but I could have faith in the way God guides my life, through the force of good. This force, while it might sound a little too Obi-Wan Kenobi for many traditional believers, seemed perfectly credible as a God who could be inherent in the development of life.

The starry sky didn't inspire me to believe in the way that it may have affected David Hume. What I discovered is that science does call into question much of the traditional dogma, such as a literal understanding of Genesis, in which the universe is created in seven days, but isn't inconsistent with a more metaphysical understanding, and a more metaphorical language, regarding God. Science, as I learned, can't prove there is a God, but it doesn't claim to disprove the notion either: partly because, as Karen Armstrong has pointed out in *A Case for God*, most religions have affirmed that God isn't knowable the way things in the world can be known.

It's interesting to contrast this emerged understanding of the deity with the model I had created for myself as a little boy laboring in the middle of the night, reaching in to touch deadly electrical switches hot with voltage. That little fellow needed the supportive power of a superman who would descend from the sky to protect me. But now, while I feel the force of goodness, which I call God, I also sense an increased personal responsibility for embodying that force, rather than expecting it to arrive in my life from somewhere or someone else. Fully aware of the unimaginable scope of the universe, in the reality of this world we inhabit, I know my role may be microscopic yet I believe what I do matters. This is a new kind of faith: that my behavior actually means something in ways I might not fully grasp at the time. Looking at the world with these new eyes, I see the impact of good people on their own lives and on the lives of others and I understand now that this is how God intervenes in the world, through the choices of good people. I respect what they do, and that respect becomes inspirational. That's how goodness works.

For most of my life, my relationship to God hasn't represented an *understanding* of the deity. It's been an acquaintance, a friendship, a direct awareness of God's presence, which can become especially pronounced at certain times. My training in the Silva techniques put God back at the center of my life, but it didn't exactly give me a conceptual understanding of God. Over the years since then, I've had moments of heightened awareness, which I associate with God. These epiphanies are inescapably tangible, as real as the sound of my alarm clock in the morning. It's the difference between the two French verbs for knowing: *savoir* and *connaître*. One is about knowledge. The other is about acquaintance. We're so insistent on the first sense of knowing: knowing in the head. We need more of that other version of knowing: the knowing of the heart. I've known God in my heart, and yet even now, by writing these words and this book, I'm determined, maybe foolishly, to squeeze him into my head—and *yours*.

The most common awareness of God, for me, is simply a heightened awareness of beauty. In Vail once, visiting with close friends, Barbara and I found ourselves listening to a performance of the New York Philharmonic. As I was listening to Beethoven's magnificent piano concerto, I could see over the heads of the performers to the distant mountains in Vail. Behind that music, the beauty of those silent mountains surprised me with a quiet joy, not entirely different from the effect music usually has, but far more overwhelming. I felt almost a sense of levitation, of being completely released from the burden of having a body.

I have had, as well, similar encounters with a distinctly different sort of peace and tranquility. In Chautauqua, hearing some two hundred voices in the choir singing in harmony, or at the Church in the Rocks outside Sedona, or at one of my favorite churches, Grace Cathedral, near the hotel in San Francisco where I've stayed on business trips. I have experienced special moments of love with my wife and son and grandchildren that are extraordinarily selfless and exhilarating. I have certainly acted on occasion out of compassion, but far more often I've been the recipient of compassion from others. After all, I wouldn't have been reborn on American soil without Frances Bolton's help. I wouldn't have had the start in life I had without the help of Bill Saltonstall and Arnie Arbuckle and so many other people in my career who gave of themselves to help me, with nothing to gain by helping me. These personal experiences have served for me as evidence of the force I call God. God acts in the world, He intervenes, through the goodness of individual human beings.

Barbara and I have been to India many times on business. We fell in love with the country and its subtle energy and majesty. On one particular trip, we drove from Cochin, on the west coast, to Chennai, the city once named Madras. We stopped in the beautiful backwaters of the delta that moves inland during the rising tide. In Cochin, we stayed in a comfortable inn; a peek over the high surrounding walls revealed a squalid struggle, with garbage piled in the streets. The people around us survived by fishing, employing a centuries-old process of tossing huge nets into the tide and hauling in thousands of fish, at sunset.

As we drove eastward, the land was dotted by what appeared to be beautiful vineyards, a sea of green, yet they weren't fields of grapes but tea plantations. On the way, we stopped in Maduri and visited a temple to Vishnu—the preserving, sustaining God in the Hindu trinity of Brahma, Vishnu, and Shiva. This temple, fragrant with incense, reminded me of my childhood and the smoky interior of my grandfather's Orthodox church. At one place there was a special statue of Vishnu, in female form. We'd arrived punctually, having been warned that we had to steer clear of processions of worshippers with offerings of flowers, food, and other goods.

Observing all of this, feeling the power of the growing throng, sensing the collective prayer and meditation around me, I spotted a young man in his thirties, a few inches taller than five feet, dressed in a loose robe. His face struck me. It was the face of a man completely transported. It's a word we usually use for descriptions of sex, but his heightened state of consciousness was anything but erotic. It was what the Indians call *samadhi*, a communion with God in which the disciple becomes virtually unaware of his surroundings, at one—in this man's case—with Vishnu. Krishna is the familiar incarnation of Vishnu, for most Westerners. He happens to be the deity that George Harrison of the Beatles chose to worship. I saw the passion in this one man's face, the totally unadulterated rapture of his faith in Vishnu, something I'd seen in the faces of the most devout Christians in my grandfather's church. I was astonished by this man's fervor, similar to what you might see in a Pentecostal church in America, but without the noise. He was deep in meditation, consumed with love, and standing there, not seated, in a totally motionless posture. His eyes were half closed, yet he saw nothing of the world around him. I realized his God was indistinguishable from mine.

I witnessed the same kind of rapturous, emotional embrace of spirituality on a visit to Trinity Church in Chicago. This was the parish of Reverend Otis Moss III, a brilliant young preacher. We had first met him in Chautauqua. We were excited to be able to attend the service because Joan Brown Campbell was going to preach that day. This was more than enough incentive and gave us the nerve to play the role of upper-middle-class white believers in a largely black crowd. We arrived at the church, where we were warmly greeted. To say *warmly* doesn't quite convey the love. We were hugged, kissed, fawned over, and generally treated like members of the family before anyone even knew our names.

After we found seats, I went back to the entrance and watched the people as they arrived. It was a warm and pleasant day. It was as if our Casual Friday culture, which has overtaken every day of the week now it seems, had happened on some planet in a distant galaxy. Everyone looked as if they'd stepped out of a scene from early in the previous century. They were elegantly dressed, with brightly colored hats, coats and ties. One young man was escorting his wife to the door and spotted an elderly lady slowly climbing out of a car, he excused himself and rushed back to help her make her way up the steps.

Finally, the place was packed with nearly two thousand people, and a choir of what must have been several hundred, all in robes of many different colors, creating a stunning human rainbow. When Rev. Moss stepped up to the pulpit, he asked everyone to welcome his or her neighbors. Again, we found ourselves in a hive of kisses, hugs, handshakes, and words of affection. These weren't air kisses, and the hugs were bear hugs.

Once the choir began to sing, the congregation became vocal, animated, overflowing with emotion. Theirs was a more demonstrative, cheerful, and garrulous version of what I'd seen in that Hindu temple. They were sensing the sound, in a big way. Everyone here could easily connect with a deeper spiritual level in their lives, a force above and beyond their average daily con-sciousness. It was unlike anything I'd ever witnessed in any other denomination's church service. Rev. Moss was a very close friend of Joan Brown Campbell, so we had heard him before when he came to Chautauqua to preach with his father, also a famous pastor from Cleveland. On stage, both then and now, he was a magnificent performer. He could get any crowd worked up, even white middle-aged Chautauquan adults, in an upstate New

York version of a black church's call and response. His message was clear, persuasive, and articulate, and he was unafraid to mix conventional oratory with a black church style. Otis, just over forty, is one of the most charismatic preachers and leaders of any parish in this country. In a way, it's not surprising. He took over Trinity Church, which had been President Obama's church, when the notorious Rev. Wright resigned.

Our morning at Trinity confirmed everything I'd seen in Chautauqua when Reverend Otis Moss preached there. It reinforced for me a commonality of spirituality around the world; all the trappings of dogma and religion might be different, but the centrality of love and faith was identical. This service in Chicago convinced me that what interested me most was the source, the root, of all religious practice, from which so many different rituals emerge.

I saw faith all around me and recognized it within myself, yet I was still dissatisfied. I felt God's presence. I lived with God's support. But I couldn't quite understand how all of this jibed with the traditional faith of my childhood. I was uneasy and maybe a bit worried that I was fooling myself somehow. Even with all of this persuasive evidence of God's crucial presence in my own life and the lives of others, I still couldn't see a way to maintain my hold on God without seeking permission by casting nervous glances over my shoulder toward the Orthodox dogma of my childhood. I'd begun to realize I couldn't contort my adult faith into the straitjacket of the dogma I'd been taught as a child, and this bothered me, because I remained, at heart, a Christian. How could I be a Christian, though, without an interventionist God who answers prayers and dotes on every living creature? I worried that maybe I'd become like a member of some cult who is convinced he has found the true way, but is as far from it as anyone can get.

Science didn't seem to be making this any easier for me. My confidence in scientific method, and my sense of the world it revealed to me, made it impossible for me to believe in the God on Michelangelo's ceiling, bearded and bulked up as a professional wrestler. The God of the Old Testament seemed nasty and capricious to me, like an individual who suffered from multiple personality disorder. One of the ironies of my spiritual struggle has been that the Bible, during these years, became a stumbling block. The more I delved into the Old Testament, the more I disliked its temperamental God; there were so many petty rules, so much wrath from on high, so much punitive stoning. This was an all-powerful individual who seemed more in league with Stalin and Pol Pot, rather than the fellow who had fathered Jesus. I wanted to love the Bible the way I did as a child, but Jehovah kept getting in the way.

It can be a worrisome thing to light out onto this sort of individual path. The Bible is, after all, the Bible, not only holy but possibly the most powerful and influential collection of words ever printed between two covers. This unique book and the principles it espoused, which had helped keep me alive during seven years of servitude in Romania, also had taught me Jesus was God's *only* son, and my *only* path to salvation, and that He rose from the dead, and that God would cast into hell those who didn't believe in this prophet . . . and on and on. Who was I, the runt of the family, the mischievous little prankster my mother doted on, to question these scriptures and the vast religion cantilevered around it?

I'd come out of my experience in the Silva program with a firm, confident commitment to a higher power that seemed to transform my life every day. Emotionally and spiritually, I was in better shape, but rationally, not so much. I didn't have an intellectual way of making sense of my new relationship with God. All of this weighed on me. I was still sitting at the Exeter Harkness Table, feeling compelled to defend my stance to the skeptic in myself, unsatisfied until I could support my intuitions with an unbiased inquiry into the foundations of dogmatic religion. So I investigated various religions more deeply, thinking maybe there would be a philosophical or theoretical framework, unfettered by the axioms of any individual religion, which would give me a way of thinking about the presence of this new force in my life. It was fairly easy to find confirmation of my experience in what I read about the practice of meditation and yoga, or the philosophy of the Upanishads and the Buddhist sutras. I would always run up against dogma in the organized institution built around these practices and writings.

So on I would go, investigating one religion after another, until I eventually realized, with Karen Armstrong, who followed a similar path in her own life, that at the basis of them all was simply compassion and wisdom. The way I found myself understanding this was to see it most perfectly expressed in a dictum for human behavior: the Golden Rule. Love your neighbor as you love yourself; do good unto others. All the various religions had even more in common, from the experiential side as well as in the common wisdom of their mystics, but I was more interested in action. I favored works over contemplation, behavior more than states of being. Jesus Christ was, and still is, the religious figure that means the most to me, primarily because of the way he lived his life, and yet the religious dogma built on the Bible was still getting in the way of my faith.

———

On a visit to Syria in June of 2009, I found a way to put my qualms about the Old Testament to rest. I met a kindred spirit by the name of Daniel Fleming who said some things about the Bible that came as a relief to me. Dan was chair of Hebrew and Judaic Studies at New York University. In his latest book, *The Legacy of Israel in Judah's Bible*, Dan provides meaningful insight into the sociopolitical factor, in the region that affected the nearly 400 years of the writing and editing of the Old Testament.

He's good-looking, with some premature balding of his red hair, and he has a ginger beard and blue eyes. My personal quest strikes him as fairly typical of the way Americans now search for God. While the buffet-style tendency to pick and choose what you like from various spiritual traditions has invited more than its share of mockery, Dan seems to think it's an especially appropriate way to find a spiritual practice now in this melting pot of diverse faiths America has become.

"So you don't believe in God as a person?" he asked.

"No."

"That's a crucial choice," he said. "Everything else you think about deity is defined by that moment. So you explore. You collect evidence. You reason it out."

"Which is why I'm here," I said. "I don't argue with dogma. If it works for you, fine. It just doesn't work for me."

Dan continued, "You are trying to think your way through to a system that you then intend to live by. And at the same time, you hold yourself responsible to come up with all this, without an inherited religious system. Polling in America shows a large number of people participating in churches and yet they are extremely eclectic in the way they actually think. Even in Christianity, people are all over the map. This trend in American culture fits what you're doing; you're consciously stripping away the institutions and what you call the dogma, and yet there's a way in which people in America today are doing something like what you're doing. What immediately stands out in your approach is the desire to find a God that embodies your focus on the good and the beautiful. Someone could build a philosophical system around that without any notion of deity, like for instance, Socrates. What's intriguing is that you do bring with you from a previous mental life the category of deity that you can't shake. You know that all the stuff you think about doesn't require a God, but you already have this category of God you don't want to give up. The idea of God comes from outside the reasoning you are doing now, in a way. I think there is an enormous number of people in your shoes, despite all your uniqueness."

I asked him about the authority of the Bible and how literally this collection of writings is meant to be taken. "In Syria, you told me these stories of Jews that ended up in the Bible were stories of their culture, subject to many mutations. They were memorized and spoken until finally scribes wrote them down until they were edited and compiled," I said.

Dan said, "To some extent, the Old Testament itself is just an accumulated charter for a diverse community. The earliest stories trace back to 900 BC, and a version of the selected stories was finalized in Jerusalem around 512 BC. It was not about establishing a religion, but rather a way of preserving a culture. It was political. It wasn't dogmatic so much as communal: something the Jews used to define themselves as a people. What kind of God they imagined wasn't dogmatic. They didn't even think twice about it. It was a given. They might ask, How many Gods are there? Even the Hebrew word for God is plural. I'm still not totally sure why the Hebrew word for God is plural. It seems to reflect the transformation of polytheism into monotheism, that all gods are embodied in this one plural word."

"When Jesus appeared, the first Christians just considered themselves followers of Judaism, who were allowed into the fold by Jesus," I said. "If it weren't for circumcision, there wouldn't be Christianity, there would be only Judaism. Men didn't want to be circumcised, so Paul decided to abolish it in order to gain converts outside Israel, and this meant the sect was no longer Jewish, because circumcision had become culturally essential to Judaism, right? There were also major questions at that stage about the Messiah. For the Jews, the Messiah was simply going to restore the integrity and independence of Israel. Again, it was political. It was about restoration for the Jews, a recovery of their lost homeland. Being restored to their place in the world. Somehow God would come back and set things right. Even Paul saw Jesus in those terms, and they saw it as still being a Jewish issue. The dogma said this and that, and you can't violate this and that and still be a Jew. So we got Christianity."

Dan said, "Yes. A couple hundred years ago there was a movement to analyze the text of the Bible and understand how to read it. More recently, we gained more historical knowledge about the origin of the text and how it was produced. We gathered all the evidence and reconsidered the nature of the writings."

"This is essentially what you're doing yourself, isn't it?" I asked him.

"I'm trying to create a bridge between the Bible and what we know historically, and from archaeology. What Israel meant was a collaboration of a group of people who would act together as a unified nation and culture. Most people don't realize that Israel originally occupied a part of Jordan. Being Jewish isn't racial. It's social, cultural. Genetically, the Jewish community was diverse."

For days after our conversation, I realized that what Dan had told me changed the way I thought of the Old Testament. It wasn't so much a dogmatic charter for a religion as a founding collection of writings meant to hold together a racially diverse culture and community. Its urgency was political rather than spiritual. It wasn't a way of saying *This is what I believe as an individual.* Instead it was *This is who we are, as a people.* As such, I thought more about the questions this raised and how fluid and provisional it made the Bible seem. After all, the Bible was simply a collection of stories that somehow survived the selection process of countless people who had chosen and edited what would be included. I wanted to do something completely contrary to this new sense I had of the utility of the Old Testament. I wanted to do something peculiarly American, as Dan might have put it, to get to the heart of what mattered to *me*, as an individual, about the Bible.

---

This was all encouraging. This perspective on the partly random and heterogeneous way in which the Bible was assembled—meaning that the doctrines of various churches shared that same kind of contingency—helped ease my mind. It reassured me that what matters is faith and practice, not doctrine.

Yet, back here in Chautauqua, I want to make sure the selective way I've approached the Bible really does hold up to the scrutiny of someone who's made Christianity a mission. Being here in Chautauqua is the perfect place to be on a quest like this. Almost everyone is on some kind of like-minded quest, and people who have made this sort of preoccupation their life's work find a home here in the summers. I know I have the opportunity to sit down with someone I've known for many years, someone I consider the embodiment of the Christian way of life, and I intend to put my views to the test with him.

On a particularly sunny day this summer in Chautauqua I met with Albert Pennybacker, who has had a close relationship with

the Chautauqua community and has often served as a spokesman for contemporary Christianity. My first encounter with
Albert Pennybacker was in a wonderful French restaurant outside the Chautauqua gates for a dinner with Joan Brown Campbell, Karen Armstrong, Barbara, and Albert. I noticed early in
the conversation how Joan kept referring to him as "Penny."
Soon enough, he became Penny to me as well.

When I was in my twenties, I read *Diary of a Country Priest*,
by Georges Bernanos, the story of an unacknowledged saint who
serves his parish in the French countryside, quietly and without
recognition, following in the footsteps of Christ. When I got to
know Penny, I thought, *Here is the country priest!* When Joan
Brown Campbell changed her life and decided to become a minister, Penny stepped up and became her private tutor in the Bible.
He was essentially the person who enabled her to find her new
calling, her own one-man seminary. I knew nothing about him in
our early years at Chautauqua, but often when we would have
dinner with Joan, she would say, "Could Penny come along?
He's my trusted guy." I had no idea who he was and didn't ask
any questions, because our view was the more, the merrier. Yet,
at our meals, he rarely asserted himself and didn't interject his
views very much. Finally, Joan explained what a crucial role he'd
had in her life, and how he had devoted himself to his small
congregation for many years. He'd played a significant role with
the National Council of Churches and had been director of the
National Clergy and Laity Network. The more I got to know
him, the more I loved him and what he stood for. Like me, his
view of the Bible was that the essence of being a Christian is in
following the example of Jesus, not in subscribing to a certain
set of doctrines.

My faith had become quite simple: to be a Christian, I
needed to get to know Jesus and learn how to treat others with

love. And I didn't think this required an organization. I asked Penny what he thought of this.

"Let me tell you a joke," he says. "Jesus asks, 'Who do people say that I am?' He gets various responses. 'Some say you're Elijah.' 'Some say John the Baptist.' Peter says, 'You are the Christ, son of the living God, light of light . . .' and he goes on to quote the whole Nicene Creed. There's a moment of puzzled silence and Jesus says, 'Huh?'"

When I'm done laughing, I say, "So you're saying I'm not too far off target."

In our conversation, Penny essentially said he agreed with my entire approach.

"At the center of religious faith for a Christian is the figure of Jesus. He was a teacher, a leader. But it was really his character—the person—that is his gift to us. He's living out the character and the heart of God. Through Jesus, we know what God is like: kind, forgiving, loving. The questions are not whether he said this or that, but it's more about finding the deeper current flowing through his life. He was living out the love of God. That is the single focus. I love the Palm Sunday story. Here is the new Messiah, the new King of the Jews. But he's riding on a donkey, not a white horse. He was followed by fishermen and tax collectors, the worst of the lot in that age, and some who had collaborated with Rome, a really ragtag bunch. Wait a minute? This is the Messiah? He overturned expectations with a radical simplicity and humility. He was living out the love of God for all people."

"So his life, how he behaved, is as important as what he said?" I asked.

"Dogma is what kills Jesus. One of the repeated images in the New Testament was putting the needs of people ahead of the restrictions of the Sabbath. Religious perfection, according to the rules, is not the goal. It isn't about impressing God in order to get a reward. My job in life is to embody and act out the love of God as I understand it. Love your neighbor. Love your enemies. Love everybody. Pray for your enemies. We love our enemies because God loves our enemies."

"Here's a big question, Penny. This is going to get me in trouble. I don't see Christ as the only son of God. There were many profound messengers—Buddha, Muhammad, Moses, and many others. To me, Jesus was more than just one of the messengers. He was the supreme embodiment of God. Am I in hot water here?"

"Absolutely not. Yes, he says 'I am the Way and the Truth and the Life and no one comes to the Father except by me.' But there's a legalese way of interpreting this which is so far from the life of Jesus that I find it scurrilous."

"So I'm not a complete infidel here?" I say.

"Not at all, Peter. The key word in the Bible is the Hebrew word for love and loving kindness. Whoever is preaching this principle is essentially a Christian."

I'm still circling around my central concern: Am I really a Christian? I looked for more validation of my views, hoping for some reassurance. I first encountered Joseph C. Hough as a distinguished 10:45 a.m. Chautauqua lecture speaker—an unusual time for a religious figure to speak. But then Joe Hough is a remarkable individual: a Yale Divinity School graduate, former president of Union Theological Seminary, a dean at Vanderbilt University Divinity School, dean of the School of Theology at Claremont College, and most recently drafted as president of all the Claremont Colleges.

The amphitheater was packed but the reception was lukewarm. Joe was chiding his audience, drawing a line between how all of us live and how Jesus lived his life. Again and again, he was making the simple point that Christ's teachings and personal life story should be the focus of Christianity. He was challenging us to question ourselves and ask whether we, in our everyday lives, were following his path. It was one thing to piously attend Sunday morning services and something else to walk the walk. He kept asking, How many of us actually do that? This was not a welcome message. The long benches in the amphitheater began to feel harder and harder, but instead of writing him off, I found myself listening and taking his words to heart.

With no small degree of trepidation, I approached Joe, who listened to my views about how all religions lead to the same awakening, and he told me, "A lot of Christians are going to think you are off the reservation, Peter. Especially the people who think the purpose of religion is to purchase cosmic fire insurance and win a place in heaven." But *Joe* didn't think I was off the reservation. He told me he thought I was on the right path.

Not long after my conversations with Hough and Penny, I found myself one Sunday listening to Otis Moss III again, this time preaching to the Chautauquan congregation about "the problem we have with Jesus." He said, "We've put him into a cupboard and sanitized him. We don't want to preach what Jesus preached. We don't want someone who deals with the poor, the disadvantaged, the lepers, someone who has a different view of power. We see Jesus refusing to come down from the cross. We want him to stay up there and retain an extra-human power different from the power of love that he preached, which requires us to get into the act and do what he did: help the poor, the disenfranchised, the sick. He spent his time among lepers as an act of love; but to recognize this as the heart of his teaching requires us to do what he did, and we don't want to face that. Love was the point, not power."

God is love, not wrath. That's what I heard from all these

authorities on the Bible, and if you devote your life to love and making choices to treat others with care and compassion, then you are living a Christian life.

---

This past summer I ordered *The Third Jesus*. I finished it only a couple of days after it arrived. I was struck by how much Deepak Chopra's view of Jesus seemed to confirm the view I've developed over the years. The first Jesus, for him, is the historical figure, the man we know from the stories about his life. The second Jesus is the icon of the Christian religion, its founding God and the cornerstone of the vast theology of Christianity. The third Jesus represents a spiritual state: a "God consciousness" in which the individual can tap into a larger and deeper awareness.

Chopra's point isn't new; it's been around, in one guise or another, for centuries, and particularly in the work of some thinkers from the past two centuries. His central point is that Jesus was working to help induce in his listeners and followers a state of "God consciousness." It's a shift from a life motivated and governed by fear to one that arises out of love, compassion, and goodness. Reading Chopra was, for me, an "aha!" moment—as if he were putting into words exactly what Christ and God's other great messengers have meant to me, in the simplest possible formulation. His vision has a distinguished heritage, drawing not only from quotes of mystics in various religious traditions for thousands of years but also from the work of Western thinkers such as Richard Bucke, William James, Aldous Huxley, Jung, Joseph Campbell, and many others. The central thesis that aligns all these thinkers and psychologists was that "religious experience" is essentially a spiritual transformation, not simply the acquisition of theological understanding, or a life of obedience to an institution. This transformation, at least partially, can release an individual from bondage to his or her own ego, with all of its cravings, terrors, and dependencies.

Chopra sees Jesus fully merging his own individual selfhood into a God who also resides within each and every one of us, who is at the heart of our true identity as spiritual beings. The power of God emanates from deep in our soul and awareness. Chopra's contention is that "what made Jesus the son of God was the fact that he had achieved God consciousness." Jesus said as much over and over when he declared, "the Father and I are one." (However, traditional theologians have usually interpreted this to simply affirm part of the doctrine of the Trinity.) In Chopra's view, this enlightened capacity enabled Christ to show the world the power of the love of God in each of us. His words in the New Testament are intended as a road map to the ultimate potential of humankind as we progress from embracing goodness to a fully awakened and compassionate state.

As Deepak Chopra puts it in his book:

> Calling himself the Son of man was personal—it denoted humility and a fate in common with everyday people. But Jesus tells us much more about himself when he says, "I am the Light." Physically, light is what you see when you wake up to your soul. Light gives life, and it shows the way through darkness. Jesus had all those things in mind. More thrilling, however, is his intention to raise others up to the same status, as when he said to his followers, "You are the Light of the world." Making others enlightened was his purpose, but a huge gulf yawned between Jesus and other people—the gulf between darkness and light—so his whole life amounts to one long struggle to make people see that they were in darkness and had to wake up.

What I take from Chopra is still similar to the path illuminated for me by Penny and Joe Hough. Chopra also suggests the possibility that Christ lived at a spiritual level beyond what most of us can comprehend. Yet Chopra argues that everyone can aspire to this higher state of being, this "Christ consciousness," as he puts it. He urges people to develop this consciousness through practice, through meditation and right action. The early Christian mystics clearly were able to do that.

In my own humble exposure to the meditative experience of Silva, I too had a most modest glimpse of seeing beyond the normal boundaries of our three-dimensional view of the universe. Again, science and mathematics suggest unimaginable dimensions to the physical world, from dark matter to string theory. Perhaps all these people—the Romanian Gypsy fortune-teller who foresaw my dad's release from prison three years ahead of the event, or the Reverend Florence's knowledge of my deceased young brother, the Brazilian bouzio's sage advice, or America Martinez's impatience with me when she rightly said I already knew the answers to the questions I was asking—had reached an elevated state of being compared with most of us ordinary mortals. After all, in the New Testament, Christ promises that we too can do even greater deeds than He.

Yet, in the end, I have come to believe that the most useful path for me, and probably for many of us, is about choosing goodness and compassion. Life needs to be about the everyday mundane decision to reach for goodness in all we do. It's about the everyday choices to resist the evil tendencies inside us. Having the will and the courage to do that, with consistency, will move us and our children's children on that more enlightened path.

———————

So I had my new, evolving model. Jesus was no longer a super-hero who used his sword to separate the good from the bad. He was a loving and wise servant showing me the way. I had recon-firmed that the challenge is to activate the force of goodness in my life and serve it, to act as a surrogate of God's will, interven-ing in ways that would help me and others get closer to the ideal that the life of Jesus represented. This has been one of the central insights of my life: to realize that God is good and God is love, but only if we make this so through our actions. Every choice matters, some more than others, but the most wonderful thing is that the more often you make the right choices out of love rather than selfishness, the easier they become and the more they sim-ply become ingrained behavior.

From my conversations with people I consider wise and devoted to the truth, I feel a renewed confidence that I can hold on to the life of Jesus and ignore much of the often-confusing dogma built around it. It doesn't make me a heretic, but simply a believer trying hard to understand the essence of faith, without all the organizational trappings. The sad, tragic sagas of leading Christian institutions—from the Crusades to the Inquisition to the stories that appear now in the media with acts of hatred and bigotry against women, gays, and other minorities, as well as abuse of unsuspecting and defenseless children—are a chasten-ing lesson in what happens when spiritual teachings are warped by those who use the teachings to secure and enhance organiza-tional power. Beyond Christianity, in the Muslim world, dogma enforced by the powerful has split the religion into two warring tribes. Millions of faithful have died, as a result, and continue to die. Yet it must be acknowledged that religious institutions have also done an extraordinary amount of good, the world over. Dedicated men and women of faith are helping to make the world a better place.

My pervasive questioning and my life's experiences have returned me to a strong belief in a higher spiritual state. It is a different, adult belief, but just as powerful as my early childhood vision. The evidence for this force for good is overwhelming. While I may not be able to define the nature of this force, I have come to accept it. Doing so, for me, amounts to an act of faith. I am content in this faith and accept my current human limitation of not fully knowing. I have also come to peace with the idea that I can be a spiritual person without the need to embrace any single, complete religious dogma. That too has become a choice with which I find myself totally comfortable.

Over time I realized that the fundamental spiritual values, the ones that cross religions, become the foundation, the guiding hand for the good in human endeavor. Our world is awash in change. If we grasp the possibility that we have the power and responsibility to diminish the forces of evil within us, then we can free ourselves to more fully embrace spiritual values. If we develop the will and wisdom to do that, then the ultimate potential for us, the seven-plus billion souls on this planet, can be forever brighter. It has become increasingly clear to me that these fundamental spiritual values are the sources that inform and shape what we have come to call basic human values.

To me these basic human values—truth, honesty, compassion, responsibility, accountability—are at their essence spiritual values devoid of dogma. These are the values being taught and that exist around the world. When we follow them, good happens. They may not be recognized as spiritual or religious values, but to me that is exactly what they are. Rather than argue the point or try to prove the logic of the connection, I simply rejoice at their very existence. I have encountered countless women and men of principle who live exemplary lives and are guided by these common values. Some fill their lives with religious rituals, which help reinforce their values, and some merely adopt the best of these human values in their daily lives. These are remarkable people whose lives are filled with gifts they are able to bring to humanity. It's joyous and inspiring to observe them live their lives and carry out their wondrous deeds.

Ken Langone is one of the most successful businessmen of our generation and one of the kindest, most compassionate men I've ever met. His work on behalf of the good is truly legendary, an astonishing breadth of effort in helping the sick and underprivileged. He was a young man of modest means, very modest, who made it on his own. He fell in love and married his childhood sweetheart, and now they are still in love, still together, doing good in this world. He has achieved enormous wealth and success, and I know no one who is kinder and more generous. You'll find Ken at the 8:00 a.m. service every single day. No matter where he is, he will find a church and attend Mass. For Ken, the relationship with his God has opened doors and windows. It has given him enormous confidence and has enabled him to succeed through kindness. He's no wallflower, no fool; he's tough. But he's all heart.

Thinking about Ken Langone's faith raises an obvious question. Is there a relationship between his daily commitment to worship and what Ken does in his life? Pondering this question, I find myself thinking about how, twenty years ago, a younger senior executive at Y&R, Mitch Kurz (he was chief executive of our direct marketing company, Wunderman), introduced me to a tall, skinny, well-spoken, and passionate African American pal of his, Geoffrey Canada. Geoff had taken over an educational institution in Harlem, committed to bettering the lives of the poor and minorities. Mitch was insistent: We must help Geoffrey's cause. This is worth your effort. Already involved with an organization called A Better Chance, I found it an easy decision. So I chaired a fund-raising dinner for Geoff and his organization. But that was the end of my involvement, except for some occasional modest contributions over the years.

Yet, as I followed the organization's growth, the Geoffrey Canada and Harlem Children's Zone saga became a remarkable success story. It did not come easily. Through one experiment after another, it struggled to hit its stride. Many ideas worked, while others failed. Along the way the school discovered its motto: "Whatever it takes." It took a lot, in fact. But the kids did win. From covering a few blocks in Harlem's poorest neighborhoods, the Harlem Children's Zone now draws from almost a hundred square blocks, reaching out to some 11,000 children and more than 14,000 adults. True to their motto, the school gets involved in all aspects of the students' lives. Programs start in infancy. School hours and school days have been expanded. Parents, families, and supporters become engaged in helping their kids achieve measurable results. Passionate, committed teachers have signed up for the cause.

Arguably, the chief power behind Geoff Canada's extraordinary effort is none other than Ken Langone. Yes, some large sums of his hard-earned money are at work in funding many of the program's activities. But it's more than that; he puts many hours of his own time into making sure the program achieves its goals. When he gets involved in something like this, he's involved 24/7. I remember waiting half an hour in his car in Florida at 9:00 a.m. (past Mass) outside a café for breakfast. Ken was in full flight, discussing the most mundane issues affecting the lives of those lucky kids. I kept thinking we could easily have gotten out of the car, found a table, and ordered a glass of juice, at least, without losing the thread of his mono-logue. If he was hungry, he'd become oblivious to it. I watched his face contort in empathetic pain and then break into a smile. This extraordinarily successful entrepreneur was so totally involved, so totally consumed with the smallest details in a school's existence and the lives of the kids it helped, that he had lost all interest in ordering a meal. He was the embodiment of the school's mission: *Whatever it takes.*

And that isn't the only way in which Langone devotes himself to the welfare of others. In the spring of 2008, I remember reading my newspaper headlines, as is my custom, first thing in the morning. The New York University School of Medicine, which has a heritage going back to 1837 in New York City, proudly announced the largest philanthropic gift in the Medical Center's history—a $100 million donation from Elaine and Ken Langone.

Of course, these are but two of the countless contributions, in service to good, made by these two very special people. I will never know for sure what motivates Ken to walk the walk or whether his daily attendance at Mass leads directly to this sort of charity and compassion. The simple fact, though, is that doing good is what consumes most of his waking life now. It's hard to imagine what else he contemplates at Mass, if not an ongoing commitment to bettering a life less fortunate than his.

———

Two people in particular represent, for me, examples of how individuals can effectively serve God without actually having any formal faith in a deity or any formal association with orga-nized religion. One of these individuals I've known since I was a student at Princeton: Frank Wisner Jr., my classmate at Princeton in the late 1950s. His father worked with my father in the

OSS and helped found the CIA, the same Frank Wisner Sr. who befriended my mom and dad when they landed in the United States back in 1947. This was the same man who, as one of the founders and leaders of the CIA, cooperated with Frances Bolton and President Eisenhower to obtain our freedom from the Communist regime.

My admiration for the younger Frank grew immensely when, as a brilliant graduate, with a world of opportunity ahead of him, he chose to join the State Department and devoted the next three decades-plus of his life to the service of our country. Frank was not an occasional activist. He did more than spend weekends and evenings supporting good causes. He spent the first thirty-five years of his adult life in the cause of the good for our country, 24/7. As expected, Frank's accomplishments as one of our most senior career ambassadors and diplomats became legendary. His tours of duty as undersecretary of state and defense were equally impressive. Yet in many ways, it was a life of sacrifice.

While Barbara and I were visiting Frank in Cairo, where he spent more than six years as U.S. ambassador to Egypt, he pointed out that his wife had purchased the fabric for his office's curtains herself because the government budget would be inadequate to cover even such basic necessities. Whereas I, and most of my classmates, went on to successful business careers and were amply rewarded for our efforts, Frank labored in faraway countries, earning a subsistence income and having his life threatened with regularity. In his sixties Frank retired from the State Department and joined the business world to earn a retirement nest egg. I find it unacceptable that we pay our brilliant civil servants so pathetically. Our embassies (with the few exceptions of those in major capitals) are underfinanced and in disrepair. Our nation's budget for the foreign service is only some two percent of what we spend on defense: a lamentable ratio of soft power to share. But such was the path Frank chose. He wanted to make a difference. As another friend has put it, "There are more people employed in our military bands than in our foreign service." Frank lived a life of service to our nation with dignity, integrity, and remarkable skill, and without complaint. He was a friend and an amazing inspiration.

I consider Mark Schwartz to be another example of selflessness, a man who embraces and serves goodness, without the structure of any religious rigor and dogma. Since I've retired, I've devoted probably half of my time to nonprofit organizations, putting the business and managerial skills I learned in my years at Y&R to use in helping others. In these surroundings I have met many who have astounded me with the level of their selfless discipline and devotion. Mark Schwartz is one of the people who exemplifies our human evolutionary potential. He has had a distinguished career, with stints at MasterCard and Goldman Sachs, as CEO of Soros Fund Management, and now with Mission-Point Capital Partners. He's a self-made man, raised by a middle-class couple; his father is a dentist and his mother a teacher, in Poughkeepsie, New York. No one handed Mark his success. He achieved these remarkable things through hard work and good choices. Yet in his forties, he made a choice that changed his life. Unlike so many wealthy, successful individuals, he decided to spend his money and time helping others in a very specific way. He saw an opportunity to make a major difference and he went for it—with money, wisdom, time, energy, and passion.

I met Mark at New York Presbyterian Hospital. He doesn't simply attend the board meetings. He uses all his skills and resources to make a difference. Yet what he does here in my backyard of Manhattan is only a tiny part of his willingness to work for others. Seven years ago, he was attending a Soros

Fund meeting when six medical scientists requested a donation to develop and deploy a new device for quickly diagnosing AIDS for patients in Africa. Soros dismissed the team, saying the fund had already given generously to African projects.

During the presentation, Mark heard the scientists predict that as many as 100 million people could die of AIDS before research developed a cure, and that, in the interim, better methods of diagnosis could save many of those lives. So, after the meeting, he approached one of the scientists, Bruce Walker, who happens to be one of the most distinguished AIDS doctors in the world. Mark asked what he could do to help.

"I'm flying to Africa in a couple of weeks. You want to join me?" Walker asked.

His resulting nineteen-hour flight to Africa was the start of a journey Mark has been on ever since. He currently visits Africa for weeks at a time, working in hospitals, four times every year. After that first visit to the continent, he wrote out the first of many checks to Walker and he has since become one of the mission's angel donors. Partly through Mark's support, the group has developed a handheld flow cytometer that reduces the time for determining an AIDS diagnosis from months to hours. The fight against AIDS, which this group has centralized in South Africa's largest and most infected province—KwaZulu-Natal—has met with enormous obstacles. Indigenous healers first told the population to ignore any Western attempts to apply medicine to the problem. Victims shunned treatment because of the stigma associated with the disease. Patients were resistant to learning how to take pills, something they've never done before, on a daily basis. Yet the team members have overcome all these obstacles and are now saving countless lives through education and medical intervention.

What fascinates me is the moment in that meeting with

George Soros when Mark, as he has told me, thought to himself, "I don't want to look back on all this after twenty years and realize I did nothing to help halt this disease." The mystery of how that impulse arose in him is at the heart of this book's message. When I got to know Mark better, I realized maybe it wasn't such a mystery after all, but rather the outcome of decades of good choices. It was, quite simply, the fruit of practice, practice, practice—years if not generations of disciplined devotion. In a way, Mark's life may be an illustration of the power of epigenetics. He told me he was raised in a moderately Jewish household—his parents were conservative Jews, not orthodox and not reform—observing holidays, keeping a kosher home, and going to synagogue. Though Mark has left behind the ritualistic practice of Judaism, he has assimilated the heart of his religious heritage and incorporated it directly into his behavior. Having good parents, and being raised to see the value of compassion and wisdom, he has now, in middle age, put the rewards of his success into action, helping to make the world better.

Not surprisingly, Mark looks upon his exemplary life as simply a selfish pursuit: It makes him happy to toil in Africa. "I feel I've always been philanthropic. I know that sounds like BS, but it's always the way I've felt. Each of us is the product of our ancestors who have gotten values and passed them along. I think some people are wired to make a contribution. Other people who have resources are wired to want to buy airplanes and have four homes. That to me is a mystery of life. I've thought about it often. People who want to buy airplanes and boats and helicopters are good people, but they just aren't wired to want to change the world. It's just the way I am. I view all my efforts as very selfish. Philanthropy can be a very selfish activity. It's an enriching experience."

In my view, he's wired not only to devote himself to Africa

but also to see himself in this self-effacing way, because his DNA, and his parents' DNA, which he inherited from them, has been shaped by decades of persistent, habitual good choices. And a key part of Mark's character was the spirituality of his household, even though he doesn't see his own life in those religious terms. Formal religious dogma plays no role in his devotion to doing good.

"I've tried to live a moral life not so much because of my Jewish heritage but because of my family heritage."

God was and is a central part of that family tradition, with or without the religious trappings. And Mark's life is testimony to the power of that faith and the way it shaped the behavior of his entire family—and lives are being saved because of it. His life also demonstrates that formal religious belief can be completely absent in a person's life and yet that life can be, in essence, a life that demonstrates how God works through the choices of ordinary people every day.

Joan Brown Campbell, the close Chautauquan friend I have mentioned, is the director of religion at Chautauqua, and as a minister, she's perfectly suited for her job in this community. She radiates affability as well as a quiet attentiveness that can make you feel cheerful for the rest of the day. She listens as well as anyone I've ever met. She really sees you and hears you. She understands when you talk to her about almost any subject.

When she speaks, you hear kindness and Midwestern candor, those traces of her Cleveland childhood still there, and a hint of Julie Kavner's raspy timbre. It's a benevolent voice, full of life—regardless of what she's saying.

"You had a relationship with God long before you felt you

understood evil. The doubt you had was resolved through intellectual investigation," she says.

"It wasn't just a spiritual thing. I had to give it an intellectual dimension."

"The thing is, Peter, in all of this you never said '*There is no God.*' Even in a time of doubt there was something in you that believed . . ."

"Absolutely. Yes."

"You didn't take the baby and throw it out with the bathwater. I think you've heard my stories about Carl Sagan. Sometimes I think the noisiest nonbelievers are, at heart, believers. Otherwise, why do they care? I used to say that to Carl. Whenever I saw him, he had to keep proving to me that he didn't believe."

"The dogma is what gets in the way. The dogma is one of the biggest barriers, the orthodox dogma. People need to find their own way and quit denying God because of the dogma," I tell her.

"I found it interesting that Karen Armstrong said she just got so tired of riding on the subway and seeing posters about not believing in God that she, who isn't a believer in any traditional sense, decided to write *A Case for God.*"

"She didn't find God in a simple way in her heart. I did. She has problems with the historic God, the one we've created. But she isn't an atheist."

Joan mentions that when Karen's book was published, the author sent a copy to Joan with a note, but it sat on her desk for weeks. When she finally opened it, she was astonished to see the book's dedication page: *For Joan Brown Campbell.* Those were the only words on the page.

It's no surprise. Joan's history is quite remarkable. She couldn't find her deepest faith in God until she met Martin Luther King Jr. in the 1960s and saw how faith could be married to social activism so intimately that the two were impossible to separate.

Faith and love became equated in her life with great risks and great courage. She joined his team, working with him for civil rights, watching this messenger of God, someone who became a good friend, give his life as a result of his faith. It inspired her to work around the world for justice and peace.

As a young and well-to-do woman, living in Cleveland's exclusive Shaker Heights neighborhood, married to a successful attorney, she chose to do something that changed her life: she invited Martin Luther King Jr. to come to her church and speak. In those times when the struggle for civil rights had become a bloody and threatening movement for many who still believed in some form of segregation, the personal repercussions in Joan's life were dramatic. Partners in her husband's firm disapproved of her actions and ostracized her. Her husband resented what she had done and grew distant. She became an outcast within her circle and began more and more to identify with the black struggle—the struggle of the outsider to be recognized by the privileged and powerful, those who've been insiders all their lives.

As a mother and housewife, she had been working as a volunteer in Operation Head Start, which worked with preschool children in Clevland's inner city. She became so accepted by those she served that even during the race riots, when military tanks were assembled on the streets to keep order, she didn't hesitate to drive directly into the fray in order to show up for work. Meanwhile she began to help register voters to elect Cleveland's first black mayor, Carl Stokes. King took note, which is how she met him, and then she met Jesse Jackson. Once she had the notion of inviting King to speak at her church, she knew she couldn't shirk it, regardless of the repercussions. It was the first hint of her true calling, the first decision of her life in which her service to something higher than herself began to emerge in a way that threatened the secure world she had built around her. Eventually, it led to her divorce and ultimately to her vocation as a pastor. She became very close to King himself and remembers many episodes in the civil rights struggle when she was directly at his side.

After becoming a minister, she took a role with the Greater Cleveland Council of Churches, and then left Ohio for New York City when she became general secretary of the National Council of Churches of Christ. Six years later, she was executive director of the U.S. Office of the World Council of Churches. Soon she was swept into similar struggles around the world. Ultimately, her roles on the national level enabled her to participate on the international scene, working with such world leaders as Shimon Peres, Desmond Tutu, Nelson Mandela, and Fidel Castro. She even represented Elian Gonzalez—the Cuban child stranded in Florida years ago—against those who wanted to keep him in the United States and apart from his father. And all of this was set in motion by her choice, as a housewife and mother, to invite that heroic troublemaker into her church to speak a few words of truth to power.

It's no surprise then that she suggests I look at Martin Luther King's sermons.

"Peter, you could do no better than to read King's sermons. They're not even in print anymore. His sermon on the courage to love is all about forgiveness, and it really is, of all the writings, much more profound than Desmond Tutu's. Not that Desmond's is bad, but it's definitely not as rich. King's whole point is that it takes courage to love and believe. People would say, 'Martin, you have to start using force.' He would say, 'No, we will love these people until there's nothing they can do but love us back.' It's a huge, powerful force. Mandela says so as well. At Morehouse College in Atlanta they have the original papers, with the notes. Some sermons he has given more than once, with notes to himself in the margins. It's all in his own handwriting."

"They must have photocopies."

When lunch is over, her words about courage stay with me, as well as her suggestion that love might be more powerful ultimately than our urge toward evil and violence.

---

I'm much more comfortable now in believing there's a unity of faith, a common root, at the basis of all the world's different spiritual traditions. I'm most comfortable thinking of it as a behavioral admonition, the Golden Rule, the translation of compassion into daily behavior. This is the fundamental lesson from all the great messengers: Moses, Jesus, Muhammad, Buddha, Gandhi, Krishna, Mandela, King, and all the others. It's about action. They weren't simply philosophers. Their lives were about action, often immensely self-sacrificing behavior. For me, this is how spirituality engages with the world, not just in retreats and contemplation. Faith is tempered and proven through behavior. Action matters.

When Barbara and I landed in South Africa in 1982, Nelson Mandela was still in prison. Decades later, with our granddaughters, we visited Robben Island, where he had been imprisoned. It was one of the most moving experiences of our lives. The guided tour is given by former inmates, all once political prisoners. We saw Mandela's cell and the cot on which he slept for *twentysix years*. We saw the lime and salt rock that he and his colleagues broke up with picks during the day under the punishing sun, which blinded so many of his fellow inmates. Seeing all of this, I wonder how Nelson Mandela hasn't been designated as a saint or bodhisattva. He performed one of the greatest miracles in history when he insisted on reconciliation, not bloodshed, as a way forward from colonial oppression in South Africa, saving millions of lives from a certain civil war. It was an act of heroism, the perfect expression of the imitation of Christ. It was as great a miracle as walking on water and far more beneficent. It was the ultimate demonstration of compassion and the Golden Rule.

So when I woke up this Sunday morning, for some reason I didn't feel up to either a jog or even a short trek down to the amphitheatre for the weekly sermon. After Barbara departed, I decided, maybe a bit out of guilt, to turn to an out-of-print volume of Martin Luther King's sermons to read. I ended up reading almost all of *Strength to Love*. Even after Barbara returned, I couldn't put it down. This particular copy began its life as a hardbound, but it's so old, it's virtually a paperback now. It's a small, beguiling book that works almost as autobiography; while he tells you about his vision of God, he's really telling you just as much about his own remarkable destiny.

What's astonishing is that these erudite essays were delivered as sermons. They don't sound like sermons. They're closer to scholarly lectures. There's no heightened rhetoric, none of the poetry of his speeches. These talks are quieter, reflective and intricate in their many lines of reasoning. They would have worked perfectly here in Chautauqua on the 10:45 platform. His doctorate in philosophy gives a pedagogical edge to his thoughts about the role Christian love might have in contemporary history. In their subtle grasp of the Western intellectual tradition, and in their personal tone, his sermons owe more to Albert Camus and Michel de Montaigne than they do to the exhortations of, say, Billy Graham. Listening to him, members of a congregation would have found themselves called to reconsider their faith in the shadow of writers from the past, both religious and secular: Rousseau, Condorcet, Hegel, Darwin, Tolstoy, Freud,

Kierkegaard, Nietzsche, Jaspers, Heidegger, Sartre, Marcel, Car-
lyle, Tillich, Niebuhr, and most significantly, Gandhi. And this is
only a partial roll call of the people who shaped King's life and
faith.

These sermons show that as the 1960s progressed, King
became more and more aware of his impending peril. It's clear
that he knew the threats on his life were genuine, and yet he
never retreated from the pulpit. His pulpit became anywhere
he stood. He used his growing authority to spark a transformation in our social order that brought equal rights for American minorities and ultimately resulted, only four decades later,
in something unthinkable in his own time: the election of an
African American president. His historical importance to race
relations in America is second only to Abraham Lincoln's. You
can hear in these sermons that he might have once dreamed of
becoming an academic, an influential religious philosopher. Yet
he recognized his calling as a man of action. Staying true to this
difficult path had to be a constant choice for him, because—
as he could see more and more clearly—it led him toward the
equivalent of martyrdom.

He never once lamented the injustice and evil of the hatred
directed at him. He never hid from the danger. The menace
arrayed against his movement had been showing its face for
more than ten years. His enemies burned down his house. They
tossed bricks at his head. They mailed death threats. Yet he never
flinched and never complained about how he deserved none of
it. When urged to encourage violence against oppressors, he
declined. He continued to speak the truth and to rally hundreds
of thousands into action through principle. By studying Gandhi
and by visiting India himself, he learned *satyagraha*, which has
come to be understood, politically, as nonviolent resistance. This
is a narrow definition that reflects the two people who made the

term famous in the West: Gandhi and King. Yet it's much more
fundamental than that. It can be translated clumsily into English
as *love force* or *truth force*. More literally, it means *the power
of following the path to the ultimate Truth*. In the Hindu tradition, wisdom and compassion are how the ultimate truth, God,
shapes a human life. King's method was to unleash the power of
wisdom and compassion, in order to lead people toward God.
The path *is* the destination.

As I read about him here, in the comfort of Chautauqua's
civilized and peaceful community, I realize that *satyagraha* is a
term that comes close to describing how I now believe in God: as
the presence of goodness in human life, manifested most directly
through compassion and wisdom and in action, through choosing good. My American journey, for more than half a century,
has been partly to rediscover a new way to believe in God. I've
been searching for a way to name this goodness, which saved me
from my captivity in Romania and guarded me from then on,
guiding my steps and moving the hearts of all the people who
gave me a hand, often when I had no other way to advance.

In the book's final sermon, "Pilgrimage to Nonviolence,"
King's profession of faith in a personal God, a God with feelings
and awareness, a God who listens to his prayers and sometimes
answers them, doesn't bother me. After all my wrestling with
this issue of an anthropomorphic God, the fact that others carry
on intimate conversations with their God, who for them has a
human incarnation, doesn't strike me as foolish anymore. My
sense of comfort in my own, more abstract idea of God, more
like the Tao or Brahman or the Godhead of the mystics, has
enabled me to be quite open to the personal God who dwells in
the lives of so many other people. When King testifies that he
could see and feel this personal God at his side through his final,
passionate crusade for civil rights, it's entirely convincing. It's

almost enough for me to wonder if a personal God really does reveal himself to people as worthy as King. His relationship, his conversations, if you will, with God enabled him to say, toward the end of his life, "Unearned suffering is redemptive." He had come to terms with evil. King's trust in satyagraha represents exactly how I see God now. For me, God is both a noun and a verb. The good, as well, feels like a verb, not just an adjective. We become who we are through action and choice. With satyagraha as the animating principle behind all of his choices, King was able to see a meaning in his own suffering and accept the assassination he was certain would be his fate. Along with Nelson Mandela, Martin Luther King Jr. has always struck me as one person of the twentieth century who most perfectly embodied the teachings of Jesus. He imitated the life of Jesus, right up to the moment of his death.

----

One close friend stands out, for me, in his religious practice: Keith Reinhard. We still have our differences. He goes to church and I don't, he thinks it's important to believe in the Trinity and I don't, and he has a more traditional view of sin than I. Unlike me, he's a die-hard traditionalist, although he belongs to a congregation where dogma takes a backseat to nearly every other pillar of the organization's ritual. Contrast this with his knowledge that I probably would have been burned at the stake for many of my views five centuries ago. What he didn't realize, when I first suggested we meet for breakfast, was that I wanted to give him a chance to tell me, in all fairness, how valuable it can be to believe in God the Father, God the Son, and God the Holy Ghost and go to church every Sunday. It works in a profound way for Keith, and I wanted to hear about it.

For years, he was chairman of the board of Union Theological Seminary in New York City, exposed to people from all different faiths: Roman Catholic, Buddhist, Jewish, Protestant. "This meant I got to bounce around to a lot of different churches, so when visitors came to town, I'd pick a church I thought would appeal to them," he told me. "I actually discovered the Episcopal Church by accident. As a kid, I grew up a Mennonite in the small town of Berne, Indiana. I left home after high school and found myself in Chicago, checking into the YMCA hotel with no money. I asked the hotel manager if he had any jobs that needed doing for pay and he said yes, they needed someone to clean up the photo darkroom every night. I knew how to do that because I had spent some time in high school working with the local photographer. Then he said, 'We also need an associate religious commissioner.' He explained, 'Every Thursday night you have to conduct Vesper services and you also have to head a committee that, every Sunday morning, takes visiting guests to the church of their choice.' There were no transients who wanted to go to a Mennonite church and, at the same time, there was no Episcopalian on the committee. So I ended up taking Episcopalian visitors to their church, which I found to be a good fit for me. I'm now a member of St. Bartholomew's Episcopal Church in New York, where we take pride in what we call a *radical welcome.*"

"How does that work?"

"Whoever you are, you are radically welcomed. It's not uncommon to be at the communion rail next to a transgendered member of the congregation. Our clergy has included gays and a rabbi. Not all Episcopal parishes are this progressive, but in St. Bart's, I've found a home. St. Bart's and the liturgy of the Episcopal Church provide a framework for me in which to contemplate, reflect, receive guidance, and find respite from the distractions of the week and the day. It's really valuable to me, and I would miss it if I skipped a couple of Sundays. A lot of same-sex couples are joining us now from the Roman Catholic church because, while our liturgy is similar to that of the Catholics, we go beyond tolerance. We affirm and celebrate differences and learn from how others live and believe. It's a very important part of my life."

"I have a question about tradition. Let's say churches like St. Peter's, or St. John the Divine, weren't there already. Would you build them today?"

"I was once asked if I could define Christianity in a tweet—140 characters. My definition takes fewer characters: *Following Christ and trying to be like Him.*"

"We're on the same page there, Keith. I have another question," I said. I wanted to see if he could elaborate on the anthropomorphic God, the deity of my early childhood model. "When you pray, is your sense of deity anthropomorphic or is it undefined?"

"I believe in God the Father. What does He look like? I have no idea what God the Father looks like or is, but that doesn't matter to me. When I pray, I'm not sure who or what hears and answers those prayers. What I do know is that prayer has value. It's corny what I do. I have my own rosary that I use in saying prayers. I use the ten fingers on my hand. I clasp this thumb to pray for my wife and think about her and then my oldest son and my second son and all the way back to me, with this finger. Whether or not anyone hears that, I cannot say, but it changes me. I've asked myself to think of each one of those people."

He told a story from his childhood. "In Berne, Indiana, we had a company called Dunbar Furniture. They made high-end furniture, the best in the country. Their products furnished luxury liners and Hollywood homes. There was this old gentleman, Willy Wulliman, who left his job at Dunbar because he felt their standards of craftsmanship were not high enough. And so he started his own woodworking shop across the alley from where we lived. He didn't allow many visitors, but he would frequently let my brother and me watch him work a lathe or carve a finial. And as we left his shop, after every visit, he would say to us in his heavily Swiss-German accented English, 'Boys, be always good.' That advice stayed with me. It meant be good in what you do, be good to those around you, be good in the sight of God."

That phrase Keith Reinhard remembers from his childhood, *Be always good*, is nearly my own mantra: *Choose always good*. I'm now back to the height of what I was able to do when I was meditating an hour or more per day. The more I focus on this sense of purpose, the more I'm open to hearing and understanding what is said to me, even if I don't immediately agree. Often, I can hear in what's said a cry for help or the cry of hope, which is never expressed in so many words, but it's clearly there. Hitherto I would not have heard it or have wanted to hear it. I have a greater disengagement from the base instincts or knee-jerk reactions that have enabled the race to survive, making us self-centered. Sometimes when I don't hear from someone, I now increasingly stop thinking about the impact of that lack of communication on me and begin to worry about the other person: what, of consequence, might be happening to that other person? I find myself genuinely worried about them, rather than what their behavior means to me. It's not nearly as much about me anymore. It stopped being about what I need from this person. It's more about that person's health and well-being.

When I walk around I see other people and realize now that they have an infinite inner world as powerful and significant as mine. Its details may be different, but in the structure and principles—fear, anxiety, joy, hunger—it's identical. It's as unique and fascinating as any other life, and what makes it different is also what makes it interesting, and yet it's identical to mine in the depth of its emotion and imagination and feeling.

I've always had the knack of turning a conversation toward the other person. Throughout my life, I've done it on purpose because I knew people want to talk about themselves, but lately I do it because I'm really interested. It's no longer a social trick. It's genuine interest and caring.

After we'd said our goodbyes and Keith had left, I headed north to my next meeting, which also went well, but for the rest of the day those words linger in my mind. Keith's words could be the tagline for my entire worldview now: *Be always good.* Make the constant choice.

# CONCLUSION

FROM MY MODEST SEAT ON THIS FRONT PORCH IN Chautauqua, all decked out with the colors of Old Glory, my view on the twenty-first century is that the consequences of making the right choices are becoming increasingly crucial. The instinct of self-centeredness, which morphs into tribalism, can paralyze us. I've just come back from hearing a sermon at the Chautauqua amphitheater by the Rev. Alan W. Jones, dean emeritus of San Francisco's Grace Cathedral, and his words, like the hook from a popular song, won't let me go:

> In Greek and Latin, *idiot* means "a private person": that is, someone caught up in a private world of self-preservation and safety with no regard for the common good or obligations of citizenship. The word "idiot" was used derisively in ancient Athens to refer to one who declined to take part in public life. In our own days, we confuse this "idiocy"—the lack of

commitment to a community outside oneself—with freedom.
It's a scandal. It's one form of nihilism.

We need to get outside ourselves, outside our own individual preoccupations. A common good based on common sense matters more and more. A spiritual awareness of the nobler side of our natures matters more and more. We, each one of us, are capable of raising our game toward becoming better people as individuals, as communities or nations, as humankind.

Alas, I have to take stock of our cold reality in the public square. I have to remember our collective shortcomings that drove me to write this book. I watch the sad spectacle that now comes every two years for either congressional or presidential elections. The horrific display of evil deeds, lies, and half-truths and our willingness to demonize one another are a frightening mirror of who we are, who we might become, without a higher purpose, without a concern for the common good, devoid of common sense. The television talking heads keep telling us that negative advertising works. Never mind the lies, innuendoes, and demonizing tone. It puts the art and science of communication to the most dehumanizing use. It works. The big lie works. It makes us feel better to believe lies about other people because it makes us feel superior to them, doubly so when we get to apply that selfish trick to leaders. After all, they're not so special anyway. We seem to feel satisfaction when those whose views differ from ours get crucified by partisan press or by ugly, deceitful advertising. It's back to "our tribe versus the rest of them." We have the right and the truth and they don't. And then there are the well-dressed thieves who in their selfish behavior will use any devious means to enrich themselves and their inflated greed and egos. Don't worry that people get harmed, that financial crises can affect millions around the world. The "idiots" seem to be having a field day.

Still, the potential for humankind to evolve toward the good appears to be both extraordinary and also within our grasp. The messengers have been pointing the way for us for millennia. Here's one more shout-out of these figures who have meant so much to me: Christ, Buddha, Confucius, Moses, Muhammad, Krishna, Gandhi, King, Mandela, and all the others. They have shone a light on the path toward goodness. They have made sacrifices on my behalf. Christ died for me. Martin Luther King Jr. died for me. As I witnessed the only-too-recent evidence of the victims of Auschwitz and Cambodia, Darfur, and countless other places and times, in their deaths they showed all of us the urgency of making a constant choice in favor of the good. I believe they died because of the evolutionary imprint on our nature, which predisposes us to tribalism, violence, deceit, self-ishness, and cruelty. It's up to me, now that I know better, to accept the teachings and the evidence of what happens when compassion and goodness aren't followed. I must recognize the opportunity to do my own modest part. The possibility is there to become a better person, not just in my behavior, but maybe in my genetic code as well. I know I can become better than who I am now. And that's the mission that matters most.

What about you? Are you willing to examine your life and answer the sort of questions I've been asking of myself? If you have, are you willing to join in? Are you willing to come off your comfortable perch—or porch, in my case—and get your hands dirty? Are you willing to become involved, to speak truth to power, to try to live the best life you are capable of living for yourself and for your children—for all our children? Can you look at your own worldview and think, *Maybe in one way or another I am fallible and possibly mistaken*? Can you keep that element of doubt about your own views always in sight so that you're able to listen open-mindedly to someone who opposes you? William Blake said, "Opposition is true friendship." Where do we see that kind of intelligence in our political debates now? Can you be one of my role models? We can make a difference, together. We really can. It's possible.

---

Nearing the end of my season in Chautauqua, I've had four luncheons in a row with good friends whom I respect. They were all successful business people and deeply concerned about the future of America. In each case, over salmon or sandwiches or farfalle pasta, we talked about the enormous crisis this nation faces, on so many fronts. They were as worried as I am about our future and our ability to make the right choices now so that our grandchildren will have the future they deserve. Although difficult, none of these challenges is insurmountable. We can develop alternatives for fossil fuels, improve health care while cutting its cost, improve our educational systems, care for our planet, and solve immigration issues, all of them, with fairness and compassion.

A wise man told me that we all believe in justice, but we are seldom willing to marry justice with love. Justice without love is brutality, and love without justice is sappy. At our stage of development as humans, we must have both. What troubled and saddened me was the feeling that we don't have the will, the courage, the willingness to sacrifice, which is needed to confront and surmount the crises we face. My concern wasn't about the issues or solutions to those challenges. It was about contemporary America's lack of a unified resolve to master them.

For me, the most urgent question is whether, as individuals, we can make choices that are good for everyone—whether we can become the United People of America. The atavistic side of our nature, the survival impulses that have become destructive in the context of all our complex interdependencies as a culture, continue to insinuate themselves into our deliberations. These impulses are like an uninvited dinner guest that no one spotted as he slipped through the door, and yet somehow, before you know it, he's the one giving the toast. The ugly and self-centered selfish motives, the narcissism, the strongholds of tribalism keep governing our choices and framing the narrative of our inner-most thoughts with too much hatred, too much fear, too little love and compassion and faith, and too little drive for the good.

The perfect counterweight to these troubling meditations arrives in the form of a Chautauqua lecture from Karen Armstrong. By the time she's done, I feel reassured that maybe I'm on the right path. In 2008, Armstrong received a prize from Technology Entertainment Design (TED), an organization that arranges colloquiums every year, hosting the most creative minds from all fields to engage in conversations about the critical issues of our time, so very much like Chautauqua. It's a nonprofit try-ing to nurture new ideas for solving big problems. TED granted Armstrong $100,000 to create and disseminate her idea of a Charter for Compassion. Since it began on September 12, 2009, the Charter has been translated into more than thirty languages. Religious leaders, businessmen, and politicians are embracing her compassionate Charter. Encouragingly, leaders in the Middle East were among the first and most enthusiastic to adopt and promote the Charter.

Compassion, for Armstrong, is not a feeling but a transfor-mative power that alters a person's entire orientation toward the world and the other people in one's life. It is an existential, lifelong pledge of fidelity to putting other people's needs above one's own desires. You can't stand on the sidelines and under-stand compassion, for her. You have to practice it in order to gain even a glimpse of what the word means.

Every major religion puts compassion at the heart of its moral and ethical life. That is not to say that religions are all the same. They are not. They have wonderful differences. But they are in agreement that if your religious and spiritual life does not lead you somehow to a respect for others, a feeling of empathy with the pain of other people, it is somehow disengaged from goodness. Confucius was the first to teach the Golden Rule. Five hundred years later, Jesus also taught the Golden Rule. Muhammad said not one of you can be a believer unless he desires for his neighbor what he desires for himself. Jewish theologians said the same.

Listening to her words, I feel a warm sense of confirmation. This is exactly what I have discovered in my own life. Then she starts talking about the old brain and the new brain. My mind goes back to Paul Ehrlich and our inheritance of evil over millions of years that enabled us to survive in the wilds as we evolved into human beings walking on two legs.

Compassion is hard, Karen explains. Neuroscientists tell us that at the root of our brain we have what they call the old brain, she says. It's a very primitive brain and very, very strong. It's activated by aggression, fear, eating, and sex. These drives are powerful because they all deal with survival of the individual and are, in a sense, automatic. But we also have a new brain to rein in the old brain. We have a responsibility to take control of our minds and to push them into a more compassionate, more respectful, and quiet mode of existence. It requires sacrifice. The ego, that Me First brain, is the problem. Her talk offers strong echoes of Paul Ehrlich's work, I think.

Karen's lecture reaches a crescendo. Our mission, our duty, is to reject the old brain and choose the path to the good. Then she caps it off by saying that she is going to publish a new book, a handbook for those who want to subdue their old brain and strengthen their new one. It's titled *Twelve Steps to a Compassionate Life*. It's intended to echo the 12-step creed of Alcoholics Anonymous. It's not just a question of zipping through these steps. You must take it slowly, day by day. You work on all of them all the time because we are addicted to our pet hates and cravings. Compassion is not just a nice choice. You have to step up; it means hard work and commitment day in and day out.

This brings my thinking back to the subject I introduced at the beginning of this book: epigenetics. Karen's call to action resounds within me and within many others assembled here. I find it even more inspiring because I know that science is confirming exactly what she says. We *can* shape who we are as a species. We are not governed entirely by our past behavior. With every passing year, science itself demonstrates how much power we have, and will have, over our human nature itself—how we fight off disease, how we age more slowly, how we strengthen our bodies long past what used to be their prime, and how we can genetically alter the basic quality of various life-forms. We have powers never before known in human history, with grave responsibilities to make wise choices in how we exercise those powers. Yet science has also shown that every human being has the power to shape his or her own genetic code: Through consistent, habitual choices, each of us can pass down through later generations a propensity to make better choices, because our behavior is recorded in our own genetic structure.

Epigenetics, for me, represents the scientific confirmation of what I've spent all these years attempting to piece together from my own experience and my study: that each choice we make counts, and every time we choose good we're doing it not only for ourselves but also for our species. As we keep making the constant choices that shape us, the human condition moves steadily and quickly toward a more and more improved state of being. Slowly and steadily, we can become more like the leading spiritual figures who have inspired us by their example, and who have shown us the sort of creature we can all become, if we choose wisely.

I'm exhilarated by her talk. Back at our home, sitting in a wicker chair on the front porch, mulling over everything I've heard, I get restless. I want to get out and do something to change the world. Instead, I decide to keep working on changing myself. My old brain says, Keep sitting; don't do a thing. *You feel good. Relax and enjoy yourself.* My new brain tells me to keep moving. There's so much left to do in my life, and I won't be able to do it if I'm not in shape. So I go in, change into some shorts, and head out the door for a looping run around the village on this Friday morning. It's late in the season, only a couple of weeks before we return to make New York our home base again.

I reflect, as I often do, how lucky I am to be in the splendid surroundings that gradually recede behind me as I make another turn around the lake's contours. I think back over all my reflections this summer—from my harrowing childhood in Romania to my quest for a sense of meaning throughout my adulthood—and it all recedes. Slowly these ebbing thoughts leave room, as I run, for my sense of deity, my faith, and my reliance on goodness, on love and compassion. As I put one foot in front of the other, a sense of these last things, their presence in my life, simply grows stronger. As I approach the big hill around the tennis courts, I feel as if I'm hitting my stride, but this hill is always a challenge. I try hard to lift my knees high with every stride, but let's put it this way, I would be clocked at only slightly faster than a power walk. At this point in my loop, each step is a choice not to stop. And trust me, it's a constant choice to press on.

Yet my thoughts and emotions have settled down the way they do in a run, and so my sense of optimism prevails, and the bright sunny day, the crisp cool touch of air on my cheeks and arms, the sense that my strength is returning—it all gives me a hunch that I'm moving ahead, somehow, making progress, getting somewhere. I'm running in quite a large circle; so large, in fact, that you hardly notice it's simply leading me back to where I began. This path of mine around Chautauqua reminds me of the line from T. S. Eliot's *Four Quartets*: "In my beginning is my end . . . And the end of all our exploring will be to arrive where we started and know the place for the first time."

America is a land that gave me the opportunity to be the very best I could become. Despite all our challenges, this is still the home of unbounded possibility. We Americans, a nation of people unified by common values reflecting the freedom and equality so desperately missing from my childhood experience in Romania, can work together to reemerge as a shining example to the rest of the world. We *can* get better. Every step toward the good can, if it's chosen every day, produce an enduring goodness in our society. What I'm talking about is a sea change that happens voluntarily, in little pockets of personal life, which then gains impetus as each one of us chooses to do the right thing, again and again and again, in small ways and large, until all these choices become a collective wave, a cultural shift.

Ultimately, this sense of mission I have now, late in life, has energized me. I accept the responsibility to become an activist in the cause of the good. I am comforted by my daily choices, by the ever-growing opportunities to touch lives in a positive, constructive way. It's an endless sequence of decisions, one small step after another—many times failing to make the right choice but resolving to get it right the next time—until you discover you've made a journey you might not have thought you could finish, when you first started out.

I make the long snaking turn through some of the most majestic trees in the village and head back across Thunder Bridge, with its wooden planks that live up to their name when you run across them. I head past one of the oldest structures in the village, the Athenaeum, where Thomas Edison reserved tables strategically located so he could sneak out through an open window to avoid unwanted luncheon companions. As the sun glances off the calm water of the lake, I realize my outward-bound course is done, and now I begin to circle back home. As usual, past the halfway mark in my run, I start to gain a little momentum. Each small step works its way into my metabolism until everything catches up with my feet: my heart, my lungs, and my blood vessels. Each individual stride becomes less of an effort and, for a little while, as the poet Richard Wilbur once put it, I'm at rest within my run. I think, This is how it works, one small difficult step after another, again and again, constantly choosing to go forward until, finally, all those choices begin to create a sense of flow and your run returns the energy you've been investing in it, so that your motion, if only for a little while, seems effortless. And what was once so hard, and took so much determination, seems to happen on its own. Something within you has changed, and you think, This is how it's supposed to be. I was made for this. And then, as you near the end of your journey you're elated, not discouraged, to discover yourself thinking, *My God, I'm only getting started.*

# POSTSCRIPT

THE IMPETUS IN WRITING THIS BOOK CAME FROM MANY, many wonderfully caring people I call friends. These extraordinary people have inspired and supported me with deeds in everyday life, others with personal involvement in the process of actually creating this manuscript. Some of you have had an active role in the book. Others have impacted my life and this work through your consistent acts of kindness and generosity. To all of you, I humbly submit my grateful thanks.

This book, particularly the childhood years, was written from memory. The precise facts and recollections are left to the inevitable influence of the haze of time. Yet it is that retained memory that has influenced my life and impacted in dramatic ways the person I have become.

I have been aided along this journey by a paper written by my brother in Romanian, shortly after we arrived in New York on April 13, 1954. My brother was my pal and, along with our grandmother, a major source of emotional support during our childhood years in Romania. We suffered together and found in one another the strength to carry on. I still hope I was as much of a support to him as he was to me. Costa turned out to be a brilliant linguist and analyst. He garnered degrees from Princeton and Harvard and a PhD from NYU in Farsi and Arabic. He worked in the oil business for a few years, then taught languages and ended up working for the Central Intelligence Agency. In many ways Costa was perfectly suited for intelligence work, having been molded by international politics from childhood. He never once told me he was with the CIA; "I work for the federal government" was all he would say. Only later did his wife confirm his job as an analyst. At the age of fifty-eight, he succumbed to mesothelioma, a dreaded cancer often caused by exposure to asbestos, likely somewhere during forced labor in Romania. He left behind a lovely daughter, Kim, and her two children and a loving, caring, and supportive second wife, Gina.

# BIBLIOGRAPHY

Armstrong, Karen. *The Case for God.* New York: Knopf, 2009.

Armstrong, Karen. *Twelve Steps to a Compassionate Life.* New York: Knopf, 2010.

Armstrong, Karen. "The Mystery of Compassion." Lecture. Chautauqua, NY: Chautauqua Institution, Aug. 20, 2010.

Armstrong, Karen. "Why Compassion?" Lecture. Chautauqua, NY: Chautauqua Institution, Aug. 14, 2009.

Bernanos, Georges. *Diary of a Country Priest.* Translated from the French by Pamela Morris. New York: Macmillan, 1937.

Bocu, Sever. *Dictatura se Amuza: Articole din Publicatiile Banatene Interbelice.* Introductory study and notes by Vasile Bogdan. Bucharest, Romania: Paco, 1997.

Bogdan, Vasile. *Sever Bocu: Un Destin Zbuciumat.* Timisoara, Romania: Augusta Publishing, 1999. Passages translated for author by Ana Catineanu.

Burton, John Hill. *Life and Correspondence of David Hume.* Edinburgh: W. Tait, 1846.

Chopra, Deepak. *The Third Jesus: The Christ We Cannot Ignore.* New York: Harmony Books, 2008.

Cloud, John. "Your DNA Isn't Your Destiny." *Time,* Jan. 6, 2010.

Elias, Marilyn. "An Expert Asks: Do We All Have an Evil, Dark Side?" *USA Today,* Mar. 14, 2007.

Eliot, T. S. *Four Quartets.* New York: Harcourt Brace, 1943.

Ehrlich, Paul R. *Human Natures: Genes, Cultures, and the Human Prospect.* Washington, DC: Island Press/Shearwater Books, 2000.

"A Father Makes a Desperate Choice." *Life,* June. 8, 1953, pp. 34–35.

Frankl, Viktor. *Man's Search for Meaning.* Boston: Beacon Press, 2006, first published in 1959.

Friedman, Thomas L. "Advice from Grandma." *New York Times,* Nov. 21, 2009.

Gould, Stephen Jay. *Rocks of Ages: Science and Religion in the Fullness of Life.* New York: Ballantine, 1999.

Jones, Alan W. "In the End, We Shall Be Examined in Love." Lecture. Chautauqua, NY: Chautauqua Institution, Jul. 2, 2010.

Jones, Alan W. "Life in the Spirit: Education for Freedom." Lecture. Chautauqua, NY: Chautauqua Institution, June. 28, 2010.

King, Martin Luther Jr. *Strength to Love.* New York: Harper & Row, 1963.

Lawrence, W. H. "U.S. Expels Diplomat for 'Blackmail.'" *New York Times,* May 27, 1953.

Lissner, Will. "Wife of Georgescu Appeals for Sons." *New York Times,* May 27, 1953.

Moss, Otis, III. "How to Overcome Evil with the Love of God." Lecture. Chautauqua, NY: Chautauqua Institution, Aug. 15, 2003.

*New York Times,* "Eisenhower Aid Sought: Veteran Unit Asks Help for 2 Youths Held in Rumania," July. 22, 1953.

*New York Times,* "A Father's Choice," Editorial, May 28, 1953.

*New York Times*, "Georgescu Family Is Reunited Here," Apr. 14, 1954.

*New York Times*, "The Georgescu Reunion," Apr. 15, 1954.

*New York Times*, "Message to Boys Broadcast," May 31, 1953.

*New York Times*, "Officials See Father of 2 Held in Rumania," June. 4, 1953.

*New York Times*, "Text of Affidavit," May 27, 1953.

Ornstein, Robert, and Ehrlich, Paul R. *New World, New Mind: Moving Toward Conscious Evolution*. New York: Simon & Schuster, 1989.

Overbye, Dennis. "The Collider, the Particle and a Theory About Fate." *New York Times*, Oct. 12, 2009.

Randall, Lisa. *Warped Passages: Unraveling the Mysteries of the Universe's Hidden Dimensions*. New York: Ecco, 2005.

Schlesinger, Arthur M., Jr. "Folly's Antidote." *New York Times*, Jan. 1, 2007.

Schmidt, Dana Adams. "Rumania Frees Boys Held as Spy Pawns." *New York Times*, Apr. 13, 1954, pp. 1, 10.

Storey, Peter John. "South Africa." Lecture. Chautauqua, NY: Chautauqua Institution, July. 10, 2009.

*Time*, Foreign Relations: "The Course of Honor," June. 8, 1953.

*Time*, Foreign Relations: "The Happy Ending," Apr. 26, 1954.

Wiesel, Elie. "10:45 Morning Lecture: Morality." Chautauqua, NY: Chautauqua Institution, July. 27, 2009.

Wright. Robert. *The Evolution of God*. New York: Little, Brown, 2009.

Zimbardo, Philip G. *The Lucifer Effect: Understanding How Good People Turn Evil*. New York: Random House, 2007.

# ABOUT THE AUTHORS

PETER A. GEORGESCU ARRIVED IN AMERICA IN 1954, AFTER years of forced labor as a child in communist Romania. Today, he is chairman emeritus of Young & Rubicam Inc., which has more than 300 offices around the globe, vice chairman of New York Presbyterian Hospital, a member of the Council on Foreign Relations, and a graduate of Phillips Exeter Academy, Princeton University, and Stanford Business School. His lifelong quest to answer the question "Why does evil exist?" led him to ongoing philosophical and spiritual study and an integrative view of morality, religion, and our power to do good and change the world.

David Dorsey is the author of *The Force*, a critically acclaimed nonfiction narrative, and has written for a variety of national magazines. He was Peter Georgescu's collaborator on *The Source of Success*, which provides five drivers of a successful business. He lives with his wife in Rochester, New York.

For more information, please visit
www.theconstantchoice.com.